D0918857

Organizational Design

THEORY AND PRACTICE

O * P * S

Organizations, People, Society

A series edited by
Professor A. B. Cherns

Already published

Organizational Design

THEORY AND PRACTICE

PETER A. CLARK

LONDON: TAVISTOCK

ASSEN: VAN GORCUM

First published in 1972
by Tavistock Publications Limited
11 New Fetter Lane, London EC4
in association with Van Gorcum & Comp. N.V.
Printed in Great Britain
by Butler & Tanner Ltd
Frome and London
© Peter A. Clark 1972

SBN 422 73580 9

Distributed in the USA by Barnes & Noble, Inc.

Dedication

The Azimuth Group

Contents

Part Five: Implications

Preface

This book is largely based on three years' work undertaken by a team of university-based social scientists who worked in collaboration with a specially constituted design team which had the overall task of thinking through the technological and social facets of the design and introduction of a new production factory that would employ several thousand persons. We have disguised the company and the design team.

The central premiss is that social and behavioural scientists can play a valid role in representing the human aspects when major technological decisions are being introduced. This is not a study of the social consequences of technological change. Rather, the book outlines the principles and major concepts that the social scientist requires, and then illustrates the problems that arise in their development and application.

We have heard much about the need for more applied work from social scientists. To date, this has been an intermittent and precarious activity, and one that is made more difficult to imagine because of the absence of useful accounts of attempts to obtain 'applications'.

The book has been made possible by the thought and ingenuity of both individuals and groups, to whom I am grateful. For reasons of anonymity it is not possible to thank directly certain individuals for their skill in making the project possible, and for generously contributing to a mutual experience of learning. It is, however, possible to thank my colleagues in the Centre for the Utilization of Social Science Research at Loughborough University of Technology. Chris Eling, Bernard Leach, Doug Spencer, and Pauline Earnshaw all contributed in a direct way. Without the analytical and administrative skills of Albert Cherns the project would not have been possible.

Finally I must thank my wife, Jennifer, for patiently reading the first draft and for so patiently easing my thinking out of the day-to-day involvement in the project. Her commonsensical comments on behalf of the reader greatly helped the increase in clarity. The mistakes, misinterpretations, and other defects are, of course, my responsibility.

Throughout the book I refer to 'behavioural scientists'. The reasons for this will become apparent in the second chapter, but I must stress that I have selected that label because of its simplicity, and to avoid referring individually to each of the disciplines and interdisciplinary areas.

Peter Clark
The University of Technology, Loughborough
Autumn, 1971

PART ONE

Organizational design

CHAPTER ONE

Applying the behavioural sciences

AUDIENCES

'Organizational Design' has been written for three audiences. First, there are students of the behavioural sciences and organizational behaviour undertaking university studies and advanced education. Second, members of enterprises – industrial, military, welfare, including administrators, managers, management scientists (e.g. operational research and work study), and personnel specialists. Finally, there are students following courses in the sociology of organizations. The book will also be of interest to practitioners, researchers, and teachers in this field.

Behavioural science students will find both the case study and the theoretical chapters accompanying it of particular relevance. The book is based upon the application of theories and ideas from the various behavioural sciences to the problems of the design of a new factory for a 'green-fields' site. Such a problem raises most of the issues which are crucial to the application and development of a theory and practice of organizational design. As the title suggests, the focus is upon the role of the behavioural scientist in design (Clark & Cherns 1968) and the case study presents and examines part of an ongoing consultancy which commenced in 1967. Whereas much of what is taught in the organizational behaviour courses tends towards an individual perspective, this book includes an organizational perspective showing how the work of theorists like Perrow (1970) can be utilized in practical situations.

For members of enterprises the book has a particular interest and relevance. Many people are interested in the behavioural sciences, but find behavioural scientists strange and awkward. The book tackles this aspect by showing how members of 'CCE Ltd' became involved in a joint project with behavioural scientists. The problems which arose are frankly pointed out and the tensions are revealed. Both members of CCE Ltd and we ourselves sought to manage the consultancy in different ways, and this aspect is typical of many contacts between managers and behavioural scientists. The study is interesting because the eventual pattern of the consultancy was not in a direction that had been planned by either 'side'. Eventually we formalized those aspects of the consultancy which were minimal requirements into a flexible approach to organizational design which we call the 'Alternatives and Differences Approach' (Chapter 10).

Sociologists studying organizations as a special topic will find much which is pertinent to the study and explanation of phenomena in organizations. The relevance of investigating the ways in which the social sciences and social scientists are utilized in enterprises has been sharply demonstrated by Bendix (1956) in his study of managerial ideologies. Gouldner (1957) has argued that sociologists have totally failed to tackle this aspect of organizational processes. The reasons for this are in part the feeling that to study applications is in itself some kind of 'sociological sin' (Clark & Ford 1970). Much of what is said about applications is naïve and largely non-sociological. Among the interests of the Centre for the Utilization of Social Science Research is the sociological study of applications. To us this seems a vital area with both considerable sociological relevance and social importance. For example, part of the applications work seems to make certain assumptions about factors external to the enterprise such as the family and the local community. There is an urgent need to explore this area in greater depth (Clark, Ford, & Eling 1969). Again, the sociological study of applications raises a number of important theoretical and methodological problems. These do not form central themes in this book, but there is much else of relevance that does. The case study indicated some of the misunderstandings that arise when sociologists look at practitioners (see Brown, R. K., 1967).

Each of these three audiences will find different aspects of interest. In a later section of this chapter the structure of the book is outlined in a way that makes selective reading convenient and profitable.

ORGANIZATIONAL DESIGN

Sociologists and behavioural scientists have frequently observed that the real design of jobs and organizations is in practice largely allocated to those who are not social scientists. Examples would include the systems analysts, operational researchers, and work study officers. Though behavioural scientists have been quick to raise doubts about the validity of the principles underlying, for example, work study, they have not yet sufficiently thought through alternative approaches that satisfy the criterion of an organization that can survive in its environment and simultaneously take account of the aspirations of the members. Those who seemed to have made the early running (e.g. Argyris 1957) in raising criticisms do not yet seem to have formulated new directions. Certainly we have moved from horizontal job enlargement to job enrichment, but we are still a long way from organizational design as a conventional activity. The author's experience in a department of industrial engineering that was sensitive to ideas from the behavioural sciences (see Acorn Hosiery, in Scott & Lynton 1952) provided many instances of where the design of working situations could have been improved. Initially my observations were at the level of the design of work groups for the technological innovation of band-saw cutting of fabrics and similar examples. Then the focus shifted to noting the implications of method changes (Clark 1963), and then the consequences of mechanization and automation for the existing forms of reward system (Clark 1964). Later, attention was focused upon the problems of adapting to a change in the market and the required changes in management structure to cope with it. This is described in more detail in Chapter 2. These experiences gave indications of the role which a behavioural scientist within an enterprise could perform as part of the planning and development function of the enterprise. In the early 1960s there was little interest in Britain in this kind of activity and what interest did exist was essentially naïve.

These experiences pointed towards two requirements for researchers in the behavioural sciences and for practitioners. First, it was clear that there was a wide disparity between social phenomena within industrial enterprises and the *descriptions* of these in texts of industrial sociology. Second, it was also noticeable that there was a need to develop a 'technology' for approaching problems on the human side. It hardly seemed likely that changes would accrue from sending people on short courses. The most profitable approach to adopt was to bring behavioural and social scientists into enterprises and give them a recognized position (Clark 1963).

This book is about organizational design. In Chapter 2 organizational design is distinguished from planned change. We attempt to show what kinds of role a behavioural scientist can play in organizational design by examining three years' consultancy work in the light of certain basic ideas about designing (Chapters 2, 7, and 11). The basic contention is that behavioural scientists do have a role (Clark & Cherns 1968).

The consultancy was undertaken in a large British firm that was planning to build a new factory. We became involved shortly after the start of the design work, and the case study shows how we attempted to make our advice and ideas relevant and influential. In some senses what we have to say will be disappointing to those who are imbued with the 'new thinking in management'.

THEORY AND PRACTICE

Much of the work of behavioural scientists is associated with certain key names: McGregor, Herzberg, Maslow, Argyris, Likert, Bennis, for example (Rush 1970). Members of enterprises learn about them through journals, seminars, and short courses at management colleges. Until recently very few of the people who teach these ideas have been responsible for establishing their implementation. Indeed it has usually been sufficient for a teacher to claim 'industrial experience' in order to be able to teach them and be regarded as credible. We entered a situation in which some of these ideas were being considered, and the design team of engineers and production men designing the factory that forms part of the case study were interested to know how this 'new thinking' could be implemented.

This book leans away from the emphases both of the 'human relations' (classical and neo-) and of the 'human resources' approaches to organizational design. In part, it emphasizes the work of the structuralists as it has been developed by, for example, Charles Perrow. Until recently his work was available only in article form, but now he has produced a book on organizational analysis which is cogent, well-illustrated, and important to practising managers and students (Perrow 1970). It may be noted in the index of names of this book that the weight of referencing is away from the 'new thinkers' and towards the *structuralists*. The reason is that in design situations there are realities that cannot be swept under the carpet and labelled as 'new thinking'. For example, Likert has argued the case for System 4 management, first by 'proving that it is most effective and, second, by citing studies in which it has been introduced as evidence of its success. Fortunately, the detail of the success stories is good, even though the analysis would seem to be faulty. For example, Likert (1967) refers to structural factors, but discounts their influence, as do Marrow and his colleagues (1967). Both writers provide ample evidence of the importance we give to the structural approach. However, this approach also requires supplementing, and we explore the contribution that an analysis of the culture of the enterprise should make in the design and implementation of the new organization.

The structural approach is explained in certain 'theoretical' chapters, and the case study shows how we set about introducing it as part of a *joint investigation* with an internal design team. We argue that the strategy for getting the perspective of the behavioural scientist diffused, and then adopted, must be built into the design of the project from the start. It cannot easily be added later.

The focus of organizational design is upon the whole organization, or at least a large segment of it. This means that decisions made about one part of the enterprise have to be accounted for in other parts. Solutions that may seem adequate at the level of individual departments may prove not to be feasible when viewed in the light of the total organization. Therefore theory and practice have to take account of the way in which the design team draws *boundaries*.

Any technical design team will group sets of equipment and organize workflows to optimize technical criteria. These subsystems may be thought of as a network of boundaries of the technical system. In practice the people who have to 'operate' the system may experience the boundaries in a quite different way, and their boundaries for the technical system may be different. What is certain is that the boundaries for groupings of people will be neglected and go unrecognized (Miller & Rice 1967). The significance of this point will become more evident when we reach Chapter 6.

THE CASE STUDY

The case study is presented in a chronological form. This shows both the development and the changing directions of the consultancy and also emphasizes the cumulative effect of making decisions in the right order. Any design team has to think far ahead and prepare the ground for future developments. This is especially true for the behavioural science practitioner. This may mean doing things which may seem scientifically senseless, but are sociologically and politically sensible. The chronological development of the case studies illustrates the changes in the terms of reference of the contract and the relationship between the clients and ourselves.

The focus of the case study is not upon results. You will find no references to enormous savings in money or fantastic increases in happiness associated with, or following, our activities. These may have occurred, but they do not form the core of what we want to say. The emphasis is upon *processes*. That is to say, upon the relationship between the consultants and the clients, particularly upon the ways in which behavioural scientists and their clients can achieve a higher level of understanding and accommodation. This does not mean either being in the pocket of the other since the relationship may be expected to include forms of confrontation and disagreement (Chapter 5). The emphasis in the first part of the case study is largely upon design, whereas in the second half it is much more upon research and investigation. The change in emphasis also resulted in a change in relationships between ourselves and the client (Chapter 10).

Another distinctive feature of the case study is the emphasis given to the behavioural science *perspective*. There are three major activities that behavioural scientists might undertake: counting, categorizing, and propositioning.[1] Counting is the most popular, but makes the least good use of the behavioural scientist. Categorizing is so rare as to be almost unknown, but it is becoming increasingly important. Its importance may be ascertained by noting that the way in which the managers and management scientists currently define their work constitutes part of the stock of knowledge of the enterprise for which they work. One of the major gaps in this stock of knowledge is that there is no satisfactory language for examining and talking about organizational systems. Such language as there is exists primarily in the universities and similar institutions. Thus it is important to achieve a reorganization of this knowledge so that it may be more widely utilized. An important part of this wider stock of knowledge is the definitions and concepts (Schon 1967), or categories, used to define reality. Categorizing plays an important part in the case study. Finally, there are propositions: for example, high morale equals high performance. Other propositions may be taken from the approach of the structuralists, and this is illustrated in the case study.

The case study does not attempt to be exhaustive and all-inclusive. It does present the variety of activities and relationships undertaken

---

[1] I am grateful to my colleague, Barry Turner, now at Exeter University, for making this distinction.

and the range of events and incidents that occurred. In this way it illustrates the problems that arise in utilizing the behavioural sciences.

The book is based upon a real problem. It reports consulting work undertaken in Britain by a team from the Centre for the Utilization of Social Science Research, Loughborough University of Technology. The clients are a large firm in Provincial City who are planning a new factory. We have given the firm the name of CCE Ltd. The firm intended to build a factory which would be the 'most modern of its kind in the world'. The proposed changes included widespread mechanization; automation in parts; integrated information control systems; vastly reduced throughput time; the merging of three autonomous production units, each of which had distinct traditions; the transferring of a large sector of the workforce to the new site; new forms of reward system; the disappearance of some occupational groups and the dramatic alteration of others; an alteration in the skill hierarchy and changes in the relative significance of the maintenance workers. In addition to these changes the company were interested in the 'new thinking' and a variety of other administrative changes. For the workforce the new factory implied a new place of work, a shift system, and new kinds of relationship.

Thus the study has some of the characteristics of technological innovation coupled with a mini-merger and movement to a 'greenfields' site. What kind of role can the behavioural scientist play in this?

ORGANIZATION OF THE BOOK

The book is in five parts. The first introduces the topic of organizational design (Chapter 2) and outlines the distinctions between design and research. The second and fourth parts consist of the case studies (Chapters 3, 4, 5, 6, 8, 9). Part Three, which separates the two case studies, draws together the analytical frameworks utilized in the preceding four chapters and points to considerations arising in the next two.

Chapter 10, which opens Part Five, formalizes some aspects of the study in the light of the original definitions and suggests an approach to organizational design – the *Alternatives and Differences Approach* – which is flexible and useful. Chapter 11 examines the kinds of 'knowledge' that were applied in, and generated by, the study and Chapter 12 scrutinizes the 'relational' aspects of the consultancy. A final brief chapter highlights the major points.

Chapters 7, 10, 11, and 12 constitute a development of the theory and practice of organizational design outlined in Chapter 2.

Some of the chapters are more demanding than others, but the book has been organized so that there are variations in pace and depth. Since there are three different audiences for which it has been written, no single one of them will be completely satisfied. Indeed, managers are likely to find the weight of referencing in a couple of chapters to be heavy and perhaps superfluous. On the other hand, these chapters are likely to be of real interest to students of the behavioural sciences, and are thus relevant to the manager because they bring together just the kinds of idea he will be facing in the future.

CHAPTER TWO

Organizational design

INTRODUCTION

Behavioural science practitioners have largely been excluded from the shaping of the organizational systems of enterprises, firms, and institutions. Consequently, the case study which forms the core of this book is in many ways unique, but should be regarded as a fore-runner of future developments.

Typically, administrators associate behavioural science practitioners with smoothing the introduction of technical change; with reducing 'resistance to change'; and with measuring and increasing the involvement of the members of enterprises in their working activities. All this may be included under the general heading of 'planned change'. Current definitions of planned change either place organizational design in a subordinate role or exclude it altogether. We shall argue that organizational design is a distinct and critical activity. In practice, organizational design is usually the unplanned consequence of the design of the technical system and a mixture of utopian and traditional ideas about what is feasible for the organizational system.

The aims of design are distinct from those of research and from those of managing ongoing production systems. An important requirement of design is the generation of a range of alternative designs. Such an exercise is not easy to establish in enterprises because the current emphasis is upon experts collecting facts – a 'weak' scientific approach – rather than creating alternative solutions. We shall describe in the later chapters how we attempted to tackle this problem.

Organizational design is a new activity which is hard to imagine because of the paucity of the existing stock of examples. Many of these concern small-scale changes. The emergence of organizational design, as distinguished from work design in industrial engineering, has been greatly helped by the observations and insights of Eric Miller (1962) on the design and building of a new steel works. These comments provide an outline job description for the behavioural science practitioner, the contents of which will be presented and examined. The role is illustrated by reference to a case study written by the author of an enterprise's attempt to adapt its organization to changes in market and technology.

The design of new organizations to replace existing ones means that the differences between the existing situation and the alternative designs for the future have to be identified. Technical experts are interested in the differences so that they can detect where new kinds of skill will be required (e.g. control instrumentation mechanics). The behavioural science practitioner is concerned to see how plans for the future affect the existing social system, particularly in its requirements for social relationships. This kind of knowledge may be used in both training and design.

In practice, organizational design relies heavily on the ability of the behavioural science practitioner to relate the systems of organization to their market, social, and technological contexts. For example, changes from mechanized to automated working production systems require a change from a hierarchical segmentalized workforce to a system of cooperation within and between 'teams' which is horizontal rather than vertical, yet still has elements of hierarchies of authority and knowledge. This horizontal cooperation in automated technologies has been described as 'horizontally hierarchized cooperation'. The nature of this form of cooperation requires social norms and personal involvements that are quite distinct from those required in mechanized technologies. Thus features of the technology and the existing customs and traditions have to be accounted for in the process of selecting from the alternative designs.

At all stages in the creation and selection of organizational designs, the existing frameworks of ideas about how one should organize have to be modified. We shall suggest that the behavioural science practitioner should take the ideas held by the clients about appropriate principles of organizational design and use them as 'lay hypotheses' to be tested (Gouldner 1957). At CCE Ltd there was a controversy surrounding the suitability of principles of organization derived from 'participative management philosophies', and we were able to contribute by attempting to clarify the dimensions to which these principles referred and to examine particular parts of the enterprise, in existing and planned states, to show how far these principles were in operation at that time and would be in the future.

All our work over the first thirty months involved elements of research and development. We have been reluctant to formalize our method of operating in case this prevented us from being sensitive to the demands of the problems being tackled. There are, however, two main strands to our work: the emphasis upon creating alternative organizational designs and the identification of differences between the existing social system, which members of CCE Ltd know and can talk about, and the future social system that they are attempting to move towards. We have called this approach the 'Alternatives and Differences Approach'. It is described in general terms in this chapter and illustrated in the case study.

Major changes in forms of administration, in technology, and in the environment, are commonplace happenings for enterprises in every field – the military, hospital construction, organized religion, education, industry, and commerce. In general terms we may state that there is a switch from the 'economies of scale' as the major means of reducing unit costs to the 'economies of coordination' (O'Connel 1968). This switch implies the existence within enterprises of experts who possess an ability to make a precise conceptualization of the methods of coordination as currently used, and to decide whether these can be improved. There are obvious signs that the major enterprises are developing this capability. For example, Feld (1964) demonstrates that the American military have become much more interested in using ideas developed in other enterprises than they were fifty years ago. It seems likely that all enterprises will acquire more precise terminologies for describing the organization. Evidence of this may be discovered in conceptual schemata for describing types of manager in the Managerial Grid (Blake & Mouton 1964, 1967, 1969), and for relating types of manager to the kinds of tasks he is organizing in the 3-D approach of Reddin (1970). Chapple and Sayles (1961) argue that the future survival of enterprises in the face of increasingly turbulent environments will depend upon the existence of in-house experts whose major function is the conceptualization of the organizational system, and the application of this analysis to organizational design. There is some evidence to indicate that in Holland a number of the major enterprises have already become experienced at incorporating the terminology of the behavioural sciences, and are becoming proficient at making a discriminating use of the behavioural science practitioner.

PLANNED CHANGE

During the 1960s a number of new fashions emerged, including 'organizational training', 'organizational development', and 'planned organizational change'. Much of what we have to say concerns the first two ideas but we shall concentrate upon the third. We shall suggest that the whole notion of planned organizational change reflects a relationship between the behavioural science practitioner and his client(s) that both limits the value of utilizing the behavioural sciences and ignores a great deal of what we already know about behaviour in enterprises.

Warren Bennis argues that planned change is a method that employs social technology to help solve the problems of enterprises and he indicates that it aims to create intelligent action and choices (Bennis 1964). It is based upon the disciplines of the behavioural sciences in the same way as medicine is related to the biological sciences, and proceeds by converting variables from the basic disciplines into 'strategic instrumentation' and change programmes. Bennis stresses that in his definition the behavioural science practitioner and the client are in a 'collaborative' relationship in order to make a deliberate and systematic application of 'operable knowledge' to the client's problems. In this definition 'collaborative' is the key idea and it refers to the mutual setting of the goals of the consultancy by both client and consultant. Planned change is distinguished from situations in which the goals are set by one side with the other as an agent carrying them out. Later we shall examine the problems that we faced in establishing the principle of mutual goal-setting in CCE Ltd. It will be noted that, typically, enterprises utilize consultants to implement predetermined goals (e.g. install Management by Objectives).

For Bennis, planned change is based on research data, and this is a further distinguishing factor. Research results may be based on studies done on the client, as in the early feedback of attitudinal scores to accountancy departments by Floyd Mann (1957), and the more recent activities arising from the 'institutional learning' experiments initiated by Revans (1967) in ten London hospitals. Alternatively, the results may be from widespread studies done on a particular problem. In this case the results are utilized to form a 'package' which can be introduced into an enterprise to solve particular problems or achieve some objective. Examples of packages would certainly include the 'Managerial Grid' and 'Job Enrichment'. Both are based upon the results of research and are distinctive because, as packages, they include the 'strategic instrumentation', that is, the procedures, necessary for their installation. Thus Bennis has in mind that 'operable knowledge' (see Chapter 11) would draw upon the findings of scientists studying a wide range of circumstances, as well as specific data collected from the client enterprise. Strictly speaking, planned change would refer to the cases where the decision to implement a 'package' was itself based on knowledge about the client that had been collected to establish its appropriateness in that instance. In practice, Bennis seems to include 'packages' as part of planned change irrespective of whether the decision to install was based on the consultant's diagnosis. We shall refer to this aspect later when we examine the problems of matching administrative 'packages' to organizational problems. For the moment, it is sufficient to emphasize that we know far too little about the failures of packaged behavioural science; until we do there are considerable dangers (Lippitt 1965; Greiner, 1967; Clark & Ford 1970).

The general theme of the work of Bennis and his associates is in the direction of, what they call, 'more authentic relationships' (Bennis 1969). They tend to see their work as introducing meaningful interpersonal relationships into a working environment that they feel is characterized by all the features of the popular image of bureaucracy – impersonality and hierarchy (Bennis 1969). In some ways Bennis may be seen as the man who is spearheading the attempt to create a social technology for the implementation of McGregor's Theory Y. To highlight this point, we now turn and examine another, somewhat different, definition of planned change.

Garth Jones (1969) rightly points to the increasing belief that change can be structured, coordinated, and controlled in a systematic and planned way. Planned change is defined as a movement from one state of affairs to another, including the devising of a change programme before the inception of action. It involves the designing, devising, and evaluation of new performance programmes that have not previously been a part of the repertory of the enterprise. The idea of 'a repertory of performance programmes' is a useful one and we shall elaborate on it briefly. It may be argued that enterprises learn to cope with changes in their internal and external environment by developing a range of organizational structures, or performance programmes as March and Simon (1958) term them, and that there are rules which indicate which programme should be applied when the situation changes. We may therefore think of the enterprise as having a stock of performance programmes that are applied by a programmed switching of rules. Thus in this definition the consultant is one of the agents in creating a new programme. This new programme is required because it cannot be created by switching the existing repertory.

The definition by Jones does include the devising, design, and evaluation aspects and is more detailed than that of Bennis, but the focus is essentially upon planned change rather than upon organizational design. This emphasis accurately reflects the current situation with respect both to the practice of behavioural science and to the expectations of administrators. Typically, the expert advice on the nature of the organizational system itself is not seen as a distinctive competence which the behavioural science practitioner can offer. We shall be arguing that organizational design is separate from – though related to – planned change, and the mixing of the two has resulted in an underutilization of the behavioural sciences.

We shall suggest that administrators and experts inside enterprises primarily expect the behavioural science practitioner to be concerned with planned change. For example, administrators are increasingly turning to the behavioural sciences to provide advice on easing the introduction of new technologies such as computers and automation, on reducing resistance to change, and on increasing the commitment of employees to the enterprise.

Technical innovation has been a favourite area for research studies by behavioural scientists (Touraine 1965) and many 'before' and 'after' studies have already been published. A large number of the authors of these studies have included what they consider to be helpful advice to the administrator involved in technical change. For example, Mumford and Banks make suggestions about the social data the administrator should collect to help him to decide which is the smoothest means of introducing the change (Mumford & Banks 1967). Their suggestions are of interest because they epitomize the nature of 'scholarly advice'. The basic suggestion is the collection of attitudinal data which are then examined to decide where the change will create the most opposition. We shall suggest that attitude data of this kind are largely, though not totally, meaningless, and without value to the practical problems. Further we shall argue that any diagnosis must focus upon the dynamic interplay between individuals and groups within the enterprise.

'Resistance to change' has also been a popular area for administrators and researchers. In the early classic studies evidence was found to support the belief that if people were involved in changes then they would become committed to them and resistance would be reduced (Coch & French 1948; Katz & Kahn 1966). This belief in involvement as a panacea received considerable support both from the American business ethos and from those behavioural scientists operating as advisers to enterprises, despite the already considerable evidence to the contrary! Unfortunately, behavioural scientists have become associated in many people's thinking with the competence to remove resistances to innovation. This belief has crushed the emergence of organizational design as a distinct and significant activity, because it reduced the practitioner's role to that of hand-servant.

In a similar way there is a widespread belief that behavioural scientists exist to increase the commitment of the member of the enterprise to its mission and objectives. In fact, Bennis has observed that practitioners assume that work is a 'central life-interest' for the members of enterprises. We shall be tackling this assumption in more detail later in this chapter, but for the moment we shall observe that there is already considerable evidence to show that work is not a central life-interest for many employees (Dubin 1957). Thus any application of theories based on the general belief that it was would inevitably be doomed to failure in some situations. Further, there is increasing evidence to show that commitment to the job and colleagues is only of significance to the performance of the enterprise in certain kinds of technology and only possible if people have certain personality characteristics (Aronoff 1967).

In the preceding paragraphs, we have been attempting to demonstrate that both the efforts of practitioners and the interests of administrators have been directed towards planned change and that in this emphasis the prior and separate stage of organizational design has been excluded. The focus has been upon installing technologies and practices with the minimum of opposition. The appropriateness of these technologies and practices has hardly been seriously considered in the total design sense. Typically, the behavioural scientist has been in a research role rather than in a design role.

TOWARDS A DEFINITION OF ORGANIZATIONAL DESIGN

In attempting to develop a theory and practice of organizational design we have examined 'planned change' first to show how the definition of planned change excluded the prior stage of design. In this section, we shall attempt to formulate an initial definition of organizational design.

Organizational design is an activity in which a behavioural science practitioner advises a client on the appropriateness of systems of organization. He takes into account both external and internal factors. As an activity it is continuous. Consequently the most suitable solutions at one period may have to be scrapped because of change in the environment. Since the shape of the organization is a product of many factors, the design must be interdisciplinary. The activity involves the generation of ranges of alternative designs, through creative strategies, and their evaluation. It requires the selective utilization of knowledge both from the basic disciplines of the behavioural sciences and from investigations of the psychological and sociological features of the client enterprise. Though it is a multidisciplinary activity, the job of the behavioural science practitioner is to represent the 'human aspect'. Organizational design occurs when the practitioner is able to have his judgements included in the decision-taking process. The practitioner may be influential (i.e. his preferences are included) or powerful (i.e. he decides what the new organization shall be like without reference to others). The practitioner aims to develop a language of concepts, ideas, and propositions that link the unique characteristics of the client enterprise with the general body of knowledge about human and social behaviour.

Organizational design is concerned with making decisions about the forms of coordination, control, and motivation that best fit the enterprise. In making these decisions, it is necessary to consider external factors like the market, and internal factors like the needs and aspirations of the members of the enterprise. Organizational design is intimately concerned with the way in which decision-making is centralized, shared, or delegated and with the way the enterprise is governed.

We shall use the term organizational design to refer only to consultancies that include several levels of the hierarchy, a wide range of occupational categories, and a number of functions or departments. Thus we exclude instances that involve just a small number of persons at a similar level in the same function.

At CCE Ltd the consultancy was primarily concerned with the organizational aspects of designing a new, advanced, technologically integrated factory that was destined to replace three semi-autonomous factories. We made use of the study by Eric Miller of the building of a new steel works to provide a model of the kinds of ideas we had about organization and the ways we should proceed to utilize them (Miller and Rice 1967). In contrast to the Miller study, the whole of our consultancy takes place within Provincial City and involves people who are already employed by the Company.

We consider that definitions of 'planned change' have typically been constructed to exclude a separate consideration of organizational design. This separation is critical because it allows the BSP to play a new and significant role. At CCE Ltd design was an ongoing process in which we played a variety of roles, including those of critic of existing proposals and suggester of alternatives. An important part of the consultancy was the way in which we were able both to clarify the existing factory social systems and to show how they would be altered by the proposed technical and administrative designs. Because of this emphasis we feel that organizational design is best thought of as an 'ongoing dialogue' in which the BSP is representing the human organizational aspects as a functional equivalent to the engineers on the technical side (Gouldner 1964). In the dialogue at CCE Ltd we did not aim to push particular human-organizational solutions as a matter of principle, but rather to carry out pieces of investigation that would form the basis for decisions. We were not therefore aiming to introduce any particular 'package', but we were attempting to develop a range of alternative sociotechnical designs and to appraise them in the light of technical, social, and financial evidence. This approach became gradually more formalized and became known as the 'Alternatives and Differences Approach'. It is discussed in a later section.

In organizational design the BSP has frequently to show how decisions made in areas apparently totally disconnected from the organizational side impinge upon it. It is necessary both to examine the market and technological circumstances of the client (Aguilar 1968) and to draw upon research studies that demonstrate the linkages between, for example, product change and organizational structure (Lorsch 1965). The use of these studies requires the BSP to decide which theories the client must understand for the consultancy to be successful. In our work we did emphasize inputs from various analytical frameworks, for example, the 'environmental certainty–structural specificity' theory of Charles Perrow (Chapter 7), but we did not consider it necessary for the user to understand all the same kinds of 'valid knowledge' on which the BSP relies.

Organizational design for a new factory requires the linking together of experts, managers, and representatives from both the technical and the organizational side. The idea of interdisciplinary work and 'management services' is an attractive one. We hope to be able to present some of the problems arising in this kind of work when experts from different areas meet. It has been suggested that the ideal model is one of 'collaboration', but if this excludes confrontations we would want to reject it (Beckhard 1967). There are many good and sound reasons why BSPs and, for example, operational researchers should be in disagreement; in many ways their goals are in conflict (Bennis 1966). The role of the BSP is to focus upon the human-organizational aspect and to advise to the best of his ability.

STRATEGIES FOR ORGANIZATIONAL DESIGN

In our definition of organizational design we have given some considerable emphasis to the developing of alternative designs. We now briefly consider the strategies for achieving this and point forward to the ways in which we attempted to generate designs in the case study.

Many approaches to organizational and technical design are influenced by the strategies for research rather than designing. This is a critical distinction and one which indicates our doubts about researchers' recommendations to managers. Typically, academic researchers and 'management scientists' emphasize the collection of data. For example, a large part of the formalized syllabuses for teaching work study are concerned with devising means of recording the existing system, rather than with generating alternatives. These ideas are variations on the research strategy.

The research strategy may be crudely described as observation–hypothesis–testing–conclusion. The purpose of research is to arrive at general laws and theories which interrelate phenomena. It may be seen that the purpose and the strategy are appropriately matched, but are they useful strategies for *design*? Nadler (1966) has observed that current strategies of design are remarkably similar to those for research, yet the purposes are totally different.

In design strategies one of the critical differences is the shifting of emphasis away from the breakdown of components for analysis, which is typical of the 'management science' approach, to a 'wholeness' of thinking.[1] The aims of design are creative rather than analytical. This does not mean that research is excluded, but it does mean that it is not the main thrust.

Within enterprises the design aspect is typically approached by a research strategy. Also design is made difficult because it does not easily mesh with the strategies adopted by managers concerned with operating and controlling the existing system. Their strategies emphasize familiarity with the objectives of the system; preparing resources to operate the system; measuring performance; comparing performance with objectives; and taking action if required (Nadler 1966).

Thus we shall argue that the design process requires particular strategies which are distinct from those adopted by researchers and managers. In the consultancy at CCE Ltd we made a series of attempts to establish the joint designing of social and technical systems. These are described and examined in the case study.

ORIGINS OF ORGANIZATIONAL DESIGN

Organizational design did not really emerge until the mid 1960s. Prior to this period the work of BSPs had been focused either upon techniques for changing the attitudes of individuals, or upon small-scale alterations to parts of larger enterprises. The movement away from a focus upon the individual arose because of the realization that, however effective the techniques adopted in the training situation, when the individual returned to his work he returned to his previous role and re-entered surroundings in which his colleagues already had established expectations of his attitudes and behaviour. The chances of long-term individual change under such conditions is minimal. Gradually the emphasis moved towards the ideas of 'training organizations' and of 'organizational development'. This development reflected an awareness that human relationships and

---

[1] For example, in a seminar at Loughborough in 1970, Professor Louis E. Davis (University of California, Los Angeles, USA) argued that automation would provide a new opportunity to design jobs and organizations to facilitate a higher level of psychological satisfaction for the individual.

attitudes are structured and that this systemic quality of organizational life could only be transformed by a systemic approach. One such approach which was developed to meet this circumstance is the 'Managerial Grid' (See Chapter 12), a five-year programme involving the total organization (Blake & Mouton, 1964).

During the 1960s a small number of BSPs moved outside the conventional career of teaching, research, and scholarly advice to administrators, and began to carry out experiments on changing parts of the enterprise through systemic means. This work brought them into contact with other specialisms such as Operational Research, Research and Development, and Production Engineering, each of which was designing a part of the enterprise and was indirectly influencing the organization's structure. These first-generation BSPs noted that in industrial enterprises the technology has an important influence upon the deployment of people about a factory and the possibilities which exist for communication and coordination (Trist & Bamforth 1951; Meissner 1968). They attempted to develop a language for analysing the organizational structure in a way which took account of the technical system. This work led to the suggestion that in the designing of organizations the BSP must view the technical and organizational aspects within the perspective of a single system and seek to optimize both. We trace these developments through two studies done at the small-group level to one example where the BSP was able to observe the designing of a totally new steel works (Miller & Rice 1967). This last example represents, we feel, a significant development in that it both suggests a role for the BSP in organizational design and indicates the problems arising. Later, in our case study, we shall present and eamine in detail the problems arising in organizational design. We shall show how we attempted to establish the design process.

Chapple and Sayles (1961) examined a number of production problems in factory and clerical settings and suggested that the critical variable which was not sufficiently understood was the 'workflow'. They noted in one particular case that the nature of the discrepancy between the master schedule devised by the production planner and the actual requirements for coordination between departments to cope with day-to-day variation was the major source of conflicts. Following this analysis, they advised the restructuring of the planning department and the rerouting of materials. This case is an example of the BSP improving an existing system by diagnosing the relationship between variations in workflow and the 'management control' procedure of production-scheduling. Though they do not state this, they are in fact applying their own theory about the form production control should take in different situations. In this country similar work has been undertaken which may broadly be said to provide the BSP with a framework of ideas for matching control systems and workflows (Woodward 1958, 1964, 1965, 1970; Turner, B. A., 1968).

In the next example, Van Beinum (1964) applied a particular theory about human motivation to part of the Dutch PTT[1] to change the employees' strong negative attitude towards work. Three changes were introduced to some 180 persons working on postal accounts – stabilization of the groups; increased authority at the lower levels; and the installation of a communication system linking them with different levels of management. It was predicted that these changes would reduce frustration and increase satisfaction. The results indicated that the changes had contributed significantly to a change in attitudes, but were differently perceived by different levels. This point is useful because it emphasizes an aspect neglected by some BSPs. This is that there are differences in orientation to work between groups in the same place of work.

A large number of researches have shown that the meaning of work to people varies widely and that it cannot be predicted from characteristics of the technology (Goldthorpe *et al.* 1967). This is an important point because it means that the BSP must investigate the details of any particular work situation to discover what the characteristics and aspirations of the workforce really are before redesigning the organization. If this is not done, then changes in organization that are perceived by management as 'job enrichment' may be perceived by the recipients as productivity bargaining.[2]

The two previous examples are of changes to parts of existing and ongoing situations. The final example concerns the building of a new steel works on a 'green-fields site' (Miller 1962, 1967). Eric

---

[1] The Dutch Postal and Telegraph enterprise has had a strong interest in re-designing work situations to facilitate greater satisfaction and meaning (private communication from its Director).

[2] Practitioners in job enrichment state quite clearly that it should not be confused with productivity bargaining (e.g. Paul *et al.* 1970), but several personnel specialists have observed that those experiencing job enrichment have sometimes interpreted management's intentions as the opportunity to engage in productivity bargaining. There is, of course, no reason why management's definition of the situation should coincide with that of other groups.

Miller was able to observe the way in which the management of one company actually went about organizational design, or, perhaps more accurately, did not! The company had two goals: the building of a new steel works and the rebuilding of the company. In practice the major emphasis was given to the technological problems, and in summarizing his observations Miller notes:

— the design of the plan, technology, and factory building was started first and proceeds more quickly than the design of the organizational aspect. When the organizational design does start it usually consists only of manpower totals and neglects the social-structural and people aspects. For example, no consideration was given to the ways in which existing craft categories and groups would be affected by the changes in technology. (This neglect is somewhat similar to the way in which, it is reported, the design of the automated colliery at Bevercoates occurred. The labour problems there are an outstanding example of what can happen.)[1]

— it is possible for the BSP to anticipate and identify some of the problems that the technical design will create and to suggest alternative forms of organization for tackling the change and the final situation.

— the design of the technology and the organization should be concurrent and should be linked with the 'building' of the new organization and factory. The process is best considered as a whole: 'in other words, by integrating plant design and organization design, it becomes possible to take account of constraints and to anticipate and work out many of the problems of accommodation (between the technology and the organization) at the early drawing board stage' (Miller & Rice 1967).

Miller's ideas can be presented in diagrammatic form. In *Figure 1* the conventional and suggested approaches to organizational design are outlined. The conventional approach is characterized by organizational design starting so late that it is merged with 'organization-building'. It is impossible to optimize the technology and the organization jointly and the organization has to adapt to the task arrangements created by technologists. In the suggested approach the stages of plant and organizational design start simultaneously

[1] It was once suggested by a columnist in *The Sunday Times*, 1966, that the involvement of a social scientist could have saved a million tons of coal!

and are linked to one another and to the following stage of 'building' the new plant and organization.

In the case study of CCE Ltd we were able to start on organizational design almost concurrently with the plant design, and were able to keep options open about the technical aspect until the organizational design had been established.

Figure 1 Building a new factory: organizational design (after Miller & Rice 1967)

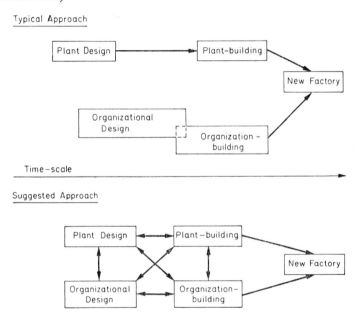

BEHAVIOURAL SCIENCE PRACTITIONERS

The analysis by Miller of the absence of organizational design in the case study just examined suggests that there is a role for behavioural science practitioners to play in working with, for example, members of management services on the organizational aspects of administrative and technological innovations. Their absence has led one social scientist to remark: 'Every time a production engineer makes a decision about such matters as batch size he influences the pattern of relations on the shop-floor' (Woodward 1964). A similar observation is made by Mumford and Banks (1967) following their investigations of the introduction of computers into two British enterprises: '... great time and affection is devoted to the systems aspect of change. ... This incomplete kind of analysis is, of course, due to the kinds of specialists traditionally brought in to advise ... for usually these are engineers or systems experts.'

There are very few behavioural science practitioners. That is to say, people who are prepared to work on the everyday and long-term problems within enterprises. There is more emphasis upon such developments: 'Increasingly in the future we would like to see the sociologist and social psychologist working side by side with the technical expert' (Mumford & Banks 1967).

The case study of CCE Ltd which forms the core of this book examines the activities undertaken by a small team of BSPs in advising one large and well-known British enterprise that was planning the building of a new factory. As a case study it is in certain important respects unique. There are few reported occasions of BSPs being involved in the design of a firm employing several thousand people and containing various functions and levels. The problems created and tackled in this work highlight most of the issues which face members of management when thinking about how the behavioural sciences can be applied. Perhaps most important was the effort made to 'work through' management ideas about 'participative management'. The study is unusual in so far as we were not concerned to recommend 'participative management' or any similar philosophy, but rather we were concerned to work with the internal experts from the technical side in deciding which theories of motivation were most appropriately applied to various types and groups of employee.

We see the BSP playing an active and interventionist role in enterprises and it may be his/her task to suggest that a particular proposal (e.g. the introduction of Likert's System 4) is impracticable. The BSP may be expected in the future to obtain a much closer matching between the objectives of management, with reference to their human resources, and the realities of the situation in which the enterprise is immersed.

PRINCIPLES OF ORGANIZING

The focus of our case study and this section is upon the factors that affect systems of decision-making in organizations. We shall argue that any system of decision-making within an organization is a product of the interaction of the exigencies (constraints) introduced by marketing, technical, and financial policies and conscious attempts to design systems of decision-making in accordance with an identifiable set of principles such as scientific management. In this section we briefly examine two sets of organizing principles: scientific management and human resources.

The industrial engineer and the BSP are both concerned to identify the human tasks which will have to be performed to operate a production system. They are both concerned to find means of recording these human tasks and a language to describe their main characteristics. The major differences lie along two dimensions. First, the industrial engineer is primarily concerned with the size of tasks, measured in time, whereas the BSP is concerned to discover which among various forms of relating people (roles) to tasks will optimize performance criteria and human satisfaction. Second, the BSP has a theory of coordination based on studies of systems of decision-making between people, whereas the industrial engineer typically adopts models based on the operation of machines rather than people.

The principles of organizing adopted by industrial engineers have been identified as those of scientific management by researchers (Friedmann 1955, 1961) and by practitioners (Davis, L. E., 1955). These principles possess the following main tenets:

— create the maximum specialization by limiting the number of tasks in a role
— reduce the variety of tasks in a role
— maximize repetitiveness and eliminate challenge
— minimize training time
— treat the employee as an isolated individual without ties to colleagues
— assume that the sole motivation for people to perform well is financial.

The same points have been made many times (Mouzelis 1967; Krupp 1961; Foster 1968).

These ideas appear to have been widely held in a diffuse form by management and by management scientists and represent in an idealized form what many industrial organizations have been attempting to achieve. In recent times some modifications have been suggested, for example, that if the operative is able to rotate jobs then he/she will find work more satisfying. There is little evidence to support this. What evidence there is suggests that job satisfaction increases with the length of the work cycle and the amount of variety in the job (Wyatt & Marriott 1952). However, these attempts to increase satisfaction represent an attempt to counter the findings of some journalists and researchers who argue that scientific management produces jobs which are 'psychologically crippling'. We now turn to examine this evidence.

Friedmann (1955) has documented scores of examples of the kinds of roles (jobs) created by the application of the scientific management principles. He suggests that the operator's individual discretion and caprice have been replaced by learnable rules of behaviour. This process may be termed rationalization (Bendix 1947) and it affects both the skill–occupational hierarchy of the enterprise and the personality of the individuals in the roles (jobs). The effects of both of these may have consequences for the outside community. Warner and his colleagues have shown how changes in methods of production in a shoe factory deskilled jobs and contributed towards a strike and a cleavage within the local community (Warner 1947). Friedmann (1955, 1960) describes the case of a Dutch factory manufacturing dresses. The production process had been broken down into more than 60 separate short-cycle tasks, each carried out by a separate individual. Apparently this particular factory used a very simple selection test for job applicants. This was designed to polarize candidates into those who were 'awake' and those who were 'asleep'. The firm selected only those who were 'asleep'. This tale can be quickly supplemented by scores of others, but perhaps a couple from Argyris will emphasize the point. He tells of one factory which employed monkeys to stuff pillows, a job previously done by humans, and of another factory where his investigation of the intelligence scores of one department, which the managing director regarded as ideal, showed the average level to be slightly above that of the educationally subnormal.

These stories illustrate some of the suggested concomitants of scientific management. However, the observations tend to be anecdotal and unsystematic. The attitude of social scientists to work study and similar approaches is best described as hostile. Much of the so-called research on applications of scientific management is in the form of social criticism rather than systematic and imaginative investigation. Sociologists have, for example, manifestly failed to examine work study and its application in a scientific manner. They have presumed that the worker is a passive respondent to the application of these principles and, more seriously, they have not investigated the extents, locations, and variations in application. Had they done so they might have noted that there are considerable variations in applications of this approach. Also they might have noted that the workers' control over the situation is more affected by technology and workflow than by the activities of industrial engineers and work study personnel.

Until the last decade the main alternative set of organizing principles at the shop-floor level was that of the 'human relations school' (Krupp 1961). In an early form this tended to emphasize that supervision, which was seen as the critical role linking management and men, should be 'general' rather than 'close' (e.g. Katz 1955). These principles were initially taught to managers through lectures. Treadgold (1963) describes some of this early period in postwar Britain. It was found that the impact of lecturing on behaviour was small and soon dissipated, so alternative techniques, such as role-playing and group experiences, were adopted. These had a higher impact on the individual, but a marginal impact upon his performance when he returned from the teaching situation back to work. Gradually it was realized that the man's performance in the working situation was influenced by the prevailing social norms and social relationships and that both these were *structured* (Katz & Kahn 1966). This realization was one of the important factors leading to the idea of training organizations rather than individuals (Bennis 1969).

The human relations principles tended to emphasize styles of supervising and to accept the pre-existing systems of decision-making. A more radical departure came with the work of the Tavistock practitioners in England and later with the applications of the principles derived from the studies of motivation by Herzberg (1958) in America. These ideas from Herzberg were formed into a procedure (a strategic instrumentation) and applied through the ideas of job enrichment. The recent application in ICI is an excellent and relatively well-documented example of this (Paul, Robertson, & Herzberg 1968). We shall not deal directly with job enrichment in this chapter.

The Tavistock practitioners have made some of the most significant contributions to organizational design. They were the first to identify the importance of treating the technical and decision-making systems jointly rather than separately. Thus they challenged the acceptance of the existing situation that so characterized the human relations school. They argued that for any given production system there may be 'organizational choice' and their comparison of two different forms of organization in the same technology is now a classic (Trist *et al*. 1963). This work was hailed by McGregor as being as significant as the Hawthorne experiments (McGregor 1966). Additionally they developed a language of concepts for designing systems of organization (Emery 1959; Miller & Rice 1967) and attempted to create applications of these principles through consulting in Britain, America, India, and Norway. In the 1960s they formulated a set of principles of organizing tasks that was termed the *human resources approach*.

Foster (1968) has outlined the main tenets as follows:

— create a maximum variety of tasks within the role (job)
— create a meaningful pattern of tasks involving different levels of effort and attention
— ensure that the scope of the role (job) provides for the setting of standards of quality and quantity, including the feedback of results
— include tasks in the job that are recognized as possessing a degree of respected skill
— make provision for interlocking tasks, job rotation, or physical proximity when there is a necessary interdependence of roles (jobs)
— when a number of roles (jobs) are linked together by interlocking tasks or job rotation their occupants should as a group have some control over setting standards, should receive knowledge of results, and should control 'boundary tasks' (e.g. maintenance).

It may be immediately noted that these principles for the design of individual roles (jobs) are, point for point, opposite to those of scientific management. Further, that considerable attention is given to the aspects of coordination, control, and motivation. A feature of these principles is their emphasis upon achieving a coincidence between the boundaries of a set of interrelated tasks and the creation of a social boundary. This idea may be termed 'responsible group autonomy'. It is an example of decision-making in which the primary aim is to delegate decision-making down to the 'grass-roots' level of the enterprise.

MANAGEMENT STYLES

In the previous section we outlined two major sets of principles that could be utilized in the designing of systems of decision-making. We closed at the point in which it had been noted that one of the primary aims of the human resources principles is to delegate decision-making and to create group boundaries at the level at which task and organizational boundaries coincide. We now extend the examination by taking a closer look at certain current theories about management styles.

There is today an extensive literature on management styles, particularly the notion of the participating manager. Four basic styles can be detected:

— the manager who makes decisions on his own without explanation (TELLS)
— the manager who makes decisions on his own with explanation (SELLS)
— the manager who engages in prior consultation before making a decision (CONSULTS)
— the manager who makes decisions jointly with his work group(s) (JOINS)

The term 'participation' has usually been applied to the manager who consults.

The current concern with participation is one with considerable implications for the selection of a system of decision-making and for the power relations within enterprises. Indeed, as Mechanic has argued, participation is essentially a multifaceted symbol which can be used by managers, workers, and students (Mechanic & Strauss 1965). Managers are concerned with new forms of ideology which legitimate their authority in contemporary Western society (Bendix 1956), and workers and students may be concerned with changing the general power relations within industry and education.

Participative management is more adequately understood if we make some simple distinctions between power and influence (Heller 1969). A person or group may be said to have power when as a result of his direct or indirect intervention his/the group's preferences are incorporated in the decision process. Usually power is exercised by direct intervention. A person may be said to have influence when as a result of direct or indirect intervention his/the group's preferences are considered in arriving at a decision. For a person or group to exercise power or influence they will have to gain access to the decision-making system. In the case of power, access is the first step. We may now use these aspects of power and influence and define participation as a process in which two or more parties influence each other in making plans, policies, and decisions.

If we now compare the definition of participation and the typology of management styles with the principles of the human resources approach we shall find that one situation is not covered by the four styles of Tells, Sells, Consults, and Joins. The neglected style is one of delegating decision. This is a central tenet in the human resources approach, but curiously has been neglected in the literature on participative management. This is a strange omission when one considers that one of the reasons given for adopting the participative approach is that it provides an opportunity for people to have autonomy and control over their working environment (Maslow 1954; Herzberg 1958). We can now include delegation as a fifth style.

In the section on systems of decision-making we have aimed to make introductory remarks about the problems of coordination, control, and motivation in enterprises. In recent years managements have publicly supported the general ideals of participative management. In practice, this has largely referred to the non-delegation of decisions, and the tenets of scientific management have tended to form the prevailing approach to the design of systems of organization. Given that there is increasing support for the human resources approach and decreasing emphasis upon scientific management, exemplified in for example, the ICI job enrichment programme, what are the assumptions which underlie the human resources approach?

HUMAN RESOURCES: ASSUMPTIONS AND EVIDENCE

In this section we scrutinize more closely the assumptions underlying the human resources approach (Foster 1968) to the design of decision-making systems. We shall argue that this approach makes unwarranted assumptions about human behaviour in enterprises and that it concentrates too much on vertical relations between 'managers' and 'workers'.

The human resources approach as defined by Foster has a number of basic assumptions about the motivations of the members of enterprises:

— that managers and workers are motivated to share influence in
decision-making
— that in general this willingness is underutilized
— that the willingness to share and its underutilization represent the
typical situation.

The identification of these assumptions is critical, because if it can
be shown that they are not widely applicable then it has implications
for the theory and application of the human resources approach.

Heller (1969) is currently making a careful appraisal of the human
resources approach, but it is possible to make a number of salient
points by utilizing existing published reports. For example, we have
some evidence to show that there are situations where the sharing
of decisions is established. In the shipbuilding industry, engineering
(e.g. the production of aero-products), and printing, we may speak
of shared decision-making. It is interesting to note that these are the
kind of industries where the behavioural scientists have been the
least prominent and the industrial relations advisers the most
prominent. Clark and Ford have suggested that there is a relationship between the utilizations of behavioural scientists (psychologists
and sociologists) and the managerial traditions and ideologies (Clark
& Ford 1970; Bendix 1956). Another example from a different setting
is provided by the failure of French and his colleagues (1960) to
replicate their experiments on shared decision-making. In Norway,
it was found that at the particular textile plant utilized for the study
no increase in performance occurred with involvement in decision-
making. This experiment is one in which no attempt was made to
appraise the level of decision-making before the experiment or to investigate the attitudes of the employees towards their work, the job,
and their colleagues.

Organizational psychologists have until recently been the single
most influential group in the behavioural sciences. They generally
tended to focus solely upon the situation inside the enterprise and to
neglect developments in the wider society (Clark, Ford, & Eling
1969). One of the most powerful assumptions underlying the approach of first-generation behavioural scientists has been the belief
that work is a 'central life-interest' for the members of enterprises.
A great deal of applications, particularly in America, have started
with this assumption and with the additional assumption that people
will be oriented similarly and strongly to work. In fact we have

considerable evidence to show that people are not motivated similarly (Myers 1965) to work and that many of them do not regard work as a 'central life-interest'. Robert Dubin has produced considerable evidence demonstrating that large numbers of the members of enterprises are emotionally neutral about work (Dubin 1963).

Goldthorpe and his colleagues (1967, 1970) have demonstrated that workers at three large plants in the rapidly growing town of Luton, north of London, were also neutral in their orientations. Goldthorpe initially set out to test the hypothesis of embourgeoisement. This stated that, as workers became more affluent, they would tend to adopt middle-class life styles. Luton was chosen as a strategic case because it could be argued that if the hypothesis could not be demonstrated in Luton then it would have to be rejected. The sample population were men in the age-range 20–45. Goldthorpe discovered that the affluent workers did not adopt middle-class values, but neither did they continue with the traditional working-class life style. They developed a new life style in which the family and home were the central features. The family was the nuclear family of parents and children, not the extended family of several generations which has been regarded as traditional (Young & Wilmott 1957). These men typically regarded work as a means to an end and had very low ego-involvement with the job and colleagues. Also there were few connections between their social contacts at work and those outside. This may be contrasted with the position of fishermen (Horobin 1956) and coalminers (Dennis *et al.* 1956) where there are close connections between work and community.

The Luton findings demonstrate that for some groups of employees the main interests are in obtaining sufficient money to support their family-centred activities. In fact, the absence of special induction and socialization procedures in Luton suggests that the managements were not concerned about the beliefs of their employees and did not attempt to resocialize them consciously to conform to a general set of values. These workers had in comparative–objective terms relatively low physical autonomy of movement about the workplace, but relatively high autonomy of norms, beliefs, and values. This may be contrasted with the military, where there is low autonomy of values (Dornbusch 1956). In the Luton sample the workers brought their working-class culture into the plant and its existence was of little interest to management. A similar point is made by Katz, F. E. (1968).

We have used the findings of investigations in America by Dubin, and in England by Goldthorpe, to demonstrate that the general assumption that work is a 'central life-interest' is without foundation. Consequently the assumption that workers are similarly motivated and can be understood in any unique situation by reference to general assumptions about human behaviour must be rejected. This point leads into our second criticism of the human resources approach.

Research and practice in the behavioural sciences has largely concerned itself with hierarchical relations between superordinates and subordinates (Sayles 1958; Etzioni 1961; Tannenbaum 1968). We have already indicated that this emphasis is somewhat limited and we now turn to make some specific objections and suggestions.

The emphasis upon hierarchical relations has led to a neglect of horizontal relations such as those between departments at different positions in the workflow and between the various groups within the enterprise (Crozier 1964). The weaknesses of the hierarchical approach can best be tackled by adopting a perspective which views the enterprise as a confederation of individuals and groups who form associations and pursue rational strategies designed to optimize their own position *as they define it.* In the case study we shall be illustrating the use of this approach. One of its features is that it recognizes that within any enterprise there are likely to be considerable differences in the form taken by the social structure and in the content of the cultures among different segments (Litwak 1961; Etzioni 1961). Further, that the delineation of these features and their explanation are critical pieces of data which should influence decisions made about the appropriateness of particular systems of organization.

In this section we have sought to indicate some of the practical and theoretical objections to the general application of the human resources approach. For example, the findings of the studies of the orientations to work of the Luton sample are an important warning to managements who blindly adopt a 'participative philosophy'.

TECHNOLOGY, RATIONALITY, AND CONTROL

In the previous section we examined the principles of the scientific management and the human resources approaches to the designing of decision-making systems and found that the application of any general set of principles should be based upon a knowledge of the attitudes and aspirations of the members of the enterprise and also upon the factors, internal and external, that influence these. We now turn to a consideration of the ways in which technology as a variable is thought to influence the shape and content of organizational systems. Once again the aim is to identify those aspects which may largely be regarded as 'givens' and outside the control of the designer and to focus upon the variables which are manipulable (Chin 1961).

We shall define technology to include *only* the raw materials to be transformed, the equipment, and the buildings within which the production processes take place. We exclude from our initial definition the layout of plant and the configuration of buildings. Both layout and configuration influence the social relationships (Goldthorpe 1957, 1967) but they reflect the beliefs which administrators and specialists hold about rationality and control (cf. Woodward 1965). This definition leaves open the possibility of moulding the technology in different ways.

Organizational design is based on the idea of 'organizational choice'. This may be achieved within the confines of the same technology and layout, as Trist and his colleagues have shown (Trist *et al.* 1963). However, Miller has hinted at the possibilities of altering both the technology and the organization to achieve a good level of 'accommodation' between them.

The connections between 'technology', 'control systems', and 'rationality' may be *illustrated* by examining Touraine's categorization of the worker's role at different stages in industrialization (Touraine 1966). He sets out three stages:

PRE-ADMINISTRATIVE

Exemplified by craft working; traditional systems of authority like paternalism; the absence of a formal organization to fix the role and status of the employee and his relations in the hierarchy. The actual arrangement of roles is the result of tradition and practice and is non-schematic. Discipline is based upon personal authority.

ADMINISTRATIVE

The emergence of the professional organizer who generates elaborate and detailed rules governing pay, selection, work specifications, and hierarchical relations. The professionals are the experts who want predictability in the administrative 'machine'. They are the precursors of the experimenters and rationalists who are, in the opinion of Roszak, the creators of the 'technocratic society'

(Roszak 1970). Formal rules may be found to govern almost every situation (Crozier 1964).

POST-ADMINISTRATIVE

This is rarely found, but is emerging. In this stage the management structure is rationalized, and vertical relations are replaced by horizontal ones. There are still formal rules but the administration has been decentralized. Workers speak of increased contact with colleagues though the actual size of groups tends to shrink and their physical dispersal to increase. There is increasing integration of the individual into a functionally determined system and increasing flexibility arising from less predetermined relations. Popitz and colleagues have suggested that coordination can take on many forms of horizontally hierarchized cooperation (Popitz *et al.* 1957). Communications tend to take the form of lateral consultations rather than vertical authority.

Technology has become an important variable in the analysis of organizational systems since the work of Woodward which suggested that spans of control, levels of hierarchy, and ratios of administrative to direct workers varied systematically in relation to whether the production system was unit, batch, or process (Woodward 1958, 1965). She also hinted at systematic variations in the climate of industrial relations but the supporting evidence presented was somewhat tenuous. Blauner (1964) uses the concept of alienation in an attempt to assess empirically the alienative effects of various technological and organizational structures on workers. Unlike Marx, for whom alienation was such a central concept, Blauner does not directly examine the problem of workers' participation, possibly because American workers are less interested in such issues.

It may be seen from *Figure 2* that Blauner is comparing the nature of employee involvement under three different kinds of production system. The data on which his inferences are based are drawn from the secondary analysis of survey data and special investigations which he carried out in, for example, Californian chemical plants. Blauner observes that the thesis of alienation is currently fashionable, but unlike Marx he does not examine the extent of worker control over ownership. In fact he goes on to argue that alienation is a concomitant of large-scale bureaucratic institutions in general rather than capitalism in particular. He believes that the major alienating forces are technology (especially the way it standardizes work), the division of labour, and the transformation from traditional to bureaucratic organization.

Blauner's conclusions, summarized in *Figure 2*, suggest a U-shaped movement from low alienation in craft technologies to high in mechanization to low in automation. Thus he later argues that the industry a man works in is 'fateful' because it decides the nature of his work and the meaning it will have for him. It also influences his freedom to move about and be away from supervision as well as the opportunities for personal growth and the nature of his 'social

Figure 2   Production system and employee involvement (based on Blauner 1964)

Type of production system Areas of involvement	Craft Printing	Mech/1 Textiles	Mech/2 Auto	Automated Chemicals
1. Sense of control of employee with reference to the production system	HIGH	LOW	LOW	HIGH
2. Extent of shared beliefs and outlooks among employees	HIGH	LOW	LOW	MEDIUM
3. Extent of social isolation in the factory and the community	LOW	MEDIUM (based on community)	HIGH	MEDIUM
4. Ego(self)-involvement in the job	HIGH	MEDIUM	LOW	HIGH

personality'. It is noticeable that he takes a less pessimistic view about the future than does, for example, Argyris (1958). He is optimistic about automative technologies.

The belief that under automation man will be less alienated is an interesting idea and one that is gaining increasing support. While it is certainly correct to argue that men have greater physical mobility about the place of work it would be wrong and naïve to conclude that they had greater 'autonomy' and therefore would be less alienated. The idea of autonomy is vague. It may be hypothesized that in process technologies American and European managements have been most active in attempting to obtain employee involvement.

Evidence to support this hypothesis may be obtained by examining the high degree of usage made by the petro-chemicals industry of the services of behavioural scientists particularly those introducing various forms of sensitivity experience. If this hypothesis has any basis, and we believe it has, then it may be argued that the managements of such enterprises are far more interested in the orientations to work and colleagues of their employees than were the managements of the Luton sample. In this case it is difficult to be general about 'autonomy', since we may now argue that the autonomy of outlook and of styles of interpersonal relationship are less than in the mechanized situations. An additional point with reference to autonomy concerns the implicit assumption of many behavioural scientists that everyone desires greater autonomy. There are many other possibilities. Employees may not want autonomy or they may find greater personal uncertainty in such situations.

Blauner does neglect the important question, in terms of Marx's analysis of alienation, of who will control the process of automation, or what will be the impact of the new technology upon the wider social structure. In fact it must be asserted that Blauner has not, strictly speaking, either operationalized or tested Marx's thesis. The utility of the Blauner thesis is as a 'bench mark' to the central aims of this book.

In summarizing this section it may be argued that Touraine, Woodward, and Blauner have provided various kinds of evidence to suggest that there is a systematic connection between types of production system and aspects of the social structure of enterprises. We shall take this evidence as an instructive reminder that the choice of organizational systems may be constrained by the nature of the production system. We have argued that the nature of rationality and control in mechanized and automated technologies is and should be different. It follows that the principles of scientific management are less appropriate in automated technologies (Stinchcombe 1958; Gouldner 1954; Thompson & Bates 1957), but it does not follow that the principles of the human resources approach will be any better. We may have to develop new sets of principles.

ORGANIZATIONAL PERSPECTIVE

In the three previous sections we have critically examined the relevance of two sets of general principles about designing decision-making systems and have argued that 'organizational choice' should be based upon characteristics of the members of the enterprise and the type of production system. In doing this we have gradually moved away from the traditional behavioural science perspective of, for example, the organizational psychologist (e.g. Schein 1966). We now turn to examine two case studies in which the author used the organizational perspective to analyse problems. One is a study of the impact of changes in the market on an enterprise and the other concerns the failure of a plant-wide productivity scheme.

Harp Mill manufactured knitted outerwear for a major chainstore-retailer in Britain. It produced styles which had a simple stitch geometry and were usually of a single colour. The factory had been opened some years before the case study starts and had largely recruited local people into what had generally been regarded as skilled operations (e.g. knitters). In the early 1960s the sales in one of the seasons dropped dramatically, but this did not seem to concern the management, possibly because this kind of variation was normal. Some seasons are a financial failure and this is accepted as typical. Had the local management looked into the shops of the retail outlets they would have noticed that there were an increasing number of styles which had a complex stitch geometry and were multicoloured. However, the local management did not carry out this kind of observation. Indeed they were largely insensitive to environmental developments in the marketing area. Why was this?

Marketing was largely carried out by the major retailer who placed orders with the headquarters of Harp Mill Enterprises. The orders included exact specifications for the manufacture of the outerwear. The details were so specific that they set out the number of stitches round a buttonhole and the length of brown sticking paper to be used on fastening down cartons of completed goods. The management at Harp Mill were able to use these detailed specifications to set up the machinery for knitting and to establish quality. Their existence and importance were widely known throughout the factory and management could and did use them as a support to its own authority in appealing for high-quality work.

The management at Harp Mill had no great experience of marketing or of product development and innovation. When the factory was instructed to recruit a designer and begin its own development there was considerable consternation. The new designer reported directly to the general manager and attempted to have experimental styles made up. The introduction of a larger number of experimental and short runs into the factory had a range of consequences for the operators (e.g. earnings) and management (e.g. advice and supervision). By the end of some three months hardly any of the styles had been successfully completed yet there was considerable pressure to have samples ready for the buyers from the retail chain to consider. It may be seen that the relationship between the manufacturer and the dealer had changed. The dealer was able in part to pre-empt public demand and respond to changes by switching sources. His technology and belief system were flexible to this, but this was not the case at Harp Mill.

At the factory the general gloom created by falling orders and the despair arising from the attempts at product innovation were increased when new advanced knitting machines were brought in and there were changes in the kinds of raw materials used. This later change affected operators at every stage in the production sequence. Some members of top management began to show signs of exhaustion and strain at the difficulties of handling their own internal problems in the face of criticisms from headquarters and pressure from the retailer. At this point members of headquarters staff began to intervene more actively in an attempt to stabilize the situation.

The operators, faced by a number of product innovations, found that their existing knowledge was insufficient and began to seek advice on techniques of working from supervisors, who were not usually able to provide it, and from their colleagues and other people at different stages in production sequence. This discussing of work is not unusual; in fact, despite extensive training there is still a necessity for a high degree of informal discussion when seasonal changes come in.

Management's reaction to the increased level of task-based discussion was to try to tighten up discipline and to define roles more precisely. Thus at a time when the degree of uncertainty for the operator was increased, the response by management was to remove one of the customary means for reducing uncertainty. It may be argued that in this situation the specificity of tasks and roles was being increased.

In a similar way the amount of horizontal communication within management decreased. It may be argued that the 'management system' had moved towards the mechanistic type (Burns & Stalker 1961). Was this an appropriate response? And if it was not, what alternatives were there and how could they be implemented?

The prescriptive analysis of the relationship between product innovation and management systems by Burns and Stalker might suggest that in the new situation of product innovation an organic management system would be more appropriate. Suppose we accept this as the correct diagnosis, then the next question is how does one introduce a new system of decision-making. We do not wish to take the analysis further or answer the question, but rather to use this example as an illustration of 'organizational learning' (Dill 1962). Harp Mill is a good case of an enterprise which has a limited repertory of performance strategies; when a new situation arose there was no one to advise on the kinds of response that were appropriate. Perhaps more significant, people were unable to see the kind of 'organizational perspective' presented in the previous paragraphs. The whole picture was seen in terms of personalities rather than structural features, consequently the response was at the level of personalities (e.g. sackings and replacements) rather than structure (e.g. organizational development). There was a total unawareness that if managers are located for long periods in the kind of environment of Harp Mill, they will develop only one kind of response.

The second example concerns the 'failure' of a plant-wide productivity scheme at a large manufacturing enterprise in the south-east of England. My interest in this was aroused by some doubts about the recommendations of McGregor for Scanlon-type incentive schemes (Strauss & Sayles 1957). The scheme – not a Scanlon plan, but based upon it – had been introduced to a site which contained three semi-autonomous production units. Each unit faced a different market environment and had a distinct character and history. Despite these differences, all three factories were lumped together in the same payment scheme. From the data collected we shall only be concerned with one aspect – the implication of a payment system which is based on the enterprise for relations between the three component plants. Over the period in which the plan was operating it became apparent that a whole new range of unforeseen conflicts between occupational groups and the factories was emerging. For the first time they had been exposed to each other by being connected through the payment system. These conflicts increased and, by the time the scheme was removed, it was being said that the enterprise had eroded fifty years of good industrial relations.

McGregor's arguments for Scanlon and his interpretation of their original success emphasized psychological factors and ignored organizational aspects, including the environment of industrial relations into which Scanlon originally introduced his proposals in the 1930s. Looking at the scheme from an organizational perspective, there were a number of prior requirements in organizational terms which would have to be satisfied. Strauss & Sayles have identified some of these in their study of Scanlon in two situations (Strauss & Sayles 1957). One requirement was that the scheme should bring together groups or departments which had separate or conflicting interests (from Dill 1958). This aspect is a critical one in organizational design. For example, Litwak has used the idea of 'mechanism of segregation' to indicate the ways in which conflicting interests are held apart in enterprises; Etzioni has pointed to the differences in patterns of compliance between departments and to changes in compliance over time; more recently, Lawrence and Lorsch have explored inter-departmental relations, and Hickson *et al.* have developed a 'strategic contingencies theory of intra-organizational power' (Litwak 1961; Etzioni 1961; Lawrence & Lorsch 1968; Hickson *et al.* 1970). All these researchers have identified the practical and theoretical significance of intra-organizational relations. In the case of the study of the plant-wide incentive it was found that this aspect had not been considered by the consultant installing it. In a personal interview, the consultant reported that this aspect was relatively unimportant.

In this section we have sought to indicate some features of the 'organizational perspective'. It is worth noting that when Miller and Rice developed their work on the organizational perspective they increasingly emphasized intra-organizational boundaries and their significance to the design process. At the same time they became somewhat more critical of the utility of the human resources approach. In the next section we introduce the strategy devised to handle the problems in organizational design that we have identified.

ALTERNATIVES AND DIFFERENCES APPROACH (ADA)

Organizational design involves the utilization of design strategies and research strategies. The former are required to generate alternative systems of organization and the latter to help in the selection and the planning of change.

One of the features of the research strategy in organizational design is that the practitioner is dealing with the unique characteristics of a single enterprise, whereas the ideas he abstracts from the general body of understanding and knowledge are based upon a wide range of cases and are in the form of generalizations (Lippitt 1953). In some cases the practitioner must use his judgement in areas which are still controversial. For example, the findings and interpretation of Goldthorpe about the instrumental attitudes (orientations) of workers in Luton are the subject of questioning for a wide variety of reasons (Daniel 1969). We would argue that the practitioner's role is to start with the basic question: 'how far and in what ways have the orientations of different sectors of the workforce at the client enterprise been "moulded" by forces from inside and outside the enterprise?' The practitioner also needs to know the mechanisms by which the orientations are transmitted to new members and are sustained.

We feel that the design of systems of organization is too serious a matter to be left to the whims of one fashionable mode of thought or another. The dangers of package deals are that they are applied in situations where they do not and could not work. Thus we have argued that the preference for participative management is a matter of personal and collective values, whereas its appropriateness is a matter for investigation.

At CCE Ltd an attempt was made to adopt an approach which began with a total picture of the firm and its environment. Previous studies had, directly and indirectly, indicated that there were market and technological features which in part determine the levels at which particular types of decisions are made and the content of, for example, the production supervisor's role. We sought to collect such data and to construct an 'organizational map' that we could use to locate the kinds of constraints being presented to us in the design process. Additionally, of course, we were able to utilize this 'map' to indicate to others how their choices affected the decision-making system.

Two facts about the study at CCE Ltd illustrate the importance of starting with a total picture. First, in this particular firm, the throughput time for the whole process is to be reduced from a period of approximately 100 hours to approximately 5 hours. This means that the functional interdependence of departments as they are known at present is dramatically altered. Functional autonomy is an aspect of interdepartmental relations that has been identified as an important ingredient in determining the form that conflict within the enterprise will take, though not its extent (Van Doorn 1964; Katz, F. E. 1968). We also have some evidence to show that changes in functional autonomy affect interpersonal relations within a department (March & Simon 1958). These points refer to changes in boundaries inside an enterprise. This is one aspect which traditional behavioural scientists seem to have neglected (Jones 1969) but is a feature of considerable importance, as the case study will show. The second aspect of importance is the merging together of three factories which have existed for several decades as semi-autonomous entities. Thus not only will the new factory represent a new technology with distinctive and unmet man–machine problems, but also it implicitly assumes a totally new set of social relationships. Early on in the consultancy we learnt that few people in CCE Ltd had any conception of how relations would change. For this reason we set out to emphasize the differences between the existing social structures and the one which was being planned for the new site. The intention is that this kind of information and insight will help both in the design process and in the planning of change.

Given that we believe organizational design to be too serious to be left to uninformed whim or fashion, we have, therefore, sought to develop a language of concepts and examples specifically to meet the needs of those involved in the first stages of the design process. We have tried to illuminate the existing social structure and to show how it will be transformed by the technological imperatives of the new production system, and to outline the kinds of alternative which exist. We have seen our approach as adopting two strategic areas of emphasis.

The first emphasis is upon the development of *alternative designs*. As practitioners, we attempted to see how far there were possibilities of altering the technology to accommodate different systems of organization.

The second emphasis we have called the *differences approach*. We have aimed to delineate the major social and organizational features and the established custom and practice, and to account for their origins. This has required a historical and organizational perspective. The 'map' of the present situation has then been compared with the plans for the future. Given that there are known changes in technology, it is possible to subtract these from the existing plans (Chapters 3 and 5). In this way major organizational differences may be identified and it is possible to focus upon the social and psychological issues they imply. We know now, for example, that whatever kind of organizational design is finally in operation there will be considerable changes in occupations, differentials, power relations, and the roles of production management. The aim of the emphasis upon differences is to point to areas which we consider are problem areas and so to anticipate some of the consequences of the move.

The Alternatives and Differences Approach has emerged from our work as consultants. It is one we have found to be flexible and meaningful. We have used it in joint investigations and design sessions with members of CCE Ltd at a variety of levels. In this way, we have sought to build in a social-science-using capability (Wilson 1969; Cherns 1968) and to create a body of local knowledge within CCE Ltd which is pertinent to the particular changes being faced.

SUMMARY

Organizational design is a new and emergent activity concerned with the designing of systems of organization, including coordination, control, and decision-making. It aims to tackle the whole enterprise and therefore may be regarded as systemic in emphasis (Katz & Kahn 1966). Previously the design of the organization had occurred largely as an unintended consequence of the activities of production engineers (Woodward 1964) and management (Chandler 1962). Increasingly, behavioural science practitioners are becoming involved.

There are few documented examples of organizational design to serve as 'role-models' for practitioners and managers. The aim of this book is to develop a theory and practice for organizational design. Part of the input for the enterprise will be a new language derived selectively from the behavioural sciences. Also there will be an increase in the using of 'organizational maps' (Chapter 4).

One of the most significant points about organizational design is that it is the only approach which deals with the aspects of the work situation identified by Herzberg as being critical to the performance and motivation of the employee. These aspects all concern the job itself, the possibilities it offers for control, autonomy, and advancement. Curiously these aspects have been effectively delegated to industrial engineering and similar functions. Management has retained control over the factors that Herzberg identified as satisfiers rather than motivators (e.g. payment and styles of supervision).

The behavioural scientist must relate the general body of knowledge to each particular enterprise. In each situation the job, social structure, traditions, community, and so on must be investigated before a conclusion is reached to the effect that a particular approach (e.g. job enlargement) will be appropriate. Earlier we included an example of the inappropriate application of a plant-wide incentive scheme.

It is highly likely that the position of the behavioural scientist in the design process will differ from that of, for example, the industrial engineer, and there will certainly be areas of confrontation (Chapter 5).

In the next chapter the main features of CCE Ltd are introduced and the work of their design group is explained.

PART TWO

Case study I

CHAPTER THREE

CCE Ltd and CUSSR

CCE LTD

CCE Ltd is a subsidiary company in one of the larger British companies. It was founded in the nineteenth century. At present there are more than 7,000 employees at the major site, which is located in Provincial City.

CCE Ltd manufactures a consumer good in bulk quantities and distributes it through an extensive network of wholesale and retail outlets. The brand image is well established and the Company now holds more than 25 per cent of the total market. The size of the market is static though there are signs that there will be changes in its composition, perhaps even fragmentation.

The existing production arrangements are situated in several different buildings of three-to-five floors on one site, which is cut in half by a busy road. These buildings, parts of which have been standing for more than forty years, are considered to lead to several kinds of inefficiency. Their spatial configuration prohibits the introduction of advanced means of production. Thus it would be difficult to automate the first stage of the production process because there are three semi-autonomous factories and it would not be technically sensible to separate this part of the production from the next, and it is felt that it would be inefficient to continue with three separate factories. In a similar way, the spatial configurations make it almost impossible to take advantage of new developments in mechanization, particularly in the cost-critical areas of linkages between departments. Because of the requirements of dispatch and distribution, it is necessary to arrange a complex internal distribution network to ensure that combinations of brands can be economically distributed. These points and others have influenced CCE Ltd in its appraisal of the relationship between projected demand, marketing policy, and production facilities. One consequence of this appraisal was a feasibility study of a proposal to transfer bulk production lines to a new site. The feasibility study was completed by 1967 and the proposal for the new factory was publicly announced with guarantees against redundancy.

At the chosen site CCE Ltd proposed to build a factory which would be technologically very advanced. In addition to the technological developments, the Company aims to introduce a shift system and to change the method of payment. It also has a strong interest in recent publicity given to management philosophy, particularly with reference to motivation, work satisfaction, and leisure. Interest in these subjects had arisen from contact with certain social science studies which they have noted in journals and at courses and conferences. This interest has received active and constructive support from some of the senior executives.

The headquarters of CCE Ltd, Marketing, Research and Development, and most of the production facilities are situated in Provincial City. The sales force is distributed throughout the United Kingdom and there are also production facilities situated some distance from Provincial City.

A major part of the case study is concerned with the design stage of a new factory to be built some miles from the existing site. Each of the three factories at present in operation has a similar production system, but there are important differences between them both in technology and in the kinds of products manufactured. Factory A, the smallest, produced the traditional lines on which the Company had built its reputation. It had the least-advanced technology. Factory C was the largest, produced the new lines which were helping CCE Ltd to build up its share of the market, and was the main focus for technological innovation and experimentation. Factory B was midway between A and C.

Up to the 1960s the factories had been almost totally autonomous. This position had gradually changed, with the introduction of centralized 'control' of production and manning. 'Control' is perhaps best understood as 'Scheduling', but its usage by the young (relatively!) and rising management stratum accurately reflects their beliefs about production and its problems.

The introduction of controls and measured performance criteria had gradually centralized the production decisions to senior production management. It was accompanied by a gradual loss of autonomy for each of the factories and the main departments within them.

The history of the period 1955–1970 for CCE Ltd was one of increasing predictability about the production function. The Company was steadily moving from a 'production orientation' to a focus upon marketing and technical development.

CE LTD AND THE AZIMUTH GROUP

Early in 1967 the Company formally constituted a small team of nine men who were given the task of designing the new factory. For some members of the team this was to be a full-time activity and for others it meant new duties in addition to existing ones. The members of this group were to be focal agents for the design process. We have given them the pseudonym of Azimuth. The nine members were drawn from Research and Development (3), Production (3), Industrial Relations, Finance, and Engineering Services (one each). There was no representative from Marketing.

Azimuth was largely responsible for generating, monitoring, and guiding the design of the new factory. It was directly responsible to the Board and two members of Azimuth held positions on the Board as Directors. As a group it had a high proportion of young men, mainly in the 35–40 age-range. All had had considerable exposure to specialist and general courses at a variety of management centres and all had worked in cooperation with consultants.

During 1967 the chairmanship of Azimuth was held by the dynamic General Manager for Production. He had wide experience of the Company's operations both in this country and abroad. He had also taken an interest in 'new approaches' to management and was keenly interested in the behavioural sciences, particularly the work of various American specialists. On a visit to North America in 1966 he had been impressed by the general concern he found for 'participative' and 'consultative' styles of management and had toured factories where these styles had been introduced.

The Chairman and the Industrial Relations representative were both concerned to ensure that the 'human side of the enterprise' was taken account of in the new factory. They did not find this an easy task. Their colleagues were not unsympathetic, but they certainly found it difficult to discuss ideas like 'participative management'. One of them recalled attending some lectures on ergonomics and suggested that ergonomists would be a useful additional input to the design process. In their minds ergonomists would be able to tackle both the 'man–machine system' aspect and the 'organizational system'. Following a somewhat unsympathetic and mixed reception to a first paper on the management styles for the new factory, the

Industrial Relations Manager suggested that ergonomists should be brought in to look at certain anticipated problems of noise and social isolation.

A team of ergonomists became involved in a general advisory capacity in mid 1967 and continued their work through that year. One member of the ergonomics team felt that the problems of social isolation and motivation were more in the area of competence of social psychologists and sociologists, and so invited CCE Ltd to meet Albert Cherns, who was Professor of Social Sciences at Loughborough University of Technology. Cherns became associated in May 1967, when he visited CCE Ltd to discuss the possibilities of advisory work. At the end of that meeting he felt that a useful input could be made, but that there would be a number of problems in explaining how this should be achieved.

Meanwhile the 'human side' was being approached on two fronts. Within the Company as a whole the General Production Manager was actively supporting the 'professionalization' and rationalization of the management of the three factories. Administrative changes planned and envisaged included MBO, new payment systems, changes in job titles, alterations to management structure, and changes in staff–worker status. At the same time, within Azimuth, he was attempting to obtain a detailed consideration of the management styles that would be appropriate to the new factory.

Within Azimuth and the Board these ideas encountered mixed reactions. For example, some members said that CCE Ltd had always practised McGregor's Theory Y form of approach to motivation, while others said Theory X predominated and was most appropriate. At that time, to the best of our knowledge, no one had any thoughts of using outside consultants to investigate the issue. In so far as there were thoughts of using outside behavioural scientists the thinking was mainly in terms of using such schemes (administrative inventions) as Blake's Managerial Grid.

By May 1967 the Azimuth Group had to hand a general outline of what the new factory should be like in technological and manpower terms. They had constructed a 'map' of the new technology by estimating the kinds of technological innovation which were, in their opinion, feasible. On the basis of this they had estimated the total numbers of persons required to man the new technology. The technical 'designs' had been collated and a sketch of the layout of the new factory constructed.

The General Production Manager, his deputy, and a member of the Board formed the group which represented the aims of Azimuth to Cherns and myself when we met them in June 1967. These three formed the basic link between Azimuth and ourselves during 1967. The Deputy General Manager of Production became the key linkman. This is a role which managers may find themselves playing and is one which we consider to be critical to the successful coupling of behavioural scientists and enterprises. We will examine this aspect in more detail in a later chapter. At the end of 1967 we had a double change in that the linkman was promoted to another job and a new Chairman took over Azimuth.

PREPARING TO MEET THE AZIMUTH GROUP

Cherns first visited CCE Ltd in late May 1967. At that meeting he discussed in general terms the possibilities for consultancy. Azimuth outlined the problem areas which they considered a behavioural scientist could clarify and resolve. The topics presented included amenities in the factory itself and for members of the Company in general; social isolation at work; noise; motivation; layout of plant and windowless buildings. Cherns indicated that some of the topics would be most fruitfully tackled by the behavioural scientist. Further, some problems were of more interest than others, and some could be tackled quite simply by a literature search. He arranged for the topic of windowless buildings to be examined, under his supervision, by an outside agency, and also offered to send the representatives of Azimuth a series of questions which would form the basis for the next meeting. This was arranged for early June.

Back at Loughborough there were a number of initial questions which we had to ask ourselves: could we make a useful contribution? Would a behavioural science consultancy be feasible with CCE Ltd? What did they expect? Were we interested? What would we offer to do?

We decided that we were interested in the *possibilities* the project would offer for tackling areas that we hoped were of mutual interest. Neither Cherns nor I was interested in producing reports to be placed on managers' shelves – though I am sure we eventually did – or in carrying out attitude surveys (see Chapters 8 and 9). We were both interested in the problems of finding systems of organization that were appropriate to the requirements of production technologies and that matched the social characteristics of the workforce. We could not decide on the basis of one meeting whether the project was feasible; that had to be left to a later stage.

We next prepared a set of questions so that certain basic data would be ready for us at the next meeting. There were a number of topics on which we wanted to have a general appreciation. With reference to the manning estimates for the future factory, we wanted to know how many working groups there would be and also their probable composition. This and other questions had a double function. On the one hand, these were data we required, and, on the other, we hoped that the definition of 'group' which we had included would start someone thinking about the detailed aspects of the new organization. Other questions probed the areas of the content and frequency of communications between supervisors and their work groups, and between working groups; the importance of visual control to supervision and management; the limitations set by maintenance requirements on the siting of machines; and what initial considerations had been given to systems of organization. A further set of questions concerned motivation, status, and payment systems.

MEETING AZIMUTH

The meeting consisted of a short exposition on the current activities of Azimuth and a request for clarification on the kind of advice we thought we could offer; after this, we toured one of the main factories and were shown the experimental work on new machinery being carried out by R & D. Towards the end of this tour we were shown sketch plans of proposed layouts. Finally, we returned to the conference room to discuss our observations.

Five members of CCE Ltd came to our briefing. They outlined the main changes in technology which were being proposed, including both the role of online process control and the integrated information control system. We then went out on the tour of the factory. This was particularly useful since it gave us a good idea of how the technological changes we had just been hearing about would affect the factory. In addition to suggesting a number of important questions to be answered later the tour included one important incident. Towards the end we had gone to examine the sketch layouts. In looking through these we asked a number of questions about the siting and grouping of machinery and the consequences of this for manning and organization. The answers were honest, but not very helpful to us except in revealing the criteria that had actually been used to allocate roles to tasks. At the time we did not accord a great deal of attention to the discussion.

On returning to the conference room we asked a number of questions relating to the tour. Then the Chairman intervened to report that he had heard about the discussion of the layouts. He was interested in the idea that forms of layout and manning might facilitate or hinder the achievement of production targets and 'good management-to-employee relations' and inquired whether it would be possible to investigate this aspect.

Cherns agreed that it would, but that it would take time and would only be a satisfactory piece of work if it was jointly undertaken by members of the Company and ourselves. This was in fact a critical point in our minds. We felt that we had seen a large number of glossy reports containing summaries of the inquiries and findings of academic behavioural scientists. In most cases these appeared to be placed on office shelves rather than become part of the decision-making apparatus. We considered, in general terms, that this was an unsatisfactory way of getting utilization of the competences of behavioural scientists. With regard to the particular proposal for advising on the organizational systems of a new factory, we felt that this would require a close interdependence between CCE's technical experts and ourselves.

Looking back at that meeting, the one idea which stands out is that of the 'dialogue'. It was suggested that the relationship between Azimuth and ourselves should take the form of a dialogue and that any reports and recommendations arising out of our work should be be seen as records of joint activities.

The idea of the 'dialogue' had some appeal to Azimuth, but they were clearly puzzled about the form it would take. The Company's main experience with consultants and other external groups was that of commissioning a specific piece of work which could not conveniently be carried out by their own specialists. However, it was agreed that any relationship should take the form of a 'dialogue'. This agreement did not mean that we all placed the same interpretation on 'dialogue', but this will become more apparent in the following chapters.

At the close of the meeting the representatives of Azimuth indicated a strong interest in consultancy by behavioural scientists. At the same time they clearly stated that they recognized that such a project should have some value to the research interests of the behavioural scientists.[1] Later the form the consultancy took will be examined in more detail, for the moment it is important to note the kinds of factors which were favouring a successful relationship. For example, as behavioural scientists we were working with a set of managers who had a real and significant problem to tackle. These managers and executives all occupied senior positions and were used to taking a long-term perspective. Furthermore, there was already an internal issue – participative management – within Azimuth and the Board which we could help in clarifying and resolving.

AZIMUTH'S CONCEPTION OF THE CONSULTANCY

Azimuth's initial conception of the content of the consultancy may be considered under the following headings:

Major areas of interest
— the size and shape of working areas
— the provision of artificial and natural lighting, including window-less buildings

Secondary areas of interest
— environmental working conditions including atmosphere, noise, etc.,
— design of entrances and stairways

Machinery layouts
— grouping of machines within main working areas
— design of individual machines to improve operating conditions for employees

Motivation
— desirability of separate entrances, dining-rooms, for different levels of employee
— colour schemes
— provision of tea bars, restaurants, and recreational facilities.

This was the first set of headings drawn up by one member of Azimuth. We were asked to indicate whether we could advise, how we would proceed, the assistance required from the company, and likely costs.

The headings clearly reflect the fact that the initial relationship

---

[1] Our main research interest was in the investigation of the relations between behavioural scientists and users of their competences.

which Azimuth established was with ergonomists. As advisers, the ergonomists approached problems in a way which members of the Company felt they could understand. It appeared that ergonomists could refer to a 'body of knowledge' and carry out 'scientific experiments'. Also the Company had had previous experience with ergonomists working on specific man-machine problems. CCE Ltd had usually been able to spell out in precise terms what they expected and when.

It is fair to say that Azimuth found some considerable difficulty in framing precise terms of reference for behavioural scientists. Between mid 1967 and January 1968 the terms of reference were amended a number of times. Each of these alterations indicated a move away from the ergonomic focus initially taken, to an emphasis upon motivation and organization (see Chapter 5).

OUR DEFINITION OF THE PROJECT

We believed that the critical decision facing Azimuth was in the choice of 'control systems' for the new factory. Previous researches had already indicated that management has a choice of control system, but there is a tendency to think within the bounds of existing experience when making a choice. Existing experience can in some cases be irrelevant since the known situation can be significantly altered by changes in, for example, mechanization and automation. Azimuth had in part recognized this problem, but in attempting to resolve it had turned for help to the literature on 'participative management'. Much of this literature is in ambiguous form and is difficult to utilize in practical terms. For example, members of CCE Ltd could not agree on whether the Company was characterized by Theory Y ideas of motivation or not.

The subject of 'participation' implies an examination of the decision-making apparatus of the Company. The first briefing on the proposed technological innovations and the tour of the factory had indicated that there would be considerable changes in both the content and level at which decisions were taken. The idea of 'centralized information systems' and closer linking of the departments are good examples of this. Clearly the existing management structure would be considerably altered, especially the areas of autonomy in decision-making. These changes reflected largely technological changes, but these were interdependent with changes in the relative importance of Marketing and R & D in comparison with Production.

Though some of the early literature on 'participative management' includes an analysis of market and technological factors, these two important factors had gradually become less salient in the published accounts of the success of 'participative management'.[1] In the case of CCE Ltd, both technological and market characteristics would be important in determining the kind of production system which was created and the levels at which decision-making would take place. These points are inherent in the way *we* utilized the idea of socio-technical systems, but appeared to be neglected in the design of the new factory. CCE Ltd's actual approach to design had many of the features which Eric Miller had found in his study of the building of a new steelworks (Miller 1962). The major problem is therefore one of breaking out of this traditional approach and ensuring that organizational design is concurrent with plant design and that the two are thought of as being interdependent.

In late June we expressed these ideas in the following terms:

> When we think about the processes that are involved in the light of the information we have so far, it appears to us that the critical area of organizational choice before you lies in the choice of systems of control; and in deciding among these, you will be taking into account factors which include, for example, the degree of variation in your supplies and in demand for your output; and also some aspects of the processes, in particular some of the time characteristics. So that we can more fully understand these issues, we shall need to have further discussion, particularly with your R & D and production control people.

> What we would do with this information is as follows. Starting from the brief sketch plans of the new factory and from the information which you have already given us and the further information we hope to obtain, we shall aim to trace out a kind of sketch of the activity structure that these will imply. From this we would also try to tease out the pattern of communications that will take place between operatives and between groups and from this deduce what kind of social structure is implied. You and we will then be able to compare this structure with the goals that you have set before yourselves and the criteria for adequate functioning of a system of control.

---

[1] Compare, for example, the treatment of market factors in the two studies published by Likert (1961, 1967).

It may be seen from this that the aim was to juxtapose and compare three sets of information – a sketch of the implied social system, the goals of Azimuth for their ideal social system, and the body of ideas that behavioural scientists had built up about the appropriateness of different forms of 'control system'.

This method of working required an analysis of the existing technical plans and proposals for layout and also the market characteristics of CCE Ltd. Earlier research studies had suggested that decisions made by firms about the market they will aim to supply ultimately affect the form of production system, the job structure of the firm, and other important features (Woodward 1965; Chandler 1962).

Looking at the proposed technological innovations it could be seen that there would inevitably be changes in many existing roles and also probable changes in the shape and content of the 'skill hierarchy'. These were defined as potential problem areas irrespective of the move to a new site. The transferring of people from the three separate factories to one new one could also be the source of problems irrespective of any technological changes. This aspect could be viewed as a 'mini-merger'. The combination of both kinds of change did not necessarily increase the problems, but this had to be considered.

The general aims of our work were to identify and anticipate the problems of adjustment created by the move and by the new technology. Such aims are not easy to articulate and are extremely difficult to communicate. Consequently, we were anxious to start investigating the market and technological aspects in order to locate more precisely some of the crucial problem areas where we felt we would be able to make contributions. This work began in July and was the start of the consultancy.

It is always difficult to decide where an organizational design project should start. There are three interdependent areas to be reconciled – the organization's exchanges with its environment; the internal coordination of departments and functions; the 'grass-roots' level. It is necessary to have background data on each of these before focusing upon any one. The project was initially framed in terms of the 'grass-roots' level. The organizational design process may be thought of in the following way (*Figure 3*).

This diagram shows that the design of the new departments could not be separated from the design of the management system and

Figure 3   Factory–environment linkages

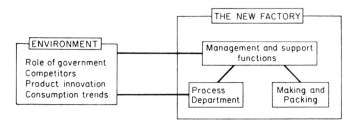

the actualities of the external environment (e.g. market fragmentation).

DIFFERENCES IN EXPECTATIONS

There were two main differences in expectations between Azimuth and ourselves. The first concerns the meaning of 'dialogue' and the second the actual content of our activities. The aspects are closely interwoven.

Azimuth had no precise idea of what the behavioural scientists were doing or could contribute. They had never used behavioural scientists before and their definition of the subject was, with one important exception, closely bound up with the ideas of Likert and McGregor.

Azimuth expected to receive reports at pre-agreed time intervals setting out the objectives of work undertaken, progress to date, and future intentions. We expected to be working *with* members of R & D and not to be involved in the collection and examination of data and in the generation of alternative sociotechnical designs.

OVERVIEW OF THE CONSULTANCY (JUNE 1967 TO MARCH 1970)

The greater part of the time in the first 30 months of the consultancy was concerned with the design of the new organization. This consisted of the critical appraisal of existing plans and the generation of alternative sociotechnical designs for the main production departments. It also included some work on the management system and the general area of 'management philosophy'. Apart from the emphasis upon generating and appraising plans for the new factory, there was a continuous process of identifying the differences in relationships between the existing and the proposed situations. This focus upon differences was intended to highlight the ways in which the forms of relations within and between groups would be changed.

The whole of this work may be thought of as extending and clarifying the ideas of the Azimuth Group. They were responsible for 'mobilizing' the motivations of people at all levels who were affected by the change. It was hoped that the consultancy would provide Azimuth with a general language for explaining the human side of the change at the stage of organization-building.

'Planned Change' as an idea has existed for behavioural science practitioners for some time. In fact, they have given more emphasis to this than to organizational design. There already exist a number of suggested routes for management to follow when considering the 'human aspects' of technological innovation. We are using the term 'organization-building' in preference to 'planned change', because the latter idea has been approached in the past with an almost arithmetical calculativeness. It has been suggested that managements can use survey data on attitudes to calculate the impact of proposed changes on particular groups. Such schemes have an air of neatness and precision which may well appeal, but they do not reflect the reality of changes which are known to managers and have been investigated by researchers.

Allan Flanders showed in the study of the Fawley Productivity Agreements that there was considerable internal turmoil associated with the change (Flanders 1964). He spoke of 'working through' the ideas in the Blue Book to gain the support of key personnel and groups. The picture he presented does not readily suggest that changes *can* be achieved without tension, as some writers have suggested (Mumford & Banks 1967).

The behavioural science practitioner rarely has the detailed knowledge and local knowhow of, for example, an industrial relations executive. Though some writers on management have suggested that there is a 'diagnostic role' for the behavioural scientist it should not be forgotten that there are in most large enterprises well-established personnel departments containing people with considerable practical experience. This in fact was very much the kind of position in CCE Ltd. Thus while it is correct to assert that part of the consultancy was concerned with 'organization-building' our role was in many ways an extension of existing competences within CCE Ltd. This is an important point because the studies of the systems of organization contained in the later part of the case study were in part aimed at 'planned organizational change'. It is important to note that the final decisions were taken by Azimuth.

In effect what we are saying is this. The case study outlines and analyses a consultancy project on organizational design and organization-building for a new factory. For CCE Ltd the major part of the design of the new factory concerned technical and financial decisions, and our consultancy was only part of the examination of the human aspect. The role we occupied is one which we see emerging in major enterprises in Europe and America. It is in part an activity for Personnel Research. We predict that all major enterprises will have large personnel research departments by the year 1975. What may seem unusual today will be commonplace tomorrow!

The consultancy may be thought of most conveniently in six overlapping phases as follows:

Dates	Length (*months*)	Principal activities
1. June–Sept. 1967	4	Establishment of consultancy; scan of main features of the environment and the Company; feasibility study; establishing the key problem areas.
2. Oct. 1967–Jan. 1968	4	A study of the impact of technological change on the female crews operating the packing machines; identification of what we meant by 'organizational design' and the 'dialogue'. A period of confrontations.
3. Feb.–June 1968	5	A sociotechnical design study of the Processing Department. Carried out on a joint basis and largely successful.
4. July 1968–Feb. 1969	8	A sociotechnical design study of the Making and Packing Departments to generate alternative designs; writing the first report on the project and feeding it back to Azimuth; meeting architects; designing a study of

Dates	Length (*months*)	Principal activities
		the social system of the existing departments in the three factories. A detailed study of management in one factory.
5. March–Nov. 1969	9	A study of the Making and Packing Departments in the three factories (a) to determine the characteristic orientations to work of different categories of worker (b) to identify the main social structural features, the aspects that were of salience and indifference to workers, and the extent of conflicting interests.
		These data were required for two purposes. First, to make decisions about the most appropriate forms of organizations and layout. Second, to plan the next phase of organization-building (i.e. the planning of change). This period included the writing of the second annual report.
6. Dec. 1969–May 1970	6	An extension of the study of orientations and social structure to an investigation of the 'indirect workers' who will play an increasingly significant role in the new factory.

In the early phases of the consultancy emphasis was given to the ways in which the proposed technological innovations would alter and in some areas shatter the existing social system. Later, increasing attention was given to the ways in which the characteristics of the existing social systems in the three factories should be considered in the design of the new and the transfer of people to the new factory.

During all these phases data were collected on the ways in which the roles of maintenance, supervision, and management would be affected.

During the design stage much of the work was a joint activity involving both 'short-life project groups' with specific tasks (e.g. the sociotechnical design of the Processing Department) and also some of, or the whole of, Azimuth. Thus there have been continuing inputs to various individuals and groups at different levels in CCE Ltd. Such a tactic is likely to create piecemeal adaptations of parts of the organization. It should be noted that we have not attempted to create an organizational blueprint. Our raw material – people – and their interface with a wide range of uncontrollable variables makes that kind of concept premature and utopian.

CENTRE FOR UTILIZATION OF SOCIAL SCIENCE RESEARCH (CUSSR)

The Centre was established at Loughborough University of Technology in 1967 by Professor Albert Cherns. Members of the Centre have one or more of the following three interests – promoting applications of the behavioural sciences in the military, industrial, educational, and hospital spheres; in carrying out research, which may be on institutions and organizations, but is primarily concerned with studying the ways in which enterprises and the government utilize the social and behavioural sciences; running a Graduate Training Centre for teaching behavioural science practitioners.

'Applications' refers to the active support and involvement given to projects involving the use of behavioural scientists in problem-solving activities. For example, in early 1970 there were two long-term projects with government departments and four medium-term projects with industrial and commercial enterprises. A unique feature of this aspect of the Centre's work is that many of the consultancies are concerned with organizational and institutional design.

'Research' covers two main areas. First, there is the small unit of three full-time Research Fellows, a Research Assistant, Cherns and myself, which is engaged in studying the uses made of the behavioural sciences by governments and enterprises. This work is financed by the Social Science Research Council.[1] Second, research includes an interest in the study of voluntary associations, organizations, and institutions. Current work includes studies of rehabilitation units and the Cooperative Movement.

'Teaching' refers to the Graduate Teaching Centre. This is con-

[1] The study of applications was made possible by SSRC grant HR. 86/1 from 1967–1971 to Professor A. B. Cherns and P. A. Clark.

cerned with postgraduate work for the behavioural science practitioner. The course takes persons qualified in the social and behavioural sciences whose interests are in solving practical rather than
theoretical problems. This is a matter of emphasis and should in
no way be considered to be less demanding than the conventional
career of research in the social sciences. The aim of this training is to
create first-class investigators with a high competence in technical
aspects as well as the intellectual skills necessary to develop new
concepts and adapt existing 'social inventions' (e.g. MBO), to new
situations. This last facility is particularly important because, as
Riley has argued: 'The applied sociologist cannot, for example, put
aside a problem merely because it does not lend itself to conventional
analysis. Instead, freed from the necessity of conforming to the prevailing orthodoxy, he is frequently under pressure to innovate and
must therefore improvise' (Lazarsfeld *et al.* 1967).

Organizational design is a central activity for the applied and
teaching elements of the Centre and is one of the areas being investigated by the research element (Clark & Ford 1970).

Seven members, past and present, of CUSSR have assisted on the
consultancy with CCE Ltd. The composition of this team has been
important for the work undertaken and is briefly examined now:

Project Director and Consultant	Peter Clark
Consultant	Albert Cherns
Investigators	Chris Eling
	Bernard Leach
	Janet Ford
	Pauline Mistry
	Barbara Appleby

Chris Eling and Pauline Mistry both graduated from the four-year
sandwich course in Humanities and Technology at Loughborough.
Eling was primarily interested in the technological aspects and was
responsible for much of the work done on this aspect during the
first year. Pauline Mistry had worked on the Internal Communication Project started by Revans in ten London hospitals, and consequently had some experience of action-research approaches
(Revans 1967; Wieland & Leigh 1971). Bernard Leach graduated in
sociology and from the Graduate Training Centre. Janet Ford, also
a sociologist, assisted with two pieces of investigation, but was not
otherwise involved in the consultancy. Both Janet Ford and Barbara

Appleby were members of the unit investigating the ways in which the behavioural sciences were being utilized in organizations.

Albert Cherns, Professor of Social Sciences, had at various times worked as a research psychologist, had had some responsibility for radar maintenance during the Second World War, had been a Principal Psychologist in the military, and, prior to coming to Loughborough, had been Scientific Secretary of DSIR and SSRC. His principal interests were in the social psychological aspects of the consultancy and in the general problems of obtaining utilization of existing research findings.

My own background was a degree in sociology, industrial experience in work study and personnel in the textile industry; a period as Research Fellow in Industrial Sociology at a residential management college, then to the Department of Social Sciences at Loughborough. During this period I had been interested in the possibilities for applications of behavioural science research. I was fortunate in my experience of industry in so far as the company I worked for was, at that time, as interested as most in the behavioural sciences. The experience there provided ideas both for subsequent research and for the utilization of the behavioural scientist. In the early 1960s the climate of opinion in industry, even in the large companies, was not conducive to the emergence of much worthwhile practical work. The early graduates of the behavioural sciences were at best employed in jobs that made peripheral use of their undergraduate training. This was in part inevitable, but the fact that the first practitioners were the occupational psychologists is of some importance.

Our team for the consultancy had more varied interests and experiences than many and has some of the competences of an operational research group. Three members of the team had carried out operational research assignments and several had important interests and competences outside their main areas of training. For example, Bernard Leach played an important part in examining the uses of technological forecasting.

This team was the main external input to Azimuth on the organizational aspects of the new factory. In the following chapters the consultancy is examined, from its uncertain start to the end of the organizational design phase in early 1970.

CHAPTER FOUR

Diagnosis

INTRODUCTION: PHASE I

The initial meetings had shown that the new factory would differ in a large number of ways from the existing three factories. Technical plans were already advanced and the Company were considering the choice of architects. It may therefore have seemed that we were entering into a situation that was already largely determined. Certainly the possibilities of sociotechnical designs would have seemed impossible if we had believed the time schedule for the building of the new factory. Cherns believed, on the basis of his previous experience, that CCE Ltd were misjudging the dates at which the new factory would be open and ready for occupation. If his assessment was correct then there was still time to develop sociotechnical designs. Our first strategy was to ensure that the options for this were kept open for as long as possible.

Our main area of expertise was in the design of the systems of coordination, control, and motivation. In the view of some members of Azimuth these areas could be tackled by adopting the 'participative management' approach, but in our minds the problems were more extensive and far-reaching than could be tackled in this way. The actual relevance of participative management as a style might itself be questionable. This question could only be answered by carrying out a study of the way in which the future production system would be connected to its environment. For example, Burns and Stalker had argued that the 'management system' which is most appropriate to a rapidly changing product market is quite different from that which is best suited to a static market.

Deciding which system of control was most appropriate required an organizational analysis of CCE Ltd and its environment. The environment includes relations with the government, size and composition of the market, behaviour of competitors, relationships with suppliers, and Provincial City. It is also necessary to know about the extent and kind of segmentation and integration between Marketing,

69

Research and Development (R & D), and Production (Lorsch 1965; Lawrence & Lorsch 1968, 1969). Once such data are available it is possible to carry out a closer analysis of the production system. The analytical frameworks underlying this diagnosis are explained and discussed more fully in Chapter 7.

The preceding paragraphs indicate the necessity for undertaking a thorough analysis of the firm in relation to its environment (Aguilar 1968). The first analysis is essentially a scan that attempts to locate the major features of the enterprise that are of concern to the BSP. The end-product of the scan is a characterization of the 'firm in action'. This is then used to plan the details of the next phases in a consultancy.

At the same time as the scan of CCE Ltd was being undertaken it was necessary to obtain data that would indicate whether a consultancy in organizational design was feasible. Most of the members of Azimuth were interviewed during this period. Questions were put to them about the experiences and expectations of consultants and their own ideas about the human and social problems of creating a new factory. The spread of the responses to these questions was pretty wide. Some members clearly had fixed impressions about what we would do, but found difficulty in actually expressing what form this might take. One member showed a keen insight into organizational analysis and three others were interested and sympathetic. The responses to these questions, which were mixed in with other questions, demonstrated that only one person had a thorough grasp of our intentions and one other had a pretty good idea. From this we knew at the time (1967) that there would be problems, but we did not quite envisage the form they would take.

The questions and discussions with members of CCE Ltd could be most accurately interpreted as showing that they largely saw human problems in manpower terms. That is to say, they were concerned to calculate the exact number of persons required for new plant. This calculation was carried out by noting how the numbers in existing jobs would be increased or reduced by the technical changes, and then adding to this an estimate to cover areas in which it seemed that totally new jobs would have to be created. This approach has the obvious advantage of providing data for costing the labour content of production. Also it facilitates some matching of available and required resources. Essentially this approach deals in terms of 'aggregates' of people and while it provides important basic data it does also require supplementing. Much of our work is concerned with examining the importance of 'organizational structures' and our emphasis upon structures may be seen as an integral part of our notion of organizational design (Cherns, Clark, & Sinclair 1970).

Apart from collecting data, the period of the scan was also an important opportunity to establish contacts with people inside the firm who had specialist information and advice. An important feature of obtaining a continuing and high utilization of the behavioural science input is to identify those persons who are influential in making decisions and in formulating opinion. The Dutch BSP Hutte (1968) has suggested that the BSP must locate the 'key power centres' in the firm in order to obtain utilization of advice. This seems a fairly sensible or obvious suggestion, but it is one with considerable implications for the shape taken by a consultancy and will be examined more closely in later chapters.

In addition to the field investigation at CCE Ltd, it was necessary to start literature searches in order to develop analytical frameworks suited to our concept of organizational design. The Alternatives and Differences Approach outlined in Chapter 2 emerged from this process of interplaying findings from the field studies with accounts of 'similar' situations published in the journals. In practice we found the reading of other case studies of technical change useful, but not usually for the reasons intended by their authors. At best they provided ideas that could be utilized to widen the perspective we had taken.

The findings from the first scan are presented under the following headings:

The Production Technology
The Social Systems of the Factory
The Environment – Markets, Raw Materials, Equipment Suppliers,
    and Provincial City
The Marketing Function
Research and Development

PRODUCTION TECHNOLOGY

The sociotechnical approach requires the BSP to make a record of the main features of the production technology. BSPs are not typically trained to carry out this activity, but fortunately my previous experience of techniques of recording for method changes used when I had been a member of an industrial engineering section proved useful. The advantage of these formalized methods of record-ing is that they provide a highly selective account of the technology. Initially this is all that is required at the first scan. At CCE Ltd we were able to obtain the assistance of the Work Study Department which supplied various charts and records of the existing and future plant layouts and flows of raw material.

It is also obviously useful to have a working appreciation of the methods of manufacturing. This was obtained by selecting Factory C, which contained the latest and the experimental equipment, and arranging to be shown round the plant by managers at different levels. This approach had the double advantage of providing several different pictures of the technology and of the kinds of variability that have to be handled. At the same time, it enabled the foremen and managers to ask questions about our activities. We found that they were very much at ease when we walked slowly round the de-partment examining the various pieces of machinery. Hence they felt more relaxed, at this first stage, than in a formal interview. More-over, by starting with the production technology and by explaining the reasons for doing so, we were able to establish a basis for future joint working.

There are three main factories at the existing site. Each possessed the sequence of departments shown in *Figure 4*.

The diagram shows that four main production departments existed in each factory in mid 1967. The Processing Department con-tained a number of large pieces of equipment arranged in a single sequence of operations that was unalterable. The actual equipment was in some parts very old and others relatively modern. Linkages between equipment were achieved by relatively primitive forms of mechanical transportation and in some cases required labouring. The Making and Packing Departments both contained individual machines that were in some instances technically advanced. The linkage between Processing and Making was mechanical, and be-tween Making and Packing the manufactured products were trans-ported in large carriers guided by various labourers.

An important feature of the existing production system was the length of time between the entry of the raw material and the dispatch of completed and packaged goods to the customer. In 1967 the time between point A and point E on the diagram was approximately 100 hours. A high proportion of this time was accounted for by the Processing stage and by the temporary storages at B and C. These storages did in effect act as 'buffers' between the departments and helped to create a degree of autonomy later shown to have had important consequences for the factory organizational system.

The general aims of the technological innovations were to automate wherever possible and to introduce various forms of mechanical linkage when it was economic to do so. The data we obtained on the

Figure 4   The production sequence

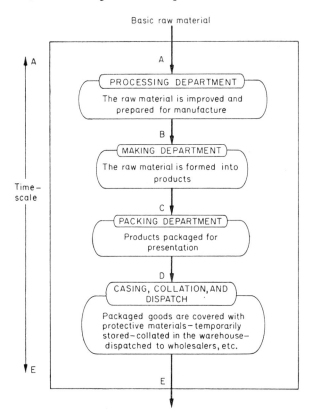

future technology demonstrated that the throughput time would be reduced from 100 hours to less than 5 hours. In more detailed terms the charts provided by Work Study indicated exactly where the time balances between stages in the manufacturing process would be altered. These charts demonstrated that the size of the 'buffer' stock between Making and Packing would be reduced from 6–10 hours to a matter of minutes. This change would have enormous implications for the intra-organizational boundary existing between the two departments.

The implications of the technical innovations would also affect the manpower required to operate the factory. The scan showed that the mechanical linkage systems into and away from the Packing Department would affect the numbers of machine operators required. This aspect is examined more closely in the following chapter.

The scan of the technology also included an analysis of the raw materials to be used in manufacturing. We know from a number of previous studies that the variability of raw materials can be an important factor in influencing the social system. Two illustrations will amplify this point. In coalmining there are, in British coal seams as compared to open-cast mining in North America, a number of distinctive features – narrow seams and faults being important examples. These distinctive features have been identified by researchers and consultants as important variables (Trist & Bamforth 1951). In a similar way it can be shown that the introduction of manmade materials into the manufacture of shoes has altered the skill hierarchy and occupational structure of firms (Bell 1966; Perrow 1967). The manmade materials have greater stability than leather and hence create fewer technical problems and require less skilled operators. Consequently, the extent of job knowledge and training is reduced. This in turn erodes the basis of craft groups. Thus it may be argued that the basis of the operators' 'influence' upon management has been reduced in the case of the shoe industry.

Changes in the composition of raw materials, particularly the extent to which they have been standardized and the sources of variation minimized, was an important factor to be investigated in CCE Ltd. The answers to the questions asked in this dimension suggested that the firm had continuously sought to reduce the amount of variation in the raw materials before they reached the factory. It was possible to trace this emphasis back over thirty years. The plans for the future included further developments in this direction. It was possible to see from these that some of the jobs in the Processing Department would be affected. This is examined in some detail in Chapter 6.

This scan of the technology enabled us to construct a 'map' of the existing and future production systems, focusing upon equipment, linkages, planned rates of throughput, raw materials, and layout. It was possible to use a great deal of the already existing data available within CCE Ltd. For example, one group of outside advisers had produced a 'map' showing how computer-based control systems could be used. This 'map' filled in a number of gaps in the total picture.

THE FACTORY AS A SOCIAL SYSTEM

From the scan of the production technology we were able to obtain a good grasp of where the major technical changes would take place. If we had been starting with a totally new labour force the next stage in the sociotechnical analysis would have been to record the 'human tasks' required to operate this new technology. This record of tasks could then be used to design the social systems. As indicated in Chapter 2, this could be achieved by applying, for example, the principles of the human resources approach (Foster 1968).

At CCE Ltd the new factory was to replace three existing factories. Thus there were already in being both the labour force to man the new factory, and the social and personality characteristics peculiar to it. In our own approach we considered the characteristics of the existing social system to be vital data. Thus we set out to make a selective record of the main features of this existing social system. The constructing of this record had largely to be undertaken by ourselves because there were no functional equivalents in the social system to the advisers and specialists on the production system. The only data to hand were statistics and a wide variety of documentation. The documents proved useful in building a background picture of 'the firm in action'.

The existing social system was important for several reasons. In a number of ways it had influenced the form in which the executives from R & D, and also from Manning, had allocated roles (jobs) to tasks. The established traditions might inhibit and facilitate different aspects of organizational design. The Company had little knowledge of how the technological changes envisaged would actually affect the social system.

There were a number of questions about the social system that had to be answered in general terms. Details could be expanded later as required. The questions included:

What is the composition of the labour force in terms of sex, age, length of service?
What are the main job categories as defined by management?

How is the labour force deployed about the factory?

What kinds of social and occupational associations and groupings exist?

What are the known characteristics of such groupings and how can they be explained?

What are the main unions, what part do union officials and shop stewards play?

What is the history of industrial relations in general terms and what variations are there between, for example, departments?

To what extent has CCE Ltd emphasized financial inducements and what forms have these taken?

What emphasis is and has been given to differential statuses by management?

What kind of 'moral' inducements are there?

What plans do management have for 'administrative rationalization'?

The following paragraphs contain a selection from the data collected under these headings.

The total labour force involved in Production as compared with, for example, Marketing, is more than 6,000 and is composed as follows:

	% *of total*	*Sex ratio* (M:F)	% *over 55*
Supervision and management	5	100M:0F	25
Staff	20	45M:55F	10 maximum
Workforce	75	40M:60F	20

Many employees have long service with CCE Ltd and a very high proportion can be classified as 'stayers'. The relative proportion of males and females varies enormously between departments. For example the entire population of indirect workers totalling approximately 1,000 is male, while in the Making and Packing Departments the females heavily outnumber the males.

The list of job categories existing at the start of the study was large and complex. The Company intended to 'rationalize' these in the future. At the time of the start of the consultancy a job evaluation scheme had been introduced which bundled a number of roles (jobs) together and 'removed anomalies' in the eyes of the management, but these developments were not always accepted by other employees.

On the existing site the labour force was scattered over a wide geographical area, and within any one building they would typically spend a large part of their time in one large room. The male maintenance workers were the most geographically mobile employees. In the existing three factories the actual density of the working population per thousand square feet was high, but though people were physically adjacent they did not necessarily have much contact. A high proportion of contacts in non-break time was based on the 'requirements' of the technology (Jasinski 1956). In practice a large sector of people were geographically fixed at their workplace. If, for example, we follow the route of a female worker into one of the factories we would find her moving through the main doors with people she did not know, climbing the stairs to her particular floor, then walking to her machine or equipment. Subsequent interviews revealed that female workers had regular 'travel routes' in and out of the factories and that their experience of the Company was very localized.

During the scan an attempt was made to locate the main social groupings (e.g. female packing crews) and to determine their interrelationship with other groups (e.g. mechanics and managers). The aim of these questions was to identify the degree of solidarity of 'occupational groups' and the likely basis for it. In the case of the female groups, the scan indicated that the female packing crews formed small cohesive groups that were part of a strong occupational group. By way of contrast there was no evidence of similar cohesiveness amongst the female workers in the Making Department.

Other questions were designed to identify the relative status of different job categories and also occupational groups where these existed. The aim here was to obtain a historical picture of changes over time. In this way it was possible also to obtain general data on major changes (e.g. a heavy reduction in the labour force of the Processing Department in the 1950s) and so gain an impression of the industrial relations background. These questions were designed to reveal ways in which relationships between individuals and groups were structured, the kinds of effect this had on levels and patterns of motivation, and the significance of these patterns for the future in the light of known technological innovations.

Two points from these questions are of immediate importance and others are included in the later chapters. First, as a general rule, CCE Ltd had adopted the 'seniority principle' for promotions. In recent times this had been queried by management, who had increasing doubts about its appropriateness to the technological demands of the new factory. Consequently a series of tests had been introduced to assess a man's aptitude for a more complex job. On the surface these innovations in administrative practice had been accepted without opposition, but in actuality the older and more long-serving employees were increasingly concerned about the implications of these and similar moves by management for their own career prospects. Second, the relative status of the Packing Department in relation to Making was high. This had been the case for a number of years. In Packing the mechanics, female packers, and senior mechanics formed cohesive 'occupational groups', and they had a history of 'influence' with management. At the existing site there was no reason to assume that this high status and preferential treatment would change. However, there had been technical changes in the making machines to allow them to manufacture a 'new' range of products introduced in the 1960s. These changes required machine operators (males) with higher skill than previously and altered the relative skill differentials and payments between members of the two departments. These changes had slow but identifiable effects on the relative status of the departments in the eyes of the younger managers particularly. The move to the new site coupled with the closer linking together of the two departments in production terms was accompanied by a proposal that each department should have approximately half of a huge open production floor. This meant that the separate social existence of the departments would be changed. One consequence of this is that the behaviour of the 'actors' in the new site would be observable (Merton 1957; Litwak 1961). We will follow through the implications of this in later chapters.

CCE's approach to rewards and inducements was also undergoing a change. In the minds of the younger managers there were ideas about 'participative management' mixed in with ideas about closer control of the production system. Management placed relatively low emphasis upon 'increments of status', though this had traditionally been a Company style. Emphasis was given to 'controls' both of a technical nature, such as integrated information systems, and in administrative terms, with the application of management by objectives.

In the 1930s CCE Ltd had been noted in Provincial City for its good rates of pay and stable employment. During that time it had attracted a high proportion of able people. Up to the 1950s there were few incentive schemes; then, during the 1950s and early 1960s, a high proportion of employees had been placed on various forms of payment by results. Current thinking had reversed this trend, and the aim in 1967 was to replace payment by results by measured performances related to standard wages. This scheme had been introduced and largely accepted. The exception and main opposition came from the Packing Department. These data were of double use. They both provided a background picture of CCE management's beliefs about inducements and helped in building the general picture of industrial relations in the factory (cf. Bennis 1969).

Changes in the system of payment were regarded as part of a 'new charter' that would modernize the Company and replace the 'old-fashioned and authoritarian management of the past' by a 'more professional management'. Part of this new charter included replacing old ideas of 'status differentials'.

CCE Ltd had an extensive system of formal committees and had additionally in the last ten years adopted the practice of small committees and informal meetings to introduce new methods and similar changes. The role of the industrial and the general unions was overtly limited to the major issues of payment and working conditions. In practice there were, as there are in many companies, close links between union officials and certain functions within CCE Ltd, for example, Personnel. Each of the factories and the departments within them had elected shop-floor representatives. It will be seen later that the roles of these representatives varied according to the sex and occupational categories they represented (see Chapter 9).

ENVIRONMENT, MARKETING, AND RESEARCH & DEVELOPMENT

The aim of questions about the environment was to learn about the market conditions and the major factors affecting them, and also about Provincial City. The focus upon suppliers of raw materials and equipment was less intense because CCE's position with both was influential, and the initial overview had indicated the forms it took.

Our decision to start the construction of the 'organizational map' by collecting data on the market and marketing caused some surprise. It will be recalled that marketing was not formally represented on Azimuth and later it will be seen that when we reinvestigated this aspect in late 1968 all the questions were answered by a member of Azimuth (see Chapter 8). We knew from published research that certain clusters of features of the product, customers, and the behaviour of competitors can influence – sometimes almost determine – the organizational structure and industrial relations (Lawrence & Lorsch 1967). H. A. Turner has demonstrated this in a series of brilliant studies of the car industry. For example, he succeeded in linking strike activity and the onset/ending of peak demand periods, and then showed a relationship between the overall level of economic activity and general elections (Turner, H. A., *et al.* 1961, 1967, 1969). The work of Burns and Stalker has provided further evidence that the rate of product innovation in a market can make some forms of 'management system' inappropriate. Earlier we looked at an illustration of this in the 'Harp Mill affair' (Chapter 2).

CCE Ltd are operating in a market that is stable in size and has been increasing only slowly during the last five years. There are a relatively small number of firms in this market and their competitive activities, while encouraged, are subject to regulation by 'the government'. In 1960 CCE Ltd held an important share of the market, but its principal products were of a traditional nature, and, in the judgement of both consultants and the Company, were going to retain a decreasing share. This was something of a local crisis and led to the establishment of marketing as a major activity with a critical role to play in CCE's future.

Following the recommendations of consultants, men were recruited to the new department from well-established brand-conscious firms. Their task was to make the firm marketing-oriented. It may be seen from this that hitherto production had been the key function.

From the interviews it became apparent that the introduction of marketing as a function had brought changes in CCE Ltd. I heard descriptions of the early reactions of the production people to this and the marketing men's responses. It was noticeable that the Marketing Department occupied a new building smoothly furnished and populated by an appropriate number of 'dollies' to redirect the 'lost' visitor. The men were different in their dress. Suits were cut in the modern style and hair was longer and shaped.

As a department the new men had produced a number of successes, which revitalized CCE Ltd and turned it into a market leader. It was obvious, however, that they had been largely encapsulated both geographically and socially from the rest of the Company. Thus we can perhaps better understand the position in 1967 as being one in which the Company had strengthened its marketing side rather than became marketing-oriented. In effect, the production people were still largely buffered and segregated from these developments and any potential clashes of belief system were avoided. This is an important point which illustrates the very important topic in organizational analysis of the ways in which task units with clearly identifiable but conflicting outlooks are related to each other (Litwak 1961). It will be seen later, in the study of the factory, that the 'mechanics of segregation' are a crucial area affecting industrial relations. In the case of marketing the different outlooks of Marketing and Production were not brought into conflict, and those who believed that the factory side was the more important could still do so unaware of the gradual changes that were taking place. At the management level, CCE Ltd had a highly formalized system of dining that has some correspondence with the officers' mess in the military. The established custom of politeness and orderly conduct, coupled with seating segregation, probably facilitated the smoothness of the entry of the 'new boys'.

The nature of the market in 1967 was that companies were competing for larger shares of the existing sales and in doing so sought out various allies, for example, the government. All companies were concerned to ensure that the market did not shrink and thus in some senses shared a common interest in stressing the advantages of the product to the consumer. At the same time each was attempting to increase its own share. One way of achieving this is to establish a distinctive brand that fits the public mood and optimism/pessimism about spending money. CCE monitored developments in consumer purchasing very closely, analysing very small changes to check if there were important trends emerging. Essentially this work was an audit. In contrast, marketing was always trying to create a new product and was constantly evaluating research in this area. Much of this work could be conducted within the marketing function. Liaison did occur regularly on both a daily basis and through product development committees. These formalized meetings involved senior management from all functions.

The previous paragraphs may now be summarized: CCE Ltd have a dominant market position in a market that is not increasing in size. They have succeeded in developing a small number of new products that have taken the Company from a position of potential decline to one of leadership. Product innovation can be handled by specialized product developments done within the marketing function and R & D. The direction and evaluation of these product developments is strongly influenced by market intelligence – the behaviour of customers and competitors. Within the Company as a whole there is a necessity to keep new products secret from competitors until they are ready for launching. Therefore marketing has to be segregated. The production side must be ready to respond to a decision to go ahead with a new product. In practice, top levels of production will have a good knowledge of probable developments. Also the factories are in some ways 'kept on their feet' by trial runs. This is part of the firm's 'repertoire of strategies' and is comparable to the rehearsing of responses or taking of initiatives in the military context (March & Simon 1958). At present the 'management system' of the firm is best characterized as mechanistic rather than organic and it may be argued, following Burns and Stalker, that this is appropriate.

There was some evidence from these first sets of interviews that the actual composition of the market might change from one in which there were a small number of brands selling a high proportion of the total, to one in which there was more fragmentation. If this were to happen it would have important consequences for the technical and social aspects of the new factory. For example, one of the assumptions underlying the design had been that the range of varieties of the basic product would be limited within a known figure. Part of the design had been done on the assumption of large runs of some lines. If all this changed then if follows that CCE would have to change its 'management system' if it was still to remain a leader in the market. Even a small movement towards a more organic system would have far-reaching implications for the norms governing relations within management in the different functions. Essentially it would require new forms of closer working relationships between people who had been largely segregated. The study of the market, and a continuing interest in this, may now be seen to be critical to the practice and process of organizational design. A change in the market has certain consequences for the technology and the social system and would bring about a treble change.

The observations made on the market aspect indicate one important rule for those involved in organizational design. That is, that it is just as 'untidy' an activity as designing the technology. Plans have to be scrapped, altered, and remade. For this reason alone the earlier emphasis upon a dialogue between Azimuth and ourselves is crucial to success.

A firm's posture towards the market is influenced by changes in the organization of its outlets (Miller & Rice 1967). Ridgeway (1958) has demonstrated how critical this relationship can be in his analysis of the manufacturer–dealer relationship in car-selling. In the case of CCE Ltd, its production policy and influence would be affected not only by changes in the public's preferences and the behaviour of competitors, but also by changes in the composition and cohesion of the outlets linking CCE and the ultimate consumer. During the scan, data were collected on this aspect and supplemented later.

In the study of the environment, Marketing is an obvious area for analysis since it occupies a critical position on the boundary of the firm. It collects intelligence reports, scrutinizes them, and passes opinions on to the 'policy development groups' (Katz & Kahn 1966). Relations with the environment are also handled by Production Scheduling and Dispatch. Both these functions were examined to check the hypothesis that the 'management system' was mechanistic. Production Scheduling carries out policies by relating sales commitments to production facilities. The form taken by this function will vary in relation to the nature of the market and the technology. It has been suggested that we can view planning as being either the programming of production or the setting of general objectives which are achieved by a decentralized arrangement of continual adjustment and negotiation. Typically, in small-batch firms there are progress chasers and similar occupations which 'negotiate' the flow of work. At CCE Production Scheduling set out detailed plans, and the relationship with production is best characterized as one of feedback and programming (March & Simon 1958). This supports the hypothesis that the 'management system' was mechanistic.

The position of Dispatch is also crucial to the successful financial performance of the firm, yet remarkably little general investigation of this function has been undertaken. Clark presents some aspects of this in the comparative studies of peak periods in organizations with reference to the supplying of cans from manufacturers to the canners during the harvesting of vegetables and fruit (Clark 1970a). In the case of CCE Ltd the existing situation of three factories on the same site, but divided by a main road, posed considerable problems for Dispatch. Each of the factories specialized, but orders contained a mix of lines and were based on customer requirements. Dispatch was the point at which the ideas underpinning the operation of the production system had to be reconciled with a different set of principles for handling the customer orders. One of the major problems in this department was the degree of autonomy from the rest of the factory.

The amount of autonomy, as measured in time, had been progressively reduced as part of the firm's policy of minimizing the volume of production in the factory and in stock. This was a major cost item for CCE Ltd, and any reduction would improve the firm's financial performance by a swift drop in working capital. The impact of this upon Dispatch and upon the motivations of people working there was not considered by members of the Company to be a source of problems, yet it was not difficult to see that any further tightening of the interdependence between Dispatch and the rest of the plant would impose severe organizational strains. The management of Dispatch were aware of this and had adopted a style of leadership and a division of labour to cope with the problems, but the important point in the construction of the organizational map was 'how critical is the existing autonomy to the running of the department?' The question is closely related to the role of centralized control in the new factory.

Finally in this section we should also note the role of Research and Development. Again this is in part a boundary function linking the firm with the latest technical ideas for economic production and for ensuring that the requisite equipment is developed and available to manufacture any product innovations.

SUMMARY

The aim of this chapter is to outline our objectives and the ways in which we set about achieving them. In this sense it is one 'model' of how to proceed and should be a useful source of ideas. Actual material has been included to show crucial features of CCE Ltd and also to illustrate the method adopted. Our objectives were to obtain a background record of the 'firm in action'; to test the feasibility of a consultancy; and to establish the consultancy. In addition to the kinds of data already indicated, we investigated the firm's previous experiences with consultants. This information was utilized to decide how best we could make known the problems in organizational design we felt to be significant. We concluded that our idea of the 'dialogue' was the appropriate kind of relationship, but that its successful achievement would be difficult. The reason for this was that the firm had typically utilized consultants to implement policy decisions in areas where the firm had no full-time expert and saw no advantage in establishing one. Examples include warehouse design and operation, changes in wage structures, Management by Objectives. In the following chapter we examine the way in which we tackled the problem of establishing the 'dialogue'.

CHAPTER FIVE

Technological change
and the packing crews

INTRODUCTION: PHASE II

The diagnosis has established that there were a number of problem areas where we believed that a contribution could be made by behavioural scientists. Also we felt that a project with the Azimuth Group was feasible, but we had doubts about the extent of their understanding of our approach. We had a number of problems in mind in 'planning' the next phase, one of which was the need to demonstrate the behavioural science perspective, including its advantages and limitations.

We felt that there would be difficulty in establishing a socio-logical and social-psychological approach as a distinctive and relevant contribution to the design process. We anticipated that we would be faced by a kind of distant appreciation and an unwilling-ness to take account of the structural and cultural features of the situation, and of the ways in which individuals and groups behave and define their situation. We also expected that there would be some difficulties in linking with the ongoing activities of the specialists engaged in plant design. We suspected that our work would be conceived of as a totally separate and only partially related exercise. Consequently we anticipated our objective of a joint investigation of the technical and organizational systems would be difficult of attainment.

We aimed to have both joint investigations, where appropriate, and joint appraisal of our findings and the way we were proceeding. It seemed highly likely, in view of the firm's previous experiences with consultants, that most of our activities would be encapsulated and we would be forced to operate within what Gouldner has termed the 'engineering model' (Gouldner 1964). Gouldner suggests that enterprises may typically be thought of as presenting the client with a request to institute a particular practice (e.g. MBO), or, to collect data, rather than to get involved in identifying and solving problems. In the 'engineering model' the consultant accepts the client's definition of the problem, collects the requested data, and returns this to the company in the form of a report or some other appropriate medium. We had a number of practical objections to this method of working since it was not considered appropriate to tackling the fluctuations and uncertainties that arise in design. It was basically a research model when a design strategy was needed (Nadler 1966). Our preference has already been described as a dialogue, and this approximates to the 'clinical model' (Gouldner 1964). We considered this strategy appropriate to the developing of new performance programmes which had not previously been a part of the repertory of the enterprise.

Even though the level of entry to the firm and the connection with an ongoing design team who were experienced in tackling abstract problems was in our favour, as was the time of our entry, in practice we anticipated a number of early problems. Existing studies of behavioural scientists were remarkably unhelpful. They described mainly the entry period as a success or failure, but with a few notable exceptions failed to detail in a meaningful way the kinds of incident that occurred, or the kinds of factor facilitating or inhibiting a joint relationship.

The anticipation of certain problems influenced the way in which we proceeded in this phase. It influenced, for example, the selection of the first department to work in; the methods of investigation; and the form of the feedback. The relationship that eventually emerged during this phase was described by one of our colleagues as 'discriminated confrontation'.

The selection of the first department or section to demonstrate the consultant's approach is one of the most critical decisions in the early phases. Dalzeil and Klein (1960) suggested, from their study of the work of consultants in a mid-England packaging firm, that when new areas of consultancy are emerging there is a high likelihood of misunderstanding between the client and the consultant. In their particular investigation they found that the client had selected the wrong category of consultant, even though the client's directors had drawn up a specification of what was required. Then, because of their confidence in the selection, they ignored a number of cues indicating that they had made a wrong choice. The consultants had, on entering, selected one department and had produced a number of recommendations for this, but were not able immediately to implement these and so had moved to another department. They selected the 'stripping' department, which had considerable fluctuations in workload and staffing. The consultants later reported that this had been, for technical reasons, a bad choice. In addition, there is evidence within that study to suggest that the initial selection is one which managements regard as significant and indicative of the consultant's abilities. This example highlights the relevance of the selection and of the need continually to clarify the objectives of the consultancy when it is a novel activity.

In the previous chapter we indicated that our approach included the reconstruction of the organizational system implied by the new technology and manpower designs. The basic idea was simple, but its practice was much more complicated. Also the comparison of the existing designs with a range of alternatives was a neat idea, but here again were problems. The actual difficulties of successfully undertaking this and at the same time convincing the client (and at times ourselves) that it was worthwhile were greater than we had imagined. When discussing the data from the scan with the linkman it could be seen that the proposed technical and manning changes in the Packing Department would entirely alter the position of the female packing crews and possibly also alter the entire hierarchy of power and statuses in the firm. The first hypothesis was that the female crews would lose 'control' over their machines. Thus it seemed that a study of the way in which technological changes would affect these groups would be one means of demonstrating that the current hopes for 'participative management' were idealistic and that in fact areas of participation (e.g. delegated decisions) may be decreased in the future.

The diagnosis suggested there would be changes in the power position of the female crews that would affect the relative balance of power in that department, particularly in relations between mechanics and other groups; and this in turn would have (unknown) consequences for the power structure of the enterprise as a whole. In practical terms far too little significance has been attached by either researchers or consultants to changes in the power relations within and between firms. This is in fact a very significant area for industrial relations in general.

There were already a number of good reasons for selecting the packing crews as the initial point of entry. The question remaining to be answered was 'would this provide a useful trial demonstration?'

At that time Azimuth were particularly interested in the possibilities of manning the packing complex of the future with one girl rather than the four or five required in 1967. They had started a series of experiments with highly modified machines to see if this was feasible. The existence of these studies provided an excellent opportunity to demonstrate the distinctive perspective of the behavioural scientist from that of the work study man and the ergonomist. We have already argued that the objective of the behavioural scientist is to represent the organizational system and to make his advice on the basis of the aspirations and needs of the members of the enterprise. This activity is quite likely to lead to sharp and important differences of opinion between behavioural scientists and, for example, industrial engineers. Thus while the problems of designing individual jobs within an engineering or man–machine framework are important and challenging, it is also equally important to give consideration to the areas of coordination, control, and motivation. In the design of organizational systems there are important advantages to management and unions in utilizing both behavioural scientists and ergonomists, but this is a process which demands considerable sophistication. Such a strategy does facilitate the scrutiny and discussion of a wide range of critical issues on the 'human aspect of the enterprise'. The importance of this is contained in Touraine's (1965) observation: 'frequently resistance to technical innovation is not directed against the technological change, but against the transformation of the structure of inter-personal relationships'.

The emphasis upon manning and upon aggregates in the experiments on the packing crews seemed to offer a useful opportunity to demonstrate the utility of an alternative emphasis – upon social structures. Earlier, in outlining the 'organizational perspective', the structural focus was presented. This may be regarded as an alternative set of ideas (paradigm) to those which guide manpower planning (Cherns, Clark, & Sinclair 1970).

GENERAL APPROACH

The approach adopted in the Packing Department was to record the existing and future production systems, and to record selected aspects of the existing social structure, with particular reference to the female packing crews. Then the organizational features for the new factory were reconstructed from the data on manning, technology, and management policy. These records of the existing and future technologies were compared to indicate the areas of major change. This was then used to compare the existing and future systems of organization. Finally, the findings were fed back at various points in time to Azimuth including a specially established subgroup. The general strategy is set out in *Figure 5*.

In the existing situation, there were a number of aspects which interested us particularly. We wanted to obtain a 'map' of the main features of the interrelated activities carried on within the Packing Department. For example, we were concerned to find out the ways in which the workflow operated through the department; the role of

Figure 5   General strategy

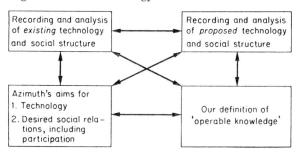

the maintenance workers; and the patterns of contact between maintenance and packing crews. We also wanted to locate the existing decision-making networks and grievance procedures and to identify the management style adopted. For example, with reference to our earlier typology of participation (Chapter 2), we wanted to learn how far the existing situation approximated the participative philosophy desired by the company. The objective was to characterize the management styles as they actually existed, not as they were desired. Additionally, we were concerned to know the attitudes of the employees of the department to, for example, their work, their colleagues, their work groups, the unions, and the firm. We will return to this aspect later. Finally, we required a record of the technology delineating the main features so that we could compare them with plans for the future.

With regard to the future, we needed to obtain two kinds of data. First, the details of the planned technical changes; this might seem a fairly straightforward matter, but in actual fact it was extremely difficult because there were a variety of technical plans whose ranking changed constantly. It was necessary to go as far as getting data on machinery purchases and other policies in order to see the way in which decisions were, in fact, being taken, though it was not believed that this was the case. In other words, we were attempting to see in which ways the company, or at least the purchasing function of the company, was closing off the options in the area of sociotechnical design. Second, we required knowledge of the company's objectives for the social system in the future. This included a statement on the managerial philosophy and management styles the company felt were appropriate to the change situation and to manning.

Given data on both the existing and the future situations, we would be able to both identify and explain the sociotechnical system and its interdependencies. This would include a historical analysis of the changes over time and a study of the way in which people were socialized into the organization. We would then compare this information with the planned sociotechnical system in order to draw out the main social differences and their implications.

We had not foreseen that our future role would include drawing together the technological side. The actual technological component, though seen in a neat box by Eric Miller, was, in our investigation, found to be enormously fragmented and we found ourselves attempting to draw together the work of the different technologists in order to complete our own exercise.

In addition to the data we were obtaining about the existing and future situations and the comparisons we were drawing, it was inevitable that there would be a conceptual input into the organization. We aimed to achieve this by meeting individuals separately and discussing with them the ideas we were using.

The strategy we adopted is set out in *Figure 6.*

METHODS OF INVESTIGATION AND FEEDBACK

The method for tackling this second phase was in two closely related parts: the investigation and the feedback. One of the principal requirements of our method of investigation was to conduct it in such a way as to ensure agreement on the accuracy of the findings and the relevance of their interpretation. We intended the feedback to take the form of a continuous dialogue with Azimuth and other

Figure 6   Details of the general strategy

MAKE A RECORD OF

Existing situation	*Planned situation*
(i) Technological features	(i) Technological features
(ii) Social features	(ii) Social features extrapolated
(iii) Most probable explanation of the social structure and behaviour of the group(s) studied	from technical designs and manpower

PART ONE

COMPARISONS AND DIFFERENCES

Compare the existing and proposed *technology* to reveal differences in:

(i) spatial configuration of equipment and machine complexes

(ii) temporal dimension of the time balances in the flow of work and

(iii) develop implications for total manning and deployment of the workforce

PART TWO

Compare the existing and future *social structures* to show how the following are affected:

(i) the existing networks of social relationships

(ii) the factors which facilitate/inhibit the continuance of the existing social structure

(iii) the existing level and content of decision-making at all levels

(iv) the existing networks and modes of decision-making for production, grievance settlement, etc.

FEEDBACK

(i) the analysis of existing social structure

(ii) the extrapolation of the future social structure

(iii) outline the principal differences in (i) and (ii)

(iv) compare the extrapolation of the future social structure with Azimuth's stated requirements for the new social system; critically examine to develop alternatives

(v) contrast the manning studies with the perspective of the social scientist to show how our work is complementary

PART THREE

groups, preferring this kind of feedback in the early stages to ensure mutual understanding of our method of working, the findings, and the analysis. At that stage of the consultancy both Azimuth and ourselves were uncertain about the precise path the consultancy would take.

There was general agreement on the value of conducting the first studies in the Packing Department. To simplify the problems it was decided to concentrate upon only one of the three factories. The initial plan for the investigation of the Packing Department includes the identification of the main groupings and the relationships within and between these. The collection of data on the existing social system was undertaken with the assistance of another sociologist, Janet Ford, and of Chris Eling, who was principally concerned with the technical aspects.

The analysis of the social system was started by gaining a general picture of the three principal groups involved in the existing Packing Department. These were the female packing crews, who were the single largest group, accounting for more than half the total population of the Department. The male mechanics were the next largest group, and the male supervisors and management the smallest. Initial impressions of the packing crews suggested that each of the five-girl teams was identifiable as a social group in which the members had a high level of mutual knowledge about one another's roles. This impression raised the question of how these solidary groups had emerged and would be sustained.

Sociologists have indicated the importance of the community in forming people's notions of occupational identity. A good example is the shipbuilding industry (Eldridge 1968). One way of identifying the role of the community in forming images of occupations is to find out the knowledge and expectations of persons joining the Company. To check this aspect we decided to reconstruct the passage of a new entrant to the Packing Department from the first interviews in Personnel through the Training Department and into the factory. The findings from the studies carried out in Training and the factory are presented in a later section.

The information about the existing technical system was obtained from direct observation, photographs, plans, various recording techniques used by industrial engineers (e.g. flow process charts), and interviews with operators, managers, and R & D executives. Our requirement was not for a detailed record of the kind used by design engineers but for the kind of highly selected and abstract 'map' used by industrial engineers.

Information about the planned technical system was more difficult to obtain because the planning was at an early stage. We decided to make an arbitrary selection of the first layout plans and to supplement them with detailed interviews with Research and Development to identify where changes were anticipated and the range of alternative equipment available to carry out similar tasks. For example, one of the technical innovations was a mechanical linking system connecting making and packing machines. Several alternatives were undergoing proving trials. We obtained information about each of these and were able to see some in operation in the experimental areas.

At that stage in the consultancy the fact that no final decisions had been made was an advantage because it provided more time to ensure that the design of the new department was seen as building a social *and* technical system. Attempts were made to identify the most probable technology by checking the machinery purchases and connections with suppliers.

Comparing the first plans of the new technical system with existing systems in the Packing Department revealed a number of obvious changes. This was an easy exercise when compared with the difficulties that arose when we began to collect data relevant to sketching out the implications of technological decisions for the new social system. We were able to see how, at the level of the transformation of the raw material into a new product, the layout plans had been 'clad' with people. It was, however, extremely difficult to imagine how the actual coordination of the new production system was being envisaged.

In order to demonstrate the kinds of problem we felt were relevant to Azimuth, we were also forced to make quite an arbitrary decision about the intended social organization. Some members of Azimuth had prepared a paper on the kind of 'management philosophy' they believed should be embodied in the new factory. This had not been a straightforward exercise and they had quite clearly found that on a practical level of policy formation much of the writing by behavioural scientists was general and woolly. However, they decided that the best means of crystallizing opinion within Azimuth and the Board was to present the ideas of 'participative management'. Accordingly, they had presented a paper to their colleagues setting out the points they considered most important. Azimuth's selection of ideas for this paper was influenced by the writings of the late Douglas McGregor and Rensis Likert. Their final paper was a source of controversy both in Azimuth and among their members of the company. Some argued that CCE Ltd had always been a Theory Y firm, while others said it never had been and there was no good reason why it should be.

We decided to take the ongoing discussions of the 'participative management philosophy' and use these in our analysis of the existing situation. We had in mind the simple fact that few managers can agree on what is a 'participative social structure'. Do managers in the printing industry participate, for example? Knowing that to 'map' the organization would provide an empirical base for discussion within CCE Ltd we decided that it would be a useful exercise to compare the amount and form of participation at present, with the amount and form implied by the design work of Research and Development.

Thus while the investigation of the Packing Department proceeded very largely according to plan, the form and content of the feedback was reformulated to link in with Azimuth's current activities. Though we had argued the need for the 'organizational design' stage and had formal agreement that this should take place, we knew in practice that all our work would be negated and neglected if it did not make Azimuth aware of the actual way in which it was unconsciously and unwittingly creating a social organization for the new plant.

We soon learnt both the personal costs and advantages of our decision. As will be seen shortly, the feedback meetings indicated all too clearly that the principles being adopted for the design of the new organization were primarily those of scientific management. At that stage we were initially concerned to reveal to Azimuth the gap between the stated and the actual goals of the social system. Later we were concerned to test the value of these principles for the particular populations that were to be transferred to the new factory.

We had planned that the method of investigation would be a joint one in which we would work alongside the internal experts. During this second phase we did establish joint investigation as a principle, and made considerable advances on the first phase when our work was almost totally a separated exercise. However, as will be seen when we turn to the third phase, the joint method of investigation was only partially established.

One of the guiding principles behind the idea of 'building in a social-science-using capability' was that the feedback would be a continuous dialogue in which our perceptions of the Company would be appraised and scrutinized. We have already indicated that we anticipated considerable resistance to this strategy, particularly since this approach departed from the established kind of relationship which CCE Ltd typically had with its consultants and external advisers. The fate of this particular ideal is documented in the following chapters and so it is perhaps relevant to consider how realistic a hope it was.

Alvin Gouldner, the American social scientist who has constantly advocated that his colleagues should and can become involved in solving problems, made a sharp distinction between the 'engineering' and 'clinical' types of relationship between the client and the consultant. We considered that the 'engineering' model was less appropriate to the kind of problem-solving that arises in 'organizational design' because many exceptions occur and the relationship is not routine or easily programmed (March & Simon 1958). However, exponents of the 'clinical' model may underestimate the range of problems faced by the managements of enterprises. For example, they receive advice from a wide number of specialists – personnel, operational research, marketing – and they have to reconcile conflicting ideas.

We would argue that the 'clinical' relationship is especially appropriate at the first stages of projects involving non-routine problem-solving affecting a variety of levels and functions. At later stages and for certain kinds of work it may not only be inappropriate, but actually wasteful of the enterprise's resources.

FINDINGS: EXISTING SYSTEMS

(i) *Technology*

The Packing Department is linked to the Making Department by a man-operated transportation system. Completed products are stored on movable container racks and transferred to Packing by a system of lifts.

Typically the transportation system contained several hours' work and was thus also a form of buffer stock. In practice, a large part of the buffer would be located in the Packing Department close to the particular machines that would do the packing. Small parts of the buffer would be in transit and in the Making Department.

One important consequence of this system was that the two departments were 'buffered' from one another and hence there was a degree of autonomy for both the departmental managers. The significance of this for the social system will be examined in the following section.

Packing machines are shaped like a squared U. The products are hand-fed by a female operator into the top left end and are hand-removed by an operator at the top right end. Each machine is technologically independent of all other packing machines and of machines in the prior and subsequent departments. If one machine breaks down, or the crew wish to stop it in anticipation of a break-down, this does not require any special coordination involving, for example, supervision.

(ii) *Social system*

As may be seen from *Figure 7* the department contains three principal 'groups'. Additional to those outlined there are a number of small groups that we excluded from the first investigation but examined in Phase Four. A good example of this would be the female quality attendants. There were also several functionally related, but spatially isolated, jobs which we neglected for the purpose of this first demonstration. We initially neglected the position of 'indirect workers' on maintenance and similar activities (see Chapter 9). We did take some account of these and gave them special attention in Phase Five, but we placed most emphasis upon the female packing crews. The reason for this decision was that it was widely accepted that they would be the one group who would be most immediately affected by the technological innovations proposed by R & D.

At the time the management expressed its concern about the impact of the changes on the packing crews by referring to the problems of 'social isolation'. This is an important observation because it helps to reveal the conception of manpower analysis held by Azimuth. As we have mentioned, the Company had developed an overall picture of the total numbers of people required to man the new factory. However, when deploying people to match the tasks 'created' by the new technology, they had relied on existing models of the methods of organizing. The actual principles being applied were those of scientific management. This demonstrates the relevance of our expectation that the 'structural features of social organization would be neglected. The neglect arises largely from the absence of operational procedures for translating the ideals of 'participative management' into an organizational structure.

Each week the manager of the Packing Department received his target schedules from Production Planning. Every day, in the late afternoon, the manager would calculate the probable production for that day, including the evening shift, and plan the following day. This would also be done by the foreman and supervisors. At the

Figure 7   Organization for the Packing Department in Factory C (1967)

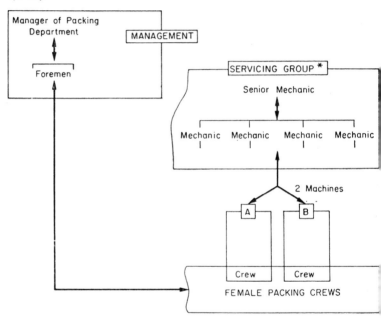

*Maintenance workers (mechanical engineers and electricians) are not included in this phase of the investigation

start of the new day the management would assess the buffer stocks and actual production for the previous day. This statistic would then be used to plan the loading of the machines for the new day and would form the basis of mid-morning discussions with the Making manager on the state of progress towards the established target.

Thus the typical day starts with the majority of machine crews knowing that they can continue to process racks of work adjacent to their machines. Each crew can start and proceed without direct reference to the departmental manager. For some crews it will be necessary to change machines, or have their machine modified to take a different product.

One of the principal activities of the management is ensuring the availability of work to the machines. The actual contact with crews is infrequent and, as we shall see, concerns only a small number of aspects of the 'internal discipline' of the crews.

We now turn to examine the female packing crews in more detail. At the time of the studies the crew consisted of five persons. The 'senior girl' (SG) is situated in the centre of the machine. She is primarily responsible for the performance of the crew and its internal operation.

One of the main features of the organizational structure of the packing crews is the principle of rotation. The four members of the crew who work at the feeding-in, the taking-away of packaged goods, and other support activities rotate their jobs every half hour. A new member of a crew would therefore experience each of these four roles twenty times in her first week of work in the Department.

The rotation principle includes the 'senior girl'. Each week for one half day a deputy takes on the senior role and is thus tried out and, if successful, given an opportunity to become a 'senior girl' when a vacancy arises.

The frequent rotation of roles is, in our opinion, an important factor in explaining the 'solidary' and cohesive character of relationships between the packing girls as an occupational grouping. The rotation facilitates the development of shared and known experiences in operating the machines. An operative can expect her observations on, for example, the state of the raw material to be meaningful to her colleagues because they are likely to have experienced similar problems when occupying other roles. Given that we discovered shared attitudes about the work, it may be seen that these provide the basis for agreement – or at least understanding – of any action taken in anticipation of faulty work or machine stoppages.

Each crew is hierarchically organized, 'control' being balanced between the 'senior girl' and the other members of the crew. Allowing for both pre- and self-selection, it can be observed that a packer leaving the Training Department enters a defined social structure. This structure is recognized and implicitly supported by management and mechanics. We explore the path of a new girl in the following section.

Each crew can be seen to be distinct, a small community possessing opportunities for an experience as varied as any expectation that these girls have about work in Provincial City, and also carrying local esteem, particularly among members of CCE Ltd. Crews have a fair degree of autonomy because the machines are not interdependent. This means that the 'senior girl' can stop and start the machine knowing that a short break in production will not affect the overall operation of the department. An important consequence of this feature of the existing production system is that it does provide the 'senior girl' with a number of areas of responsibility—crew performance and discipline, for example, and also allows her to demonstrate her control over the situation by stopping the machines.

Already this description has contained a number of clues that indicate that much of the discipline has been allocated to the crew. The packing crews are an interesting example of 'responsible autonomy'.[1] This observation has suggested that the motivation of individuals to work at particular levels was strongly influenced by the prevailing norms of the crews and the overall structure linking crews. Also within each particular crew there is sufficient 'play' to allow psychological adjustment to take place at a higher level than is the case for many female operations in factories.

The quality level of the packaged good is an important criterion of performance in CCE Ltd. We observed that in the five-girl crews the visual inspection was almost continuous. The continuous nature of inspection is important in relation to the ongoing experiment – in 1967 – on a single-operator packing machine. We shall return to this point later when examining the feedback of findings to Azimuth.

Our initial studies revealed a hierarchy of rules governing the relationship between packing crews. In the department selected for investigation there were some forty crews. One of the features of the system of rules was the existence of a rota indicating which crews would be affected by any changes in production. This particular rule, which was recognized by management and was formalized, examplifies the network of practices, which had grown up over many years, influencing the government of the department. Once we had identified the packing crews as an example of 'responsible autonomy', we asked two questions. How did this situation arise? and What are the factors that ensure its continuing?

[1] The notion of 'responsible autonomy' precisely indicates the philosophy behind that particular form of designing inter-job relations.

The explanation for the emergence of this particular social structure involved reference to the previous thirty years of the department. In the 1930s the crews had been larger than today, and it can be argued that the nature of the production system, coupled with the attitude taken by management to dealing with industrial relation, facilitated its emergence. Though this problem interested us the answer was in many ways less critical than the answer to the second question, 'How is it able to continue?' As practitioners rather than researchers, we could take the existence of the groups and their solidarity as one given in the situation and focus upon the factors affecting the continued transmission of the particular customs and practices we had discovered. To answer this question we needed to know about the way in which a new entrant learnt these traditions and attitudes. That is to say, we had to investigate the method of socialization, taking into account the orientations that new members brought to CCE Ltd. Looking at many other studies of 'planned change', it is noticeable that the transmission of culture has been neglected for far too long. Indeed, the implication of many comments upon how managers can approach changing situations is that there is a body of ideas that can be instantly applied. An example of this kind of thinking is contained in that vast body of literature arguing that management must consult to achieve organizational change. One can only assume that the researchers and authors concerned are ignorant of the political activities of all members of organizations.

We focused upon socialization so that we could show how the proposed technology would rupture the existing social organization for the packers and also make some of the induction processes that were in existence redundant. To discover more about socialization we traced the career path of a new entrant to the Packing Department from the first interview through training and into the department.

Social system: socialization of packers The socialization[1] of any new worker in an enterprise, at any level, commences with the clues that are thrown out at the first interviews in the Personnel Department. We learnt that members of Personnel regarded the Packing Department as the pinnacle for the female operator. The peak of the pinnacle was the 'senior girl'. Newcomers picked up these clues both in the interview situation and from the results of aptitude tests.

[1] The concept of socialization has been treated too simplistically in a number of studies, particularly where its problematic character is not recognized. For an insightful and cogent discussion of this, see Weick (1970).

The clues about the high status and greater skill of the female operator in Packing are sustained and emphasized in the three weeks' pre-production training. Though the principal emphasis of the training was discovered to be the technical requirements of being a competent operative, there are many indirect ways in which the trainees learn that they are joining a special group.

The final stages of this process occur in the production situation on the machines when the new girl joins an established group.

One of our findings, when conducting this particular entry, was that those persons most concerned with selection and training placed great emphasis on the *status quo* and were thus unintentionally supporting it.

Social system: interrelation of groups   We will now examine the main relationships between the three principal groups shown in *Figure 7.* Actual contact between managers and crew members was infrequent. When it did occur it was largely to do with decisions about which machines would be operated, reallocation of spare crew members, and filling vacancies in the crew. Usually the foreman would 'negotiate' with the 'senior girl' over the suitability of particular candidates. This is a good example of the way in which the established position of the 'senior girl' is maintained. The mechanics are responsible for two machines, but in practice work with the adjacent mechanics and the senior mechanics. The main contacts between crews and mechanics occur over breakdowns and malfunctioning.

Social system: conclusions   Our main conclusions from the first study of the Packing Department were selected to highlight both our emphasis upon 'social organization' and to interplay with the discussions within Azimuth on the subject of 'participative management'. As may be seen from the previous sections, we were focusing upon the existing social system and attempting to identify the factors that would be crucial to the proposed changes.

From our analysis we concluded that the relative balance of influence and power between management, packers, and mechanics was such that the government of the department is best described as 'joint regulation'. That is to say, in our opinion, a great deal of autonomy had been delegated to both the packers and the mechanics. Our investigation suggested that the senior mechanics were particularly influential in the running of the Department and their relationship with the junior management was the source of some ambiguity and tension.

Essentially, the role of management was supportive and the style of management prevailing was general rather than close. Much of the 'internal discipline' of the packers and mechanics was outside the immediate influence of junior management.

At the time of the study the department was independent of the Making Department. We emphasized this point because we considered that this situation would undergo one of the crucial changes that would take place at the new factory: a change that, we hypothesized, would transform the existing social system, and particularly the power structure and occupational identities.

Our final report introduced a number of factors we considered significant to explaining our findings. For example, we had identified the two solidary groups and had noted their recent behaviour towards management when administrative changes in the payment system were proposed. They had objected and were able to present a firm front to management, whereas other groups had accepted, or at least not offered strong opposition. Among the factors we identified were the following: the spatial and temporal characteristics of the work situation act generally to facilitate the development of solidary groups; management policy supports this by reducing the amount of intervention to a minimum; the relative balance of power is one in which the mechanics and packers will mutually support each other against management innovations.

FUTURE SYSTEM

(i) *Technology*

At the time we joined in the design exercises in 1967, there were already outline plans for the new factory. These plans were based on assumptions about the total size of the product market, and CCE's probable share of it, and also assumptions about the extent of fragmentation of the market. These assumptions did not seriously affect the proposed layout for the new factory in general terms, but they did affect the policy of introducing automatic controls on equipment and also sophisticated linkage systems between the machines in the Manufacturing Department and those in the Packing Department. In 1967 the policy of Research and Development was to assume that many of the human tasks in the Packing Department could be removed by mechanization and automation. The principal area for mechanization was in designing linkage systems between the packing machines and the departments preceding and following packing.

At that time we noted the general intention of linking machines in different departments, but focused our attention on the attempts to transfer human tasks from the packing crews to the machine. The prime concept of R & D was to have a 'singing and dancing machine' with a single operator.

(ii) *Social system*

The ideas for the social system were contained in two discrete packages. First, there were the overall figures for the manning of the new factory in general and Packing in particular. An estimate of manpower requirements had been constructed by noting where the proposed technological innovations remove human tasks and jobs and where the new technology created a need for new jobs (e.g., maintenance). Second, management had given some attention to the ideas of participative management.

In practice, the actual design of jobs was being largely left to the engineers in almost exactly the way Joan Woodward (1964) suggested in her Hancock Memorial Lecture to the Institute of Production Engineers. This is curious when one considers the interest in the work of Likert and Herzberg. In effect, there was no following through of policy decisions to examine their structural implications for the organization as a whole. Jobs were treated as isolated occurrences and thorough consideration was not given to the problems of human coordination.

For CCE Ltd organizational design was treated as an end-product of technical design, and the Industrial Relations Manager was expected to provide the means for ensuring the smooth introduction of the new technology. That is to say, the approach to the new social system was one in which the human side was treated as aggregates and the prior existence of structured relationships and patterned beliefs was neglected (Cherns, Clark, & Sinclair 1970).

COMPARING THE EXISTING AND FUTURE SYSTEMS

The comparison between the existing and future systems formed the subject-matter of the dialogue and feedback meetings between Azimuth, a special project group, and ourselves. We therefore deal with this mainly in the following section. It will be noted that during this phase we appear to be some distance from our stated intention of examining the 'systems of control'. In practice, the apparent détour was seen as a means of establishing the importance of systems of control by tackling one of the areas in which they were being neglected.

Feedback and dialogue

The feedback of the findings of investigations to the client enterprise has been one of the distinguishing features of *action research*.[1] If this were the only feature we would find that many researchers met this criterion. Perhaps the most important feature to be added is the discussion of the implications of the findings for some aspect of the client's performance. Thus the object of the discussion is the clarification or resolution of the client's problems rather than the enlargement of our knowledge about the ways in which enterprises function and are structured. In this sense our work is action research.

The most obvious characteristic of the feedback and dialogue in this phase of the project was that it was continuous and operated at two or more levels. The principal reason for this was that the project was in its early stages and we wanted to penetrate the thinking of the Azimuth Group. At the start of the phase a small project group was established. This consisted of two members of Azimuth—the linkman and an R & D executive—plus representatives from specialist groups and ourselves. In addition we had monthly meetings of a formal nature with three of the senior members of Azimuth. We did not meet with Azimuth as a whole until February 1968.

The small project group began its work in October by attempting to link the manning studies with our investigations of the social consequences of technological change for the packing crews. The manning studies had started before the sociological investigations and so their authors were ready to make initial reports on their findings. Their presentations were in the form of short papers outlining the terms of reference *given*, the methods used, and the results

[1] We use the term 'action research' interchangeably with 'consulting' in this account. It is recognized that, strictly speaking, it would be sensible to speak of action research since this is the way the project would be described by social and behavioural scientists. However, we also want to discuss organizational design with managers and experts. For many of this group the term 'research' in action research might be seen as just another way of conducting research that has no feedback to the sponsor.

obtained. The findings were not definitive, as the advising ergonomists were at pains to emphasize. However, the linkman–chairman tended to conclude that it would be possible to man the machines in the new factory with a single operator. At this point we objected that the results were far from conclusive and that the object of the project group was organizational design. The major difficulty for the chairman, who was an operating manager, was to understand the nature of design as a method (Nadler 1966). We further objected that the initial terms of reference had been too narrow and were prejudiced towards establishing a case in the rarefied atmosphere of the 'secret' experimental room. In contrast, our studies of the 'real-life' situation in the Packing Department suggested that the present method of packing was a complicated operation in which there were a number of interdependent activities that had to be coordinated.

As the discussion developed it became apparent that psychological and social factors were being ignored in general and in particular. For example, we had visited the experimental site several times to observe the manning studies and had noted observations made by the operators during the trials. These observations gave clear evidence that the experimental situation represented a strong departure from the problems typically encountered in the factories. Our main problem was to gain some acknowledgement that factors of social organization should be considered.

The major point of controversy in the meeting gradually emerged as being the difference between the meanings given by the behavioural scientist and the manager to the term 'organization'. The ideas on manning from the CCE men neglected the problems of coordination and motivation. Essentially, we were placed in the position of challenging this notion rather than offering an alternative. This fact is neatly reflected in the first draft minutes for the meeting. These state that at the next meeting the behavioural scientist 'must define in precise terms the questions to be answered in the social science field'. The significance of this extract is that it illustrates both confrontation and the attempt by CCE Ltd to respond by controlling the situation. We responded to the minutes by demanding, and getting, their withdrawal. It was however agreed that we would make a presentation at the next meeting.

The second meeting was in mid November. Like the first, it began tensely and there was considerable uncertainty. Our presentation of the notion of organization was profusely illustrated with examples from a variety of situations. Finally we used material from the study of packing to show how the existing situation would be transformed by the proposed introduction of mechanized linkage systems to and from the packing machines. At that point the R & D executive interrupted to develop the examples and suggested various ways in which our observations could be extended.

We did not know it at the time but that meeting and the support from the R & D executive had been one of the critical developments. We knew that he had understood the nature and significance of our observations, but could not assess whether the consultancy was progressing.

These two meetings with the project group were particularly important. They are good examples of the kinds of confrontation that can be expected when utilizing behavioural scientists. For our part, we had selected a range of variables different from those selected by the experts on manning. Inevitably this presents the opportunity for confrontations. Furthermore, we defined the situation in design terms. In contrast, we were met by members of Azimuth who were attempting to impose a control structure that was not appropriate to the task of the project group. The response of the chairman cannot be criticized, he attempted to be 'fair' and was always helpful, but he was somewhat uncomfortable in a constantly changing situation of continuous dialogue. Fortunately, the R & D executive was experienced in the design situation in particular and in multidisciplinary approaches in general. Part of his normal task was to liaise with Marketing over product innovation, so he was well used to changing and 'untidy' situations.

Our activities in the project group were reported to the senior members of Azimuth informally. In addition we had regular meetings with the senior members. These were largely concerned with the direction of the consultancy, for example, the choice of areas to be investigated, and the establishment of a mode of relating. These early attempts included requests for detailed network charts indicating the precise route our activities would follow and the time periods for each part. It is fair to say that we opposed these attempts, regarding them as impracticable and restricting to the design process. We were fortunate, because the points we made connected with the experience of the R & D members of Azimuth. We know of other projects where this has not been the case and the joint relationship has not succeeded (Chapters 11, 12, 13).

Towards the end of 1967 we began to summarize the findings from our studies and the meetings into a short report. This was submitted in January 1968 and fell with a dull thud. In fact, we had very little formal feedback on the document, but at an informal level there was some indication that it had been read and digested.

REVIEW

CCE Ltd is a large firm with an essentially bureaucratic pattern of relationships. The traditional and affective bonds that characterized relations within and between groups were being replaced, and the pace of change was being accelerated by the introduction of MBO and 'rational' procedures for the allocation of work, for payment, and for access to privileges. The new factory was being designed to incorporate the ideology of the rising professional management. The technical system for the new factory had many characteristics that would alter and transform the existing social system. The design process was largely being carried out by engineers and production managers who were not skilled at mapping the social structure of the firm, but they were concerned in a board sense about the impact of their designs upon people. Initially, they saw the human problems in ergonomic, welfare, and 'human relations' terms. The ways in which this base was extended is documented in the following chapters.

The company had had no previous experience with social scientists and preferred to segment problems and hand the different parts over to consultants. Consequently the 'dialogue approach' was not one they were used to.

In this phase of the project we were concerned to demonstrate the nature and content of our perspective rather than the general methods of social science. We argued that our best contribution would be to identify some of the human and social problems associated with the new factory. We made three kinds of input – the perspective, findings from studies in CCE Ltd, and selections from the published literature.

The feedback occurred in interpersonal contacts, at the project group and through its activities, and at meetings with Azimuth.

We had aimed to reveal the actual way in which Azimuth were unwittingly designing the social system and to compare this with the existing situation and the one they desired. We had also attempted to build in a 'social-science perspective' (Wilson 1969; Cherns 1969).

The client had attempted to control these inputs and the form in which they were made. We had resisted this and had found ourselves in a position of confrontation.

There were various fragmentary clues suggesting that our perspective and findings were being noted and utilized. We learnt that a sociological perspective had been perceived as one that would be useful to CCE Ltd. The most likely explanation of this rather unusual circumstance is that it is related to the recent visits made by the young, dynamic head of Production to America, where he had an opportunity to come into contact with theories of 'organizational development' and 'participative management'. He knew about the differences between individual and systemic approaches to organizational change.

The change in terms of reference presented to us at the January meeting indicated other ways in which the ideas of organizational design had been accepted. These were quite different from the initial frame of reference and came much closer to our own definition of the problems. An important change was contained in a short section on the kinds of advice and opinion that Azimuth expected.

> What CCE are paying consultants for . . . is not merely to express opinions to be weighed along with our own, but to produce data from other people's experience, so that CCE can avoid pitfalls that have already trapped others. In short, apart from any investigation that may be made . . . reports similar to that produced on the subject of (. . .) are required, which take account of as much documented work in the field as possible.

Looking at our own strategy in the first six months, we felt that we had only tenuous links with the large number of design groups that were doing parts of the plant design, many of them working autonomously. It was decided that some of these groups could be linked in an attempt to carry out organizational design. The details are set out in the following chapter.

This phase is best regarded as a *trial* by Azimuth. They had become aware of, and interested in utilizing, behavioural scientists and then had decided that it was worth experimenting – the trial. Now they had decided to go ahead and attempt organizational design.

CHAPTER SIX

The Processing Department: Sociotechnical design

INTRODUCTION: PHASE III

This chapter contains an overview of the work undertaken in the previous period and the reasons for adopting a different strategy to the investigation and to the analysis of the findings. The principal activities of this period are outlined and discussed in some detail. These activities mainly centre upon the joint investigation of one particular department. In addition, we were involved in a study of amenities. Finally, the activities of this period are reviewed and the means for transition to the next stage are outlined.

PROBLEMS ANTICIPATED

The aims of this period were to interpret the impact of technological innovation, in the form of automation and mechanization, upon the existing task and social structures as well as the existing occupational roles.[1] This included the devising of alternative forms of organization which would meet the twin criteria of adequate functioning and the management philosophy. With reference to the enterprise as a whole, a subsidiary study was undertaken, by an outside body under our supervision, on the development of amenities in the last ten years.

Certain features of our previous working styles, and of the context of the consultancy, were now seen to be important for its future development. First, we had noted a number of disconnected activities that were in many ways interrelated and overlapping. For example, the departments of Work Study, Research and Development, and Personnel were all conducting various separate studies. We saw our own role here as that of bringing together some of these activities so that separate and inconsistent designs could be scrutinized. Second,

---

[1] For a detailed discussion of the method of 'task analysis', see Emery (1959) and Trist *et al.* (1963).

we had aimed to build in a 'social-science-using capability', and though we had in fact demonstrated what social science was, we did not feel we were achieving the kind of penetration that was required. We planned to work on joint activities of investigation as a strategy for building in the social-science-using capability. This presented the potential advantage of providing the enterprise with a working knowledge of the sociotechnical framework, and our adaptations of it, as well as providing a meaningful forum within which our own work could be discussed and appraised.

We wanted to create a problem-solving situation and to move away from what Warren Bennis has called 'scholarly consultations' (Bennis 1963). That is to say, the emphasis was upon coupling an external input of social science with an ongoing group within CCE Ltd. This involved the creation of a structural mechanism into which our external input could be fed and diffused. Such a mechanism would have to have lines of feedback both to the senior group, Azimuth, and to other parts of the enterprise that were involved in the design process. These would include, of course, the departments of Research and Development, Work Study, and Personnel, as well as the Production departments.

It had seemed to us that there was considerable interest in the scholarly performance of academics and we knew that there was a real desire to obtain something 'practical' out of the project as a whole, but the difficulty was in fact to move into a role in which we could define and solve problems. A further difficulty relates to the requirements of the investigation. We had noted that our collection of technical data had been greatly simplified by the facility of different members of the consultant team for analysing various forms of data. As already indicated, it was possible, because of the previous experiences of the team, to make use of data constructed by the Work Study Department. However, we were aware of a need for a great deal more in the way of data to be gathered and evaluated, and also for economical means of doing so. Further, the evaluation would be most meaningful if demonstrated publicly rather than undertaken at the University campus. The preferred solution to this problem was to establish a joint investigatory group. We had also to contend with the reaction to our report on the packing crews. We wanted to obtain feedback on this and we were aware that a good deal had been learnt from the report. For example, at one stage, the author was talking during lunch to 'an executive' who began to explain the importance of 'socialization', and to talk in some detail about the packing crews. When the author recognized some of these aspects and inquired about their source, it was explained that there were external social scientists.

Though we were pleased to learn that this kind of diffusion was taking place, we were, as indicated earlier, concerned at the difficulty posed in obtaining public discussion between ourselves and the client. It seemed to us at the time, and subsequently, that the report had been of value, but that the clients had tended to discuss it among themselves. This was good in a number of respects but it made it difficult to proceed with the organizational design process as a joint activity. We were concerned to develop a multidisciplinary approach that would simultaneously take account of a variety of factors and facts. Again, one obvious solution to this problem is to create a *short-life project group* that would have as its mission tackling the Processing Department from a variety of aspects, including on-line process control, mechanization, method study, and production management.

Finally, we were concerned to expose more sharply the implicit assumptions held by members of the organization about the appropriate ways of organizing work, and to compare these assumptions with the alternatives that we knew existed, and with the ideas implicit in the management philosophy. We had been aware from the previous stage that, when it came to the actual process of job and organizational design, the principles typically applied were either those of scientific management *per se* or simply an extension of existing models of organization. It seemed to us that there was considerable difficulty in innovating. There were good reasons for this. Innovations have to be matched with the industrial relations situation of the organization, and the requirements of the Joint Industrial Council for that particular industry.

Our experience of the sociotechnical framework had indicated that there were a number of difficulties in carrying out a classical sociotechnical analysis (see Chapter 7). These difficulties in part arose from the simple fact that the sociotechnical framework is a product of the particular environment of the Tavistock Institute, and is best understood by them. We found a number of problems in inheriting a framework from another school of thinkers. One of these was that the data required were of a kind that could take a great deal of time to collect. Furthermore, it might be difficult to appraise their meaning. One solution to these problems was to be to create a situation in which the framework was used but supplemented where we felt it had weaknesses.

We were aware that the analysis in the Packing Department had been primarily concerned with the control of workflow. That is to say, that it was mainly concerned with the shopfloor level and only indirectly with the areas of coordination and control. Consequently, management's thinking in those areas, in terms of styles of management and the new management philosophy, had only been tackled in an indirect manner. However, as we had indicated, the form that relationships between management and other groups could take is affected by technological factors at the shop-floor level (Perrow 1967). The technological innovations planned were likely to create certain kinds of organizational structure that would facilitate some relationships and prohibit others. Thus we were anxious to move into the area of the coordination and control of departments and the enterprise as a whole.

The discussion of these problems among ourselves and with our colleagues in the client organization led us to formulate a new method of working for the Processing Department.

CHANGE OF LINKMAN

During this next period, the linkman changed. In our discussions with the first linkman, it was agreed that there was a need for a new strategy. The discussions revealed a number of areas of agreement, particularly with regard to our own feeling that the period of general education which, in fact, is the best way in describing the previous piece of work, was now over and there was a need to go for a problem-solving period. While these discussions were taking place, we learnt that our first linkman was about to be promoted and to receive experience in another factory and would thus be unable to continue. This caused us considerable concern, and we gave a great deal of thought to whom we would ideally like to carry on the next stage of the project. At that time, we were extremely nervous about what could happen because, though we had had a number of differences of opinion with our first linkman, there is no doubt that he was in a key position to inform the Azimuth group of our work and our ideas and also that he had both initially and subsequently shown support for what we were attempting to do. Further, he was sympathetic to our approach. Following discussions in which we really were not very sure about the alternatives, it was proposed that the most appropriate liaison person would be the Industrial Relations Manager. And in fact he became our second linkman. Up to that period we had had very little contact with him, apart from meetings in the initial period. However, when we went to present our ideas and to seek his support and approval, it was apparent that a good deal of diffusion had occurred in the Azimuth Group. The new man was, like our first linkman, an extremely intelligent and cogent thinker. Indeed, at times he almost alarmed us by the rapidity with which he developed our suggestions and was willing to go forward with plans that we felt were in some senses experimental.

Essentially, our aim was to work on the reconstruction of 'a day' in the existing plant as it affected the flow of work, the technology, and the persons employed. Then we would repeat the exercise, going through 'a day' as it was anticipated to take place in the new plant. We wanted then to compare the two pictures that emerged. One of our principal ideas was the notion of scenario-writing (Jantsch 1967), which we will discuss in more detail subsequently.

It was agreed that a 'short-life project group', containing members from various departments concerned with both the design and the future operation of the new Processing Department, would be gathered together. We had in mind the idea of holding a number of main meetings over a period of several months and, in between, of conducting various research and investigatory activities, both separately and jointly. The results would be brought to the next meeting for presentation and evaluation.

PHASE III OVERVIEW

The work in the Processing Department was coordinated through six major meetings spread over a period of five months in 1968. The initial three meetings were concerned with outlining and examining the old and new technical systems, including the flow and allocation of work, and the function of on-line process control. The meetings were based on papers presented by members of the R & D and Production Departments. We were all able to question these proposals and to suggest and discuss alternatives. During these meetings we aimed at determining the range of technological alternatives and indicating how the proposed technical system would affect the social system. Also we were able to obtain a valuable picture of the human tasks required to operate the new technology. We learnt that the sequence of operations was fixed and unalterable, but there were some variations in the autonomy of the parts of the total process (*Figure 8*, p. 124). For example, it was possible to vary the time balance between some of the operations on the raw material. The sequence of operations may be regarded as largely given, and the main opportunities for different technical layouts were restricted to different configurations of the same sequence. For example, it could be a straight line, a U shape, or a T shape, or an L shape.

Subsequent meetings were concerned with the examination of the human tasks and the close scrutiny of alternative forms of organization. In all this it was assumed that the market characteristics would remain as predicted at the start of the exercise in mid June 1967.

Even though the technological innovations would considerably alter both the internal social organization of the Processing Department and the manner of its coordination with other production departments and production control procedures, it must be noted that the department would still be one of the most autonomous in the new factory, in both spatial and temporal terms.

For the purposes of exposition we have focused on the six major meetings. This somewhat distorts what actually happened because a great deal occurred in between meetings, but it does provide a useful structure.

TECHNOLOGY, WORKFLOW, AND CONTROL SYSTEM

Meeting 1: Technology

At this meeting we outlined the proposed method of working. Our new linkman, the chairman of the project group, indicated that we would be adopting an approach that corresponded to the ideas of scenario-writing.

Emphasis was given, in the introduction, to tracing out the working of the department, both as a technical system and as a social system, in terms of a typical day and a typical week, making allowance for contingencies. We expanded upon the sociological and psychological aspects with which we were particularly concerned, pointing to the general principles of organization that were to be examined, and relating these to changes in management philosophy.

At this point, the notion of 'social architecture' was introduced. We suggested that the layout of machinery would create a particular social arrangement of people and that, arising from the kinds of events that occur in the department, there would emerge a structure of relationships that would contain a mixture of different tasks and consequently of different roles. Illustrations were given of this. We said there was a structure of roles existing now and there would be a structure of relationships in the future, and our aim was to compare one with the other. This involved reconstructing the future, which would be done jointly. Emphasis was also given to achieving a fit between the principles of organization and coordination for this particular department, and the rest of the factory. We then moved on to talk about styles of management and their relationship to different kinds of task (Bell 1966). Finally, attention was given to the problems of the boundaries between groups and the implications that future designs might have for the existing interrelationships of groups within the department, and the relationship between the production direct workers and the non-direct workers who were supplying services (see Chapter 9). Within 'social architecture', we included the idea of anticipating the sorts of problem that would arise in the future by finding out what differences there were between the present and the future. It was suggested that organizational design was a prior stage to organization-building. To illustrate the notion of organization-building, we took the example of the work of the Danish consultant Hjelholt (1964) on new oil-tankers.

The Research and Development executive began his exposition of the plans for the new technology. The paper he presented and circulated covered the possibilities and also the actual plans he had in mind; the likelihood of their being implemented; and a short section on the manning he envisaged.

It may be seen from *Figure 8* that the manufacture of the raw material involved seven stages. In the first two, it was anticipated that there would be very little technical change, though it was hoped there might be some innovations in the methods of docketing and auditing the batches of raw material. For the third and fourth stage, it was anticipated that there would be changes in mechanization and also the introduction of automation, including on-line process control. This also applied to the fifth and sixth stages. The final stage is one of temporary storage.

At this point, we inquired about the possibilities of locating the processes in a different sequence. These, in a sense, must have seemed very naïve questions, but I had found this to be a fruitful way of proceeding when employed in work study. Essentially the idea is to start by questioning every stage in the process, both as to whether it could be eliminated as such, and as to whether some processes might be done before others. The responses to these questions satisfied us that the process had to be sequential in terms of the current developments of the raw material and of the available technology.

Once this process of questioning the sequence of the technology was completed, we moved on to inquiring about possible configurations. Our interest here was to see whether we had a choice of, let's say, an H as compared to an L formation. It might be that at a later stage one particular configuration would facilitate a different kind of group structure from another, and perhaps even allow the emergence of more preferable types of group structure.

The representative from Production expressed considerable concern about the new technology and the ideas advanced for manning. He had obvious doubts about the suitability of on-line process control, and also expressed some fears about safety. We therefore arranged that he should liaise with Research and Development to examine this issue more closely during his preparation for the next meeting. We had in mind that the Production representative would prepare, for the next meeting, a sample schedule covering the sequence of events for the workflow for one day. This would include the position at the start of a typical day and the processing of the raw material through to the final stage of manufacture, together with an examination of the sort of contingencies that arise.

The discussion of manning also led to the exposing of ideas about the preferred form of manning for this department. The Research and Design executives had a clear picture of what they considered to be the appropriate method of deploying people to tasks. This point is evident in the way in which details were given of people's duties and the way they were finalized under the heading of 'skilled', 'semi-skilled', and 'unskilled tasks'. The mode of transposing tasks to roles reflected a mixture of the principles of scientific management and the existing situation. It quite clearly did not reflect the interest of the Azimuth Group in the participative principles of organization.

Looking back on this meeting, we summarized our own impressions somewhat as follows. We felt the meeting had actually aided Research and Development in presenting their ideas to other people, and that it created a general interest for the group. Starting with technology had been a success, because it enabled us to move from the known to the unknown. Thus we were able to create the short-life project group as an institution by beginning with things people knew about. The discussion had also been revealing in that it indicated the requirements people had in mind about the new social system and some of the problems envisaged. Finally, the meeting brought us up to date with regard to the latest technical developments and anticipated developments, and it revealed disparities of knowledge between various members of the project group.

At the end of this first meeting, tasks were allocated to members of our team and to members of the various teams from within CCE Ltd. It was agreed that some of these activities would be reported at the next meeting.

Meeting 2: Workflow

This meeting was primarily concerned with workflow. We had asked the one man who had had most experience of the production process to prepare a paper outlining the existing situation and indicated how it was likely to be affected by the technological innovations presented at the previous meeting. We asked him to construct a starting figure of orders to the department. Readers will note three points emerging during this particular meeting and the subsequent ones. The representative from Production changed his view of the technological innovations, particularly with regard to on-line process control. After close investigation, he came to the conclusion that the life of the production manager would be considerably easier, not more difficult. Moreover, he became extremely interested in the ideas about different forms of social organization, and his sympathy and support were crucial to the work we undertook in the project group. Finally, he gave an outstanding performance, demonstrating great skill, in drawing together technical and production aspects and relating them to organizational design.

At the start of the meeting we were presented with a large chart showing the seven main operations in the processing of the raw material against a time-scale for one day. The diagram contained a number of assumptions: that raw material left over from the previous day would be located in the first three operations; that the time-value for this would be four hours; that the mixing machine would contain four hours' stock; and that the variations in the finished raw material required would remain within the existing limits. This last point reflects a more general assumption referred to earlier about the state of the market.

The Production representative then related the data derived from planning schedules to the format already presented. Typically, Production Planning sent management an official plan of what was required for each of the main types of raw material. This schedule was very much in the form of a 'programme', in terms of March and Simon's distinction between 'programme activities' and 'feedback activities'. However, the production manager indicated that adjustments were required, both in terms of updating the plan and in terms of liaison with the Making and Packing Departments. Thus production management was faced with the problem of sorting out general aims and particular requirements.

Questions asked included: 'Where does management look for direction?' 'Is it to the Making Department?' 'What are the critical points in the process?' 'What is the latest time for action at any one of the seven stages within the department?' 'How will the role of management and supervision be affected by the changes in mechanization and automation and particularly by the introduction of on-line process control?' 'What variations arise from demand for raw material as compared to variations arising from breakdowns?' 'What limitations are built in by the influence of external agencies upon the rate at which the ingredients for the raw material can be made available?'

The next part of the meeting was essentially concerned with introducing contingencies. We attempted to take account of the non-availability of inputs, that is to say, of the basic unprocessed raw material. For example, if there was fog affecting transport, or holdups affecting railways, what impact would this have upon the process? This question led us to inquire into the previous history of stoppages arising from the non-availability of inputs, and here we discovered that this had rarely occurred, in fact hardly ever.

The next focus was on the difficulties arising from saturation of storage space. This led on to questions about the relationship between the primary departments and the subsequent departments. We were able to work out what contingency plans would be required for the Making Department. This raised questions that were going to be critical on the new site, and also indicated the things we should be looking at when we moved back to the Making Department later. Here we were obviously focusing upon departmental boundaries (Litwak 1961; Miller & Rice 1967).

The emphasis upon contingencies arising from inputs and outputs had considerable advantages for the general discussion. An obvious gain was that it raised the general question of departmental boundaries and interdepartmental coordinating activities. Also it focused all our attentions upon the interrelationships between the various departments and the operation of the plant as a whole at the new site. By linking the second and the first meetings, it became obvious that the exercise had made us all aware of the flexibility in the running of the Processing Department. We were now in a position to compare the underlying ideas that had influenced the manning proposals of the R & D executive with the data and experiences presented by the production manager. The latter had, by his focus upon *events*, indicated a great deal more about the requirements for 'social organization'. Considerable emphasis was placed upon this aspect in the opening chapter on organizational design.

A number of concerns had already emerged: the role of supervision and management, and the role of the computer. It was agreed that at the next meeting the R & D executive responsible for computer installations would give a paper on his particular plans, and that we would then work upon this to examine the nature of control and coordination implied in the new system. There was also the area of maintenance work and the problem of how variable would be the requirements for maintenance as compared, for example, with our other departments in the factory. We were aware of differential usage of maintenance and the implications this would have for the total social structure of the future (see Phase 6). We began to collect data on the activities of each group, and of the individuals which composed it, in the existing situation in a more sociological way. This point again directly relates to the notion we had of organizational design. We felt that the questions we had been asking in relation to the technical concept of the department had created a general awareness of the social and technical problems involved.

The next part of the second meeting concerned itself with relating the picture presented by the production manager to the manning figures contained in the first paper. Here, we began at the first operation in the process and went through what happens when each load reaches the factory and has to be handled, and what configurations of loads are likely to occur. Attention was focused upon carrying out a 'task analysis' of the interrelated activities required. We were also concerned to find the interconnected decision-taking areas.

For example, in the existing situation, certain decisions are recorded on cards, which are attached to parts of the raw material. In the new process, it was envisaged that automatic punch-recording machines might be introduced. This decision would affect the entire control structure of that part of the process. We proceeded from the first operation right through to the seventh, carrying out a similar kind of analysis. We obtained a picture of things as they are. It should be emphasized that this picture took into account the total social relationships and the tasks involved. Towards the end of this meeting, we began to arrange for the next; it was agreed that the third meeting would be concerned with the computer aspects and the fourth with the 'task analysis'.

Meeting 3: Process control

The third meeting examined the main functions to be performed by the process-control computer. These could be examined under three headings: the control of product quality; the scheduling of production; the collecting of accounting information.

The control of production quality involved the setting of the correct operating criteria; the maintenance of the correct environmental conditions; the maintenance of a smooth product flow for the seven stages; and the sequential starting and stopping of the equipment that made up each section at the beginning and end of a production run. The scheduling of production involved the interpreting of the production programme; its updating; and the revision of routing schedules in the light of variances arising, most probably, from breakdowns. The collecting of accounting information included a whole range of details. These mainly concerned various states of the raw material and it was arranged that these would be fed to a central point.

It was the functions undertaken by the computer with regard to the control of product quality which the R & D executive felt would have the greatest effect on the people working in the department. In his view, these would affect the total numbers employed. This is an interesting observation because it again reveals the idea that R & D people may typically be expected to have of the effects of technological innovation. That is to say, they think in the most manifest terms of the numbers of people involved, rather than of the social structures required for the new situation.

Meeting 4: Task analysis

The previous meetings had been primarily concerned with the technology and workflow for the Processing Department. We had used them to create a situation in which our own ideas would be understood and, we hoped, more favourably received. During these first meetings, we had been commenting upon the sociological implications and the particular psychological features of the situation that we considered to be problematical and of concern. All the time the emphasis had been upon differences and alternatives.

After the first three meetings, we were expected to produce 'the goods'. The fourth meeting was our first opportunity to examine the task aspects in some detail. The session was largely occupied with examining a record of the tasks that would have to be carried out to man the new technology. We did this stage by stage, continuing from the exploration of the unloading of the raw material right through to the organizing work done at the end when the transformed raw material went into storage.

During this period, we were able to draw upon the experiences of the industrial engineers, who were able to provide a great deal of data about the task requirements. There was close agreement between ourselves and them, in the sense that we were able to use the kinds of data that they produced. We did not at that stage think that we would necessarily come to the same conclusions when designing the organizational aspect.

A good example of differences in ideas about organizing work arose when examining the manufacturing stage, which required particular skills of a semi-craft nature. We had observed that in the existing technology the people who occupied the relevant role were seen to be of higher status than their colleagues. The task essentially was one of maintaining quality rather than undertaking any effort-type work. Although the early meetings had indicated that this process may be, in part, automated, we were not impressed by the arguments put forward and suspected that the nature and character-istics of the raw material would prevent this. We also felt there was very little understanding of that particular task. Our impression was that the discussion was strongly influenced by the historical back-ground of this particular group and by its perceived status. In prac-tice, it seemed there was somewhat of an oversimplification of the tasks; alternatively that the job was very much less demanding and strategic than management was suggesting. Following these discussions, it was agreed that we would make a film of that particular process and of the operations and the craft groups involved, and would also perform a detailed activity study. This was in part carried out by Industrial Engineering with liaison from one of our team. It was agreed that the observational aspects would be carried out by members of CCE Ltd, while the study of orientations to work would be undertaken by ourselves.

Another 'job' that was the centre of much discussion was that of the 'controller'. This is an entirely new job that arose because of the technical innovations of automation. The questions asked included: 'Are there similarities between this job and that of, for example, a signal-box operator?' 'If there are not, what kinds of special knowledge are required?' 'Is there some similarity between the kinds of knowledge of the coordination between the parts of the process the controller would require and the kind of knowledge that would be required by a foreman or manager?' This latter question reflects the 'centrality' of the process (Emery 1959). It will be seen in the section on sociotechnical analysis that one of the features of the first part of any analysis is to locate areas where it seems likely that it will be necessary to concentrate either effort or skill. In the design process, these areas may well become the points at which critical roles are located. The reasoning behind this is that, if one is to create a post with responsibility, then it seems prudent to ally this post with tasks that are widely perceived as involving responsibility and judgement.

Another problem that arose in the task analysis was the difficulty of working out the effect of technical breakdowns upon the social system. We thus attempted to identify different levels of complexity of stoppage and the kinds of social organization that might be created for tackling them. It may be recalled that earlier in this chapter, we drew attention to the work of the Danish consultant Hjelholt (1964). We had in mind here that if we obtained examples of different kinds of breakdown and of the likely role structure required to tackle them, then we could use the ideas devised by Hjelholt for dry-land training and apply them in the primary department. We will return to this point later (Chapter 10).

Another area of importance was the departmental boundary. The existing concept of boundary was critically examined. The evidence presented indicated that the Processing Department was in a number of ways autonomous in relation to the rest of the factory. In this sense, the existing boundary was more likely to remain than that between Making and Packing. It will be noted from *Figure 8* there is a time buffer between Processing and Making.

One of the important developments of this meeting was the discussion of a variety of ideas for matching roles to tasks. These ideas were characterized, identified, and then critically examined. For

Figure 8   Sequence of operations in Processing

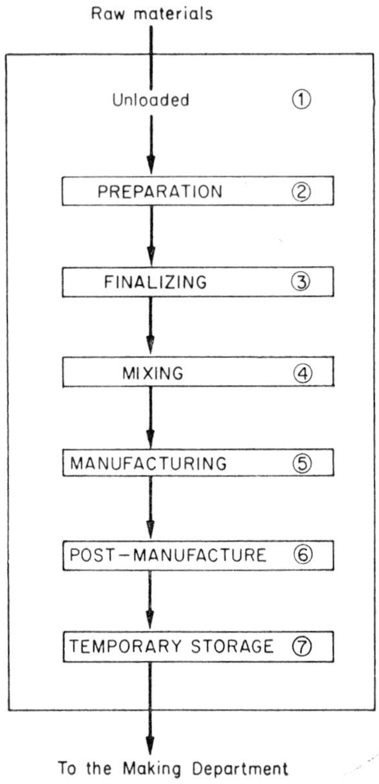

Raw materials

Unloaded   ①

↓

| PREPARATION   ② |

↓

| FINALIZING   ③ |

↓

| MIXING   ④ |

↓

| MANUFACTURING   ⑤ |

↓

| POST—MANUFACTURE   ⑥ |

↓

| TEMPORARY STORAGE   ⑦ |

↓

To the Making Department

example, the meeting discussed the idea of two teams in the department, each based upon certain operations with the leader located at the critical part of the process.

One of the difficulties we faced was that of analysing the coordination system that was likely to be required. Indeed, it was difficult to construct a satisfactory picture of the role of production control.

As on previous occasions, various activities were arranged for the next meeting. These included the study of the operators at the manufacturing stage (*Figure 8*).

Meeting 5: Organizational choice

The objectives of this meeting were threefold. First, to scrutinize the record of the tasks and task-interdependencies required by the new technology. Second, to develop and appraise alternative forms of manning and organization. The intention was to devise forms of organization that closely embodied the participative principles of management set out in a management philosophy document. Third, to inject our social-science input in such a way that it would become part of CCE's normal mode of thinking and working irrespective of our presence on site.

We hoped to achieve the 'building-in of a social-science-using capability' by making several of our analytical frameworks explicit rather than implicit, and to illustrate our thinking by examples and analysis drawn from the immediate knowledge and experience of the members of the project team. The explanation and illustration of analytical frameworks was primarily concerned with what we as behavioural scientists *recorded* and abstracted from the existing situation. A further set of problems arise when consideration is given to what use the record will be put to. For example, the same data on tasks could be used to design forms of organization embodying different principles. We wished to emphasize this by constructing one organizational design on the basis of human resources principles and another on the basis of the principles of scientific management. Both designs would then be compared and used as a base to generate a range of alternative designs.

The underlying objective was to focus upon the impact of technological innovation on the existing traditions, status, careers, and 'life styles' of members of the Processing Department.

Our plan for the meeting was a recapitulation of our previous work and the underlying themes, to be followed by an outline of the 'sociotechnical framework' and the verification of our sociotechnical record of the existing and future situations. This included data collected by ourselves and also by other members of the group. Then we planned to introduce a short paper on a group of skilled craftsmen whose activities and occupational identity had been the subject of controversy in the previous meeting. We had carried out an investigation of attitudes and behaviour, which was to be supplemented by a film and an extensive activity sample. Once these data had been collated, discussed, and agreed we planned to tackle the generation of alternative forms of manning. This would lead into an examination of the linkages between the Processing Department and its 'input' and 'output' systems. Finally, we wanted to have a review of the work of the project group, with the aim of assessing our effectiveness and deciding whether the method of working should be extended to other departments. If we decided that it should then we would need to plan a transition stage.

The first item – the presentation of the sociotechnical framework – was dealt with quite quickly. It was quite clear from the questions asked and the additional illustrative material presented to us that the underlying ideas had been grasped by members of the project group. The success of this item is important because the general response to the concept is one of blank acceptance or blank amazement. However, in this case we had outlined the concept in a general way at the start of the exercise and had structured a large proportion of the data collected during the subsequent meetings within the framework. Hence the exposition was in part an explication of certain ideas that we had been implicitly using without making them public.

Our reason for explaining the concept in some detail was that we believed it would facilitate its selective usage after we had moved on to other parts of CCE Ltd. Further, we felt it would increase the effectiveness of our meetings by helping everyone to screen out redundant information.

The explanation for the rapidity and depth of acceptance and comprehension almost certainly rests with the way in which the sequence of meetings had been planned. For example, by starting with the technological aspects, we had moved through an area familiar to members of the project group. By the time of this meeting, the project group was aware that we had a distinctive, but implicit framework for asking questions and evaluating responses. Thus the exposition of the framework was in some ways a formalization of something they had already been experiencing. We feel that this is important for the strategy adopted towards the problem of injecting social science into organizations. Our work with the project group illustrates some of the advantages of 'coupling' outside agents from universities and similar institutions to organizations. The next item on the agenda was the record of the task requirements at present and for the future. The essential feature of this record was that it indicated where, when, and how the social system would be required to 'intervene' in order to progress the flow of work through the department.[1]

Once the record had been approved, we were able to compare the existing situation with that planned for the new factory. Certain points became clear. For example, there would be important changes in the composition and shape of the skill hierarchy. Changes in technology such as mechanization removed some manual tasks like unloading and handling materials. Also the introduction of automation and on-line process control changed both the technological interdependencies within the department and the skills required to maintain maximum operating time. The new equipment required more electrical skills and also introduced a new set of tasks concerned with monitoring and controlling the processes. One of the points of earlier discussion had been how the content of the existing tasks and roles was perceived by operatives working in the Processing Department. There had been considerable controversy over the nature of the tasks undertaken by the skilled operators on the manufacturing stage. At one time this 'bundle' of tasks had been recognized as being of high skill and status, but what would the future situation be?

This question occupied the next point on our agenda. The reason for selecting this particular group of tasks and roles for special investigation was that they had traditionally represented one of the key points where attention had had to be located. In some ways the existing coordination of the department and its 'social organization' hinged on this particular group of men. We knew that in the new plant it was intended that considerable emphasis should be given to maintenance/repair, on the one hand, and to the bundle of tasks connected with the control on the on-line process control system, on the other hand. The location of coordination was likely to change and perhaps be more diffuse.

We had asked for several kinds of data about these skilled operators. First, we all watched a film that had been specially produced for the group, and compared it with the results of two pieces of intensive observation. One was an activity sample that had been conducted in each of the three factories. This indicated the main

---

[1] This aspect is developed by Emery (1959) and would seem to have been central to the most recent investigations of the late Professor Joan Woodward. See her notion of 'constrained behaviour' (Woodward 1970, pp. 5–13).

features of the job. The other was a very detailed commentary on the sequence of tasks performed during one day. This had been carried out by the representative from Production and showed that it would not be feasible to automate that part of the process.

Our own paper was designed to demonstrate the kinds of factor the project group would have to include when designing the new department. Its function was to demonstrate the same kind of point as we had made to a quite different group in the Packing Department. We viewed the discussion of the psychological and sociological aspects as an essential lead into the developing of alternative designs. In introducing the paper, we argued that the present behaviour and orientations would reflect the operators' experiences as individuals and collectively. Emphasis was placed upon historical background tradition, and customs and their significance for the future. Our introductory comments outlined the reasons for this emphasis. We have paraphrased the paper on the manufacturing operatives:

1. Before the Second World War, manufacturing contained many small machines. These were manned by a large number of operators who were considered to be skilled and were given relatively high status. They played an important role, at that time, in one of the unions.

   This position had been gradually eroded in two ways. First, the performance of the machines was continually improved by the work of skilled maintenance and R & D. This reduced the number and extent of uncertainties associated with the task. Second, technological innovation reduced the total number of men employed in the three factories to a fraction of its prewar total.

   By the 1950s, this semi-craft group had been reduced in size and was losing its critical function and prestige in the perceptions of other groups working in the department. Gradually the established career pattern of starting on a labouring job and working one's way up to being an operator disappeared.

2. The present-day operative was typically over 50, had been with CCE Ltd for much of his working-life, and had worked his way up the job hierarchy. He felt that he still had a wide knowledge of other jobs in the department and particularly of the problems of 'what to do, when, and how'. The operators considered that this kind of knowledge was necessary when relating their work to

other activities in the department. They all identified their own job as significant and were emotionally attached/committed to the task. Their self-image stressed skill, judgement, pride, plus a sense of belonging to a special group. Emphasis was given by them to the judgement of quality when inspecting the raw material. (We concluded that the neutral category of 'attendance' presented in the report based upon activity sampling was interpreted by the men as part of inspection.) Relative to other jobs and their own previous experience the operators expressed satisfaction in their present job.

3. They viewed supervision as the source of information, coordination, and occasionally direction, but not discipline. Our comments on the 'craft' nature of the job suggest that discipline was perceived as based within the group rather than externally located. In this instance, the 'craft' characteristics were organizationally induced and were not induced supportively in the outside community as would be the case in shipbuilding.[1]

Interpretation

— The job is still perceived by its present occupants as one that provides intrinsic satisfaction. These satisfactions appear to be linked with the former high status of the job and the previous experiences of the present generation of operators.

— The hypothesis advanced at a previous meeting suggesting that the job is boring and monotonous is suspect. This hypothesis did not sufficiently recognize the significance of historical factors.

— There is a considerable divergence between the project group's definition of satisfying work and the experience of the population who will be affected by technological innovations.

— What will happen when the present men, now in their fifties, retire? To answer this and the related question of how the operators are perceived by other individuals and groups a further study was undertaken of other employees in the Primary Department.

[1] For a more extended discussion of the position and persistence of craft groups in Britain, see Eldridge (1968) and Brown and Brannen (1970). We have argued elsewhere that this feature is typically neglected in the approaches of organizational psychologists (Clark, Ford, & Eling 1969). This may reflect differences in the institutional basis of industrial relationship in Europe compared with America. If it does, then there are considerable implications for the exporting and importing of 'organizational development' and other instrumented social technologies.

Additional information
Other groups of workers, particularly the younger members of the department, did not perceive that the operators were of distinctive status though they did believe that the job required skill.

Summary
Before the 1950s, the operators were a clearly identifiable occupational group whose identity was essentially a product of their collective experience within CCE Ltd. It was not supported in the outside community. They were once at the high point of a career ladder, but this has been undermined by technological and administrative changes. Their occupation of that position, coupled with their knowledge of the existing department and their own position in the authority system, has supported the hierarchy of knowledge and authority that characterize the Processing Department.

The discussion that followed this paper focused on several kinds of implication. First it was necessary to examine the relevance of the concept of craft group and the explanation of their origins in terms of inplant factors. This discussion was developed by drawing comparisons between the operators and craft groups in the shipbuilding industry (Eldridge 1969). The comparison presented the added advantage that we were able to consider the nature of authority relations in both situations. In the case of CCE Ltd, the social, technological, and economic factors that facilitated the emergence of the operators were being themselves transformed. Second, the discussion provided a bridge to the examination of the manning and organization of the new department. We had intended to discuss a variety of alternatives, but by this stage the day was drawing to a close and so we proposed that the new form of organization should approximate as closely as possible to the 'autonomous group'.

In practice this proposal provided a good opportunity to show what the participative management philosophy would imply for the Processing Department. We were able to contrast the 'autonomous group' with the earlier proposals from R & D, who were sceptical about the appropriateness of the concept for the technology and for the social characteristics of the workforce. They preferred a sharp delineation of roles and almost total role-specialization.

Meeting 6: Conclusions and transition

The final meeting has three special objectives. First, we and the linkman had decided that the whole method of working adopted in the study of the Processing Department should be extended to the next phase. This was to consist of a sociotechnical study of both the Making and Packing Departments. That decision was in part based upon the stress we had given to changing boundaries in the new factory. The first objective posed considerable problems particularly in the explaining of our method of working to a new set of people. To combat this problem, we decided to include some representatives of the new group at this last meeting. The second objective was to ensure that our input to the technical design teams would still remain salient when we had moved on to another part of CCE Ltd. One problem was the high likelihood that there would be changes in decisions made at the earlier meetings. We felt we had considered this aspect in the strategy adopted for 'building in a social-science-using capability', but we would not claim that all ideas and suggestions were accepted or relevant. Given the uncertainties about the final form of the department at the new site we felt that our best hope lay in reaffirming the points we considered to be critical. Third, we hoped that the presence of members of the Making and Packing Departments would enable the project group to examine the 'boundary' conditions between the departments.

The meeting had two principal items on the agenda. First, a recapitulation of the latest position with regard to the technology and its layout. Second, the discussion of manning and organization in relation to the tasks previously identified.

The meeting started by the R & D executives presenting their latest ideas on equipment and layout. In this second presentation, a new set of points was included. We were informed that certain parts of the layout were fixed and there were no conceivable options. This was an important innovation in the joint approach to organizational design because it indicated how far it would be possible to alter the sequence and configuration of plant and operations. Given that there were few options, we then moved to the manning aspect.

The new proposals for manning were similar in some respects to earlier totals of numbers of persons required to operate the department, but now it was suggested that the new form of organization should include interchanging of certain roles at regular intervals.

This was an important development because the proposal, which came from R & D, reflected the requirements of social organization in general and the advantages that can arise from 'mutual role knowledge' in particular.

'Mutual role knowledge' was one idea advanced in the earlier meetings to emphasize that the role of the social scientist need not be to increase the level of friendliness in the department (Emery 1959). Indeed, we might argue that there are people who prefer to be relatively independent of other people when at work. Further, we had shown in the study of the female packing crews that the most probable explanation of the cohesiveness of the crews and their 'occupational group' was high knowledge of the exact content of one another's roles rather than sociability. Transferring this principle to the Primary Department raised three questions. Was high 'mutual role knowledge' essential or important for the operation of the new technology? Was it desirable as a means of implementing the participative philosophy? Finally, how did the principle relate to the previous traditions and preferences of members of the current workforce?

SUMMARY

This chapter has presented an example of the way in which behavioural scientists can carry out organizational design by adopting the approach of joint investigation and decision-making. The focus has been upon the ways in which the sociological and psychological perspective was diffused and tested. The aim was to obtain an adoption of this perspective.

In the next chapter some of the analytical frameworks we were using 'backstage' are introduced and examined. The sociotechnical approach is scrutinized. After the discussion of frameworks, the following chapter takes the story of the consultancy to the next stage, when we attempted to apply the approach used in the Processing Department to other parts of the firm.

PART THREE

Analysis

CHAPTER SEVEN

Analytical framework for organizational design

INTRODUCTION

In this chapter some of the analytical frameworks adopted in the first year of the consultancy are identified, explained, and scrutinized. It is important to recognize that there is a distinction between the analytical frameworks that are presented by the consultant to the client and the frameworks actually used to identify and analyse problems (Clark & Ford 1970). The frameworks presented to the client tend to be simplistic, including apparently practical items like 'management controls', 'systems', and 'optimization'. These general frameworks are intended as a bridge to the client's ways of thinking. They do in part extend the prevailing level of understanding for the client, but perhaps equally important from the consultant's viewpoint is the way in which particular frameworks carve out areas of the enterprise and allocate them to particular experts (Clark & Cherns 1968). For this reason the new frameworks of thinking may cut across existing territorial boundaries between the various 'disciplines' that may be included under the general umbrella of management services. This implies that the acceptance and permanent adoption of particular frameworks are dependent upon the way in which the consultant 'fits' them to the existing configuration of relationships and beliefs of those involved. In the earlier chapters we have indicated how we attempted to establish certain limited sets of ideas and ways of looking at the human aspect of the enterprise.

The notion of 'open sociotechnical system' was one of the most important bridging ideas which we utilized to link our activities to those of the engineers, and also to provide internal links within CCE Ltd for the diverse project groups engaged on parts of the new factory. There is considerable confusion and misunderstanding about the elements of the open sociotechnical systems approach, its purposes, and the ways in which it is utilized. We therefore present our understanding of this framework and our objectives in utilizing it.

The part played by technology as a variable is clearly of importance and this is defined and examined in a separate section which
critically appraises some of the more sweeping attacks on 'technological determinism'. That section is followed by a careful exposition of the advantages and limitations of 'systems analysis' in
organizational design. This chapter formalizes some of the ideas used
in the earlier chapters, but it does not outline the major ideas influencing the latter phases of the consultancy. These are summarized
and appraised in Chapter 10.

THE OPEN SOCIOTECHNICAL SYSTEM

The notion of the open sociotechnical system is one of the devices
developed by members of the Tavistock Institute engaged on consultancy and research in industrial enterprises. It was initially suggested in a research publication by Trist and Bamforth (1951)
following the analysis of changes in the organization of underground
coalmining arising from the transformation from the 'hand-got'
method to the mechanized 'longwall' method. Trist identified a number of changes in personal well-being for the miners and postulated a
connection between these and technological innovation. Trist argued
that the various aspects of the social and psychological features
identified could only be understood by reference to 'the detailed
engineering facts and the way the technological system as a whole
behaves in the environment of the underground situation'.

This article has been of considerable importance to the study of
organizational design. It is important to note that Trist was emphasizing that his observations from the mining situation could only be
understood by reference to technological details. He was therefore
focusing upon an aspect, or critical variable, that he felt had been
neglected in previous researches. He did not state *how* this variable
– technology and production system – should be accounted for, only
that it could not be neglected in that particular study.

Trist suggested that the form of organizing the work that had been
introduced to man the new advanced form of mechanization was
based on the principles of 'scientific management' and large-batch
production, yet the situation underground was one that made the
application of these principles unsatisfactory. Similar observations
have been made by other researchers (Gouldner 1954; Stinchcombe
1958). In a close analysis of underground working, Trist demonstrated that the form of organization adopted produced considerable

strains that were dysfunctional for the miners and for management. His observations are perhaps best summarized in the statement: 'Unequal men with equal stints under unequal conditions.'

Subsequent work by Tavistock researchers and consultants developed the initial ideas along two lines. First, emphasis was given to ascertaining the part played by the technology and production system in structuring the working activities of members of work groups. Second, it was hypothesized that the features of the human system that the researchers regarded as dysfunctional could be removed by redesigning the allocation of work in terms of the principles of the human resources approach (see Chapter 2). This particular hypothesis was tested out in a wide range of settings. In further researches into coalmining it was discovered that there were two quite different methods of allocating work among three shifts of approximately 40 men. The interesting and important aspect of this finding was that two different forms of organizing were being applied to largely similar technologies and coal seams. The findings of the researchers are summarized in the title of the eventual publication, *Organizational Choice*, by Trist and his colleagues (1963). This provided extensive and important evidence that work groups of as many as 50 men spread over three shifts *could* satisfactorily organize the allocation of work among themselves. This form of organization became known as the 'autonomous group' and later as 'responsible autonomy'. It was one of the forms of organization suggested for the Processing Department at CCE Ltd (Chapter 6).

During the 1950s and 1960s the idea of looking systematically at the technical system in job design was closely linked with the prescriptive idea of responsible autonomy. Gradually these two aspects became separated. Emery (1959) made an important contribution to this process when he formalized the principal features of sociotechnical analysis.

Emery was primarily writing about work situations in which the technology is a key element and the objectives of the enterprise closely resemble those of industrial enterprises. He suggested that enterprises should be regarded as systems of interrelated parts, but he added that even when investigators and consultants had adopted the systems approach they had adopted a closed systems framework. That is to say, they ignored exchanges between the enterprise and its environment. He argued that the permeation of the enterprise by the environment is neglected, and examination of internal differentiation is totally omitted in closed systems studies. When looking at the role of the technology in open systems approaches, it is suggested the production apparatus limits the variation in the range of output markets for the product, and that enterprises seek to handle this by creating a 'distinctive competence' (Selznick 1954).

In an open sociotechnical systems analysis the consultant recognizes that the technology forms an 'internalized environment' for the members of the enterprise. The consultant will seek to identify how the system copes with gluts and lacks in its exchanges with the environment. Does the enterprise elaborate or change existing structures in order to cope? This question formed part of the focus for Clark's (1965) study of the 'peak period phenomenon' in enterprises.

Basically the open sociotechnical framework is presented as a frame of reference for ordering the collection and interpretation of facts in problem-solving work by behavioural scientists in industrial enterprises. It is not recommended for regulative institutions like prisons. The application of the approach is carried on at three interrelated, but analytically distinct, levels. These levels are: the analysis of the technology and the human tasks required to operate it; the analysis of the internal coordination and control of the departments, groups, and functions within the enterprise; the detection of relevant aspects of the environment. We shall briefly look at each of these levels in turn.

(i) *Technology and work relations*

Trist (1951) distinguished technology from social structure and occupational roles and later attempted to introduce a number of concepts for depicting the kinds of interaction between them. A major problem facing the practitioner is to find a method of recording those aspects of the technology which are relevant to organizational design. Emery and his colleagues propose a useful solution to this problem. They suggest that the analyst gathers data about some eight critical dimensions of the technology and utilizes this information to construct a matrix of the human tasks required to operate the technology. This matrix should ideally indicate the ways in which tasks are connected and Emery provides a useful language of concepts for achieving this. This matrix of tasks is then used as the basis for allocating tasks to roles. We shall look at the dimensions of the technology first and then examine the way in which this data is used to reconstruct the social structure.

The technology may be approached by collecting data on eight dimensions:

— *Raw materials* The analyst examines the raw materials being transformed in the production process to ascertain the kinds of variability that they cause. For example, some raw materials are uniform and standardized, whereas others are highly variable. The former are typically associated with mass production and the latter with craft production.

— *The spatial and temporal dimensions of production* This includes the spatial deployment of men and machines as well as the spread of operations over time. In the coalmining study, Trist (1951, 1963), shows how changes in these aspects radically affect the problems of coordination between men and management. Though Tavistock members have provided a number of concepts for analysing this area, they all recognize and emphasize the need for more and better analytical frameworks.

— *Level of mechanization and automation* Changes in the level of technology have important and sometimes far-reaching consequences for the social structure. This has been demonstrated in a wide variety of contexts, including the introduction of computers (Mumford & Banks 1967) and automation in the tinplate industry (Chadwick-Jones 1970). As the level of automation increases, so the emphasis of management may move from man-hours to machine-hours (Rice 1963).

— *Operational units* This idea is similar to the work study notational system (ILO 1960) for recording elements of the workflow and splitting the elements into sequences. The analyst identifies the main sequences and uses the data in the later design of jobs. The work carried out in the Processing Department of CCE Ltd (Chapter 6) illustrates the use of the unit operations. In practice there are a number of difficulties with this part of the framework.

— *The degree of centrality of tasks* In any technology there are likely to be sets of tasks which, relative to others, require special skill and effort. The analyst should aim to identify these and use them in the design of the subsystem as points at which the location of formal supervision can be placed.

— *Maintenance activities* Any system requires tasks to maintain the continuance of the system. Maintenance refers to tasks involving the boundary conditions of the system – atmospheric conditions in hosiery factories, for example. The nature of maintenance activities will be strongly influenced by the level of mechanization and automation.

— *Supply activities*   This refers to all tasks concerned with securing an even rate of throughput. The analyst must consider the connections between the various subsystems when examining this aspect.

These dimensions are intended as guide to the kinds of data required in sociotechnical design. Careful use of these dimensions coupled with experience can provide the analyst with a systematic picture of the human tasks required to operate a particular technology.

At CCE Ltd these headings were used, mainly by Chris Eling, to organize his own data on the technology and the human tasks and also those collected during the first three meetings of the project group in the Processing Department. In that case a record was compiled for the existing and future situations.

Once the analyst has a systematic picture of the total of human tasks and their interdependencies, he then uses this picture to group tasks together into bundles that can be allocated to individuals and groups. As indicated in the chapter on organizational design, there are various sets of principles that can be applied in the allocation process. At this stage, however, it is more important to emphasize the need for a framework of concepts to describe the different kinds of task relationships. Without this framework sociotechnical design involving behavioural scientists and engineers is almost impossible.

Emery and his colleagues have made a number of suggestions about the ways in which tasks can be described. We found the framework useful in CCE Ltd, but we would not be confident about its continued usage there when we leave because it is necessary for one internal specialist to be familiar with the framework and be continually gaining experience in using it. In the method suggested by Emery tasks are initially subdivided into independent and dependent. Independent tasks do not require cooperation except for boundary and support conditions. Dependent tasks may be further subdivided into simultaneous and successive dependence and so on.

The analysis of tasks, including their characterization, is difficult and somewhat arduous when undertaken with specialists from non-behavioural science areas. The aim of the next stage is to transpose the information on the tasks on to a constructed network of roles (jobs). Thus the demands for human tasks which the technology requires are met by creating roles and a set of relationships between them that is based on known tasks. This process depends for its success on a guiding theory that identifies the most likely consequences. Earlier we noted the important differences in focus between the guiding theory of scientific management as compared to that of the human resources approach. In practical terms they both represent a gross simplification of the problems and both exclude one critical aspect. This is the 'needs and aspirations' of the members of the enterprise who are to be affected by the new organizational design.

In presenting sociotechnical design methods, Emery carefully emphasizes that the network of 'work relationships' created by the design team will not explain either individual feelings about work, colleagues, and company, or provide an understanding of any existing patterns of work relationships. So, for example, the explanation of the orientations and behaviour of the female packing crews requires reference to many variables and a consideration of the recent history of that group in its relations with other groups.

The aim of Emery's method is to give prime emphasis to the creation of a 'role culture' in which there is a mutual testing-out of one another's understanding. He is very critical of designing organizational units on the basis of personal relations and is specifically critical of the 'friendship theory' (Homans 1951). Emery argues that there is considerable evidence to show that men will carry out their tasks without reference to personal relationships if roles are well connected to each other. If we look at the female packing crews (Chapter 5) again, it may be noted that the allocation of tasks coupled with the systems of rotation and promotion facilitated a high level of mutual knowledge about the total tasks among members of the group. Thus there was a fund of knowledge within the crew about the role behaviour appropriate to various contingencies. The important aspect for organizational analysis is the emergence of standards within the group. This point influenced the final recommendations about the most appropriate form of organization for the Processing Department.

(ii) *Internal coordination*

The major problem that arises here is the extension of the sociotechnical concept to the whole enterprise. This problem was considered by Emery and his colleagues, but their published work up to 1960 does not give an indication of how they would proceed as analysts of the internal structure of coordination and control. Subsequently Miller and Rice became involved in a number of projects in which this aspect was central (Miller & Rice 1967).

A selection of major guidelines are set out by Miller and Rice in *Systems of Organization: The Control of Task and Sentient Boundaries* (1967) and will not be repeated here. It may be noted however that as the level of analysis moved from the design of the workplace to the design of the organizational unit as a whole, so there were increasing doubts about the general applicability of the 'autonomous group'. The new emphasis has become the detection of internal and external boundaries. This may seem a somewhat theoretical and obscure emphasis and it is, as we shall hope to show later, an analytical approach that is difficult to comprehend without effort and practice. However, we hope we have already demonstrated the importance of boundaries in the examination of the sentient group of female packers and the examination of the consequences of changes in task boundaries between operations and departments for the management of the enterprise as a whole. This aspect will be further examined in the chapters following the second half of the case study. For the moment we shall note that the requirement for coordination and control varies systematically in relation to the nature of the enterprise's methods of transforming its raw materials.

(iii) *Enterprise and environment*

The analysis of the relations with the external environment has played an increasing part in sociotechnical analysis and design. In the early accounts, which were mainly about shop-floor design, the external environment was not extensively characterized though its importance was clearly recognized. The focus was upon the 'leadership function' and the 'mission' of the enterprise (Selznick 1957). While this focus was significant, it was also difficult to link the various levels of analysis. This problem has been illuminated and partly resolved by the approach of Miller and Rice and the theorizing of Emery and Trist (1965) about connections between the external environment, dimensionalized in terms of random/organized and active/placid, with the internal structure.

At CCE Ltd we attempted to characterize the market and socio-political environments of the company in order to determine some of the main sources of variability for the enterprise. We assumed – hypothesized – that the formality of CCE's structure on the production side was largely explainable by reference to the rate of product innovation (Burns & Stalker 1961; Woodward 1958, 1965; Lorsch 1965; Crozier 1964; Perrow 1967). We also attempted to give public recognition to this hypothesis in design process, but found this a hard point to establish. Later it may be seen that we were able to reactivate this issue by linking it to 'perceived' changes in the composition of the market.

SOCIOTECHNICAL ANALYSIS AT CCE LTD

In the previous section the main elements of the sociotechnical analytic approach have been outlined. It is important to note that this is an approach developed by a small number of researchers and practitioners in response to particular problems. No completely satisfactory account or statement has as yet been published. It is to be hoped that this will soon happen, otherwise certain current misconceptions will be perpetuated. The reader should always bear in mind the purposes of the practitioner using the sociotechnical approach.

We would suggest that the notion of sociotechnical system is only useful if it is considered to be a general framework for ordering observations and analysis. Its specific usage will vary with the problems faced. In CCE Ltd the focus upon technology by social scientists was one of the bridges between ourselves and the Azimuth Group. With the help of members of that group were we able to link in our work with theirs under the theme of sociotechnical design. Thus it was used equally as a social linkage and as an analytical framework.

Our approach differs in some respects from the classical usages of the concept. We were not specifically committed to designing the organization from the bottom upwards, but argued that design is a fragmentary process in which piecemeal solutions and approximations require the continuous linking of levels of analysis. We were certainly not committed to any particular 'solution' such as the autonomous group. Rather we set out to show how that idea was relevant to the management philosophy but made difficult by certain technological factors. Perhaps our major difference lay in the ways in which we utilized the concept and our focus on the human side of the enterprise.

Given that all members of the Loughborough team had some experience and knowledge of technology, we felt the important facts were only those which related to the design process. Thus we decided against a study of the technology by ourselves only, preferring instead to have it examined in the group situation where those involved in the design and operation of the new plant had access to each other's work. In this way we avoided becoming unnecessarily knowledgeable about the technology and so were able to spend the maximum amount of time on the aspects we knew best – the human side.

Unlike many users of sociotechnical analysis, we did not accept any general postulates about 'the nature of man', but where relevant, went out and investigated particular situations (Chapters 8 and 9). Examples include the packing crews and the skilled male operatives in the Processing Department. Much of our emphasis was sociological rather than psychological. Our approach may be described as a mixture of an emphasis upon enterprises and an emphasis upon occupational groups. Essentially we were attempting to draw the attention of engineers to the ways in which they were structuring the lives of individuals and groups in the new factory. We were critical and always attempted to widen the range of factors and information that was considered relevant.

It might be argued that sociotechnical design is always taking place. At CCE Ltd the aim was to ensure that the 'socio' part was included in the design rather than as an unintended consequence.

CRITIQUE OF SOCIOTECHNICAL ANALYSIS

In this section some of the limitations of sociotechnical analysis are identified. The main emphasis is upon the following areas: the extent of discretion in roles and flexibility in organizational structure; the influence of the aspirations and orientations of the members of the enterprise on organizational design; the notion of system and its relevance to organizational design. This critique is based upon experiences at CCE Ltd and it must be acknowledged that the problems we found may not be relevant to the original creators of the sociotechnical concept, but they are of general relevance since they probably reflect the difficulties faced.

(i) *Flexibility and formality*

The major strengths of the framework are in the focus upon technology and the typology of task interdependencies, but one of the weaknesses is that roles and relations between roles are viewed in static terms. There is very little recognition given to predictable and patterned changes in the discretionary content of roles and role-relationships over time. This is in one sense a surprising omission because there are many examples of changes in structure over time. The sociologist Etzioni (1961) has made a subtle and important analysis of the changes in control relationships between superordinates and subordinates in relation to changes in tasks. He cites the examples of seasonal working, the holiday industry, political parties, and the military. Clark (1965, 1970) investigated changes in the management control system, employee involvement, and the application of discipline in relation to the onset and ending of peak periods in supermarkets and factories. Crozier (1964) demonstrated that the rigidity with which rules were applied by the supervisors in a French clerical agency varied consistently with the patterns of input of work to be completed. Burns and Stalker (1961) illustrated how different rates of product innovation were associated with changes in the discretionary content of roles.

Variations over time have considerable practical implications. In Chapter 2 we noted the example of Harp Mill, where the management found it hard to understand why the typical response to a market change did not enable the enterprise to cope with difficulty. Another recent example involving a project on organizational design from CUSSR occurred when the enterprise was at the start of a five-year development and production cycle. In the particular sub-unit in which we were working the management were facing the uncertainties of product development with one system of roles and relationships while attempting to design a system appropriate to a new factory and new technology.

In order to clarify the problems involved in examining the flexibility/formality aspect, we shall start with some simple assumptions. It will be assumed that any enterprise has a repertoire of strategies – performance programmes – which it applies when it recognizes appropriate patterns in the environment. This repertoire of performance programmes may be learnt through interaction with the environment (Dill 1962) or through rehearsal, as would be the case with the military. Thus we start with elements – performance programmes and rules for applying and switching them. We shall assume that the degree of specificity of the performance programme varies, but it will include measures for internal coordination and control.

The critical point to determine is the likely degree of specificity in role content and in role-relationships. March and Simon (1958) suggest that the extent of role discretion will be determined by the nature of the problems facing the role-bearer, and the kinds of search process undertaken to solve the problem. In making this suggestion they are indicating that the structure of the enterprise, that is its degree of flexibility/formality, is strongly influenced by the techniques of searching which are applied to the problems by the role incumbent. This idea has strongly influenced Burns and Stalker, who have taken this point and suggested that the main problems influencing the discretionary content of the role-relationships in management arise from the nature of product innovation. If this is infrequent, the performance programme of the enterprise will be stable and tasks within can be subdivided and allocated to specific categories of persons. Burns and Stalker argue that the role content will be routinized and the boundaries of role relationships highly specified, with each member learning to tackle one small part of the overall task. It may be expected that there will be a recognized hierarchy of knowledge, authority, and power, and each level will be more knowledgeable than the lower level. The case of a rayon-spinning plant is cited as an illustration.

Burns and Stalker argue that, when the enterprise is faced by continuous innovation, the positions in the management hierarchy will almost certainly be defined in terms of technical qualifications and abilities to solve the immediate problem. In this situation the existence of a common set of beliefs and a sense of common purpose is crucial. Thus the basis of role boundaries is different and there is less fragmentation of the overall task.

In the opinion of March and Simon large areas of activities in enterprises are routinized: 'Most behaviour, and particularly most behaviour in organizations, is governed by performance programmes.' Thus the typical situation is one in which the enterprise is faced by frequently experienced stimuli and responds quickly with a performance programme selected from the repertoire. In this case there is virtually no search process. The less frequent situation is one in which there are new stimuli which can be handled only by a search process. This requires the formulation of the definition of the problem followed by search activities aimed at discovering alternatives from which one is selected as a response.

The notion of discretion is then used by March and Simon to consider relations between subunits in enterprises. They argue that the interdependence between subunits varies between stable and unstable situations. If the enterprise is able to anticipate and predict contingencies then there is increased toleration for interdependence between subunits. When predictability decreases then problems of coordination arise. The critical variable is the ability to absorb uncertainty.

Uncertainty is a key variable for a number of investigations that contribute to the flexibility/formality aspect. In a comparative study of the construction industry and mass production, Stinchcombe (1958) demonstrated that there was a low degree of development of bureaucratization in the construction industry. There were fewer clerical workers, absence of an administrative apparatus, less specific instructions from superordinates downwards, and more involvement of the man in the enterprise. Stinchcombe suggested that the most likely explanation lies in the great seasonal variations and product mix experienced by the construction industry. Thus there is a need for skilled employees who can perform their skills without direction and who are guided by craft standards.

The relationship between discretion in the form and content of roles and 'uncertainty' is the central theme of an important theoretical formulation with practical implications by Bell (1967). Following a careful analysis of earlier theories, he concludes 'the amount of discretion workers exercise is a key feature which is causally related to the degree of formality of organizational structures'. Discretion is, as Jaques (1958) demonstrated, present in all tasks. The total amount of discretion may be ascertained by examining which tasks, and by which methods and in what sequence, are performed by the worker.

The extent of discretion is determined by the predictability of work demands, management controls, and professionalization. When the worker is faced by situational demands that are unpredictable he will have to use personal judgement. With regard to management controls, Bell postulates that managements will encourage workers who have unpredictable jobs to use their discretion. Professionalization refers to the amount of technical training. Where professional training is high, discretion also may be expected to be high.

Bell composes all these elements into the following set of ideas: discretion will be high when there is high unpredictability in the demands of the job coupled with loose management controls and high professionalization. High discretion will reduce the rigidity of lines of authority and vertical lines of communication will increase, facilitating an exchange of ideas between supervisors and men concerning the solution of unique problems. High discretion and unpredictability lead to the dividing of links between departments and thus places them in parallel. Consequently the problems of coordination are reduced. Finally it is postulated that high discretion is associated with high personal involvement of the employee with colleagues and supervisors.

Bell's formulation provides a good link with the ideas of Charles Perrow (1967). He suggests that the techniques adopted to transform the enterprise's raw materials (things, symbols, and people) at the 'grass-roots' level strongly determine the kinds of interaction between employees and this in turn determines the flexibility/formality of structure.

Perrow's analysis is focused upon identifying flexibility/formality at two levels within the enterprise. In general terms the enterprise is divided into three main activity areas – goalsetting (board level), support services (marketing, engineering, accounts), and production. Perrow examines relations within production and between production and support services. If the raw materials being transformed at the production level are well known and highly stable then the operatives carrying out the transformation process will experience few exceptional cases and be able to solve those that do occur by a quick response from the established repertoire of performance programmes. In this example the search process would be very simple. It follows, argues Perrow, that the techniques for transforming the raw material could be highly specified. In this circumstance the amount of discretion in role performance will be low and the structure of relationships will be highly formalized.

Clearly, this proposition is strongly influenced by ideas from March and Simon, Burns and Stalker, and Woodward, as well as resembling the kinds of theory advanced by Bell. The interesting point is that Perrow extends the analysis to a detailed consideration of the forms of coordination and control that may be expected to characterize the enterprise.

In practice we have made use of the ideas drawn from March and Simon and subsequent theorists to extend areas of the sociotechnical framework which we felt required development. The whole issue of flexibility/formality is central to organizational design and crucial to decisions made about appropriate forms of management style. In this section we have attempted to indicate their relevance to organizational design. Later we shall examine their significance for management education. It is perhaps most important to emphasize that these ideas represent *some* only of the resources on which the behavioural scientist may be expected to draw in the course of his work.

(ii) *Aspirations, orientations, and structures*

As indicated earlier in this chapter, we felt that one of the important and underemphasized parts of the sociotechnical concept, as we knew it, was the analysis of the 'socio' aspect. The importance of this has, in fact, been underlined by Trist and his colleagues (1963) in their study of two different forms of social organization for the same technology, and the emphasis given to the pre-existing traditions of multi-skilled operators and autonomous self-regulating groups. At CCE Ltd the study of the female packing crews focused attention upon the complex character of the existing social system. Our study of the machine operators in the Processing Department had a similar emphasis.

At the stage in the analysis when tasks are allocated to roles and role networks, the behavioural scientist is applying an implicit set of assumptions about the individuals who will occupy these positions and their expectations. The orientations of workers are influenced in an important respect by their aspirations and demands for control over the job. The proposed technological changes at CCE Ltd might affect the levels and forms of creative activity and control over the job. However, we are not arguing that there is a quasi-mechanical link between the technology and social behaviour: 'A change, therefore, has always a symbolic value; and because it is the result of a decision, it alters the relationship of power or influence' (Touraine 1965). Thus orientations to work 'must be considered as autonomous elements subject to their own system of logic' and they cannot be considered to be a 'subjective reflection of the manner in which work organizations function' (Touraine 1965). In studying orientations the behavioural scientist's task is to identify and discover the ways in which the members of the enterprise define their own situation. We may expect that the situation at work is an experience in which the context and behaviour form an interdependent whole. The individual's own plans for his life – his project – together with his expectations will determine the meaning that the work situation will

have for him. Different workers will get different degrees of satisfaction in the same situation.

Touraine's observations raise a further set of questions relating to
the relevance of research on behaviour in organizations undertaken
in one society for applied work in another. We know from cross-
cultural studies that findings from North America are not readily
transferred to Europe or elsewhere. For example, Whyte (1963) has
shown in investigations of Peruvian workers that they react favourably to close supervision whereas comparable US workers respond
in the opposite direction. Crozier suggests that the nature of interpersonal relations in governmental bureaucracies in France is
closely related to French cultural perspectives on work and to the
political system. From a different viewpoint, Heintz observed that
differences in reaction to technical change are based on different
experiences during childhood socialization. For example the worker
will be more favourably disposed if he has strong feelings of in-
adequacy with regard to the values he has learnt, or if the principle
of authority existing in the family and internalized by the child is
generalized to all relations to authority.

The issue of the relevance of American conclusions for the European scene raises the more general problem of the part played by
technology in influencing the social system. This issue is known as
'technological determinism'. According to the various critics of
researchers and consultants who have emphasized technology as a
variable, the latter are guilty of arguing that technology determines
the social system at the level of the enterprise. This is an important
criticism in the light of the sociotechnical method of operating.
Clearly Tavistock members are excluded from this attack because
they simply insist that technology is a variable that must be considered by designers in certain specified situations. They do not
specify what the kinds of interdependence will be, but rather provide
a way of exploring this aspect that will be of value to the designer.

The critics of the 'technological determinism' approach never seem
quite to agree on what its main features are, or on what is being
determined (e.g. Hickson *et al.* 1970). Goldthorpe suggests that
theorists emphasizing technology as a variable crucial to the planning
and understanding of behaviour in enterprises are in effect stressing
the extent to which work relationships may be structured independently of particular persons, and are arguing that the pattern of social
relationships is significantly influenced by the way in which the

actual processes of production are organized. Technology may be seen imposing certain minimum constraints on the structuring of relationships and possibly forming these into particular patterns or networks of activities and interactions.

Goldthorpe identifies a number of aspects of the technical organization which are posited to affect the formation of solidary work groups as follows:

Positive and facilitating factors
    Degree of interdependence with others in the same occupational
      group
    Degree of control over work processes
    Degree of freedom of movement
Negative and impeding factors
    Spatial constraints in informal group relations
    Other constraints such as noise
    Frequency of deployment for the labour force involving changes
      in the location of work.

These sets of factors are applied to a sample of workers from three Luton factories and Goldthorpe concludes that the formation of solidary work groups in these factories was prevented by technological and spatial constraints: 'It was also evident that technical organization importantly influences the pattern of social interaction in work in the shops and departments in which we were and could thus, for instance, inhibit the formation of solidary work groups or restrict the amount of contact possible between supervisors and the men in their charge.'

Thus Goldthorpe examines the content of the 'technological determinism' approach and suggests that the organization of the production (and the way it is designed by the production engineers) does reduce the possible forms that patterns of activities and interactions can take. He then develops his analysis by asking: 'to what extent are the orientations of the members of the enterprise determined by the technology?' He concludes, on the basis of a sample of 250 workers in three firms in one town, that there was no direct association between the workers' orientations to work, to colleagues, and to the firm, with the characteristics of the technology. Goldthorpe found little systematic association between the workers' experience of the work situation as technologically determined and the range of orientations and behaviour they displayed at work. In fact,

Goldthorpe suggests that the most striking feature of his study was 'the similarity of their attitudinal and behaviour patterns, despite the very different technological environments in which men in these groups work'. His general observation was that the Luton workers were overwhelmingly characterized by a similar orientation to work, colleagues, and firm. In this case the orientation was typified by a calculative approach to work coupled with low personal involvement in the job. Additionally there was low and neutral involvement with colleagues and the firm. This particular orientation is given the generalized title of 'instrumental'. In a number of ways this conclusion agrees with earlier theoretical and research studies. Etzioni (1961), who was attempting to develop a broad analytic framework applicable to all forms of enterprise – industrial, religious, custodial, military – observed that in industrial enterprises the generalized orientation was instrumental. Further, that this orientation was generated outside work in the family and society so that in one sense the enterprise was 'more pervaded than pervasive' (Etzioni 1961). A similar conclusion is reached by Katz (1966), who argues that the managements of industrial enterprises are not directly concerned to change the central values of the working-class culture possessed by the skilled and non-skilled employees.

Goldthorpe develops his own conclusions in the direction of tentative predictions about the ways in which workers with different orientations will respond to a given technological environment. He argues that orientations will vary and this is a mediating feature between the work situation as objectively considered and the worker's response to it. For example, Goldthorpe suggests that, in instances where technological constraints prevent collaboration between workers and inhibit the formation of solidary work groups, this will not be a source of frustration and continuing discontent among workers who have an instrumental orientation. We shall return to this hypothesis later, since it has considerable implications for the designing of organizations. It has a relevance to the work at CCE Ltd. By adopting the Alternatives and Differences approach we have been able to identify the existing and planned technological systems, noting the ways in which these facilitate or inhibit the formation of solidary work groups. In the Processing Department we sought to identify the existing orientations to work so that an estimate could be made of the likely responses to the new technology. In the next chapter this emphasis is developed and plays a central part.

(iii) *The systems concept*

The systems concept has been fashionable for the last two decades in management thinking and for even longer in biology, economics, and sociology. In thinking about the enterprise, researchers and practitioners have claimed to adopt a systems approach to problems and have recommended it to other audiences, including administrators. In this section the utility of the systems concept to diagnosis and organizational design is briefly considered. The general tone adopted will be one of scepticism and questioning.

The systems approach generally emphasizes the interrelated nature of phenomena in entities. Advocates of this approach, like Seiler (1966), frequently illustrate the importance of recognizing the interrelatedness of elements by giving an example of a study in which a change was introduced and resulted in unforeseen consequences in another part of the enterprise. The example is usually then followed by a biological analogy aptly demonstrating the utility of the systems concept.

The major contribution of the systems approach is that it refocuses attention from matter to *organization*. The examination of the organization of mechanical, biological, and sociocultural phenomena is a crucial area of development for the basic sciences and for those involved in the technology of applications. Two important points now must be emphasized. First, in what ways, if at all, is the entity being analysed a system, and what measures of systemness are being applied? Second, what are the variables in the system? It must be recognized that the variables adopted by the operational researcher and the behavioural scientist do differ (Bennis 1967).

The concept is probably better considered to be a loose analytical framework of questions and ordering of responses. The analyst should be asking 'in what ways, if at all, are the elements being examined interconnected?', 'to what extent and in what ways is the enterprise differentiated?', 'to what extent and in what directions are there linkages between variations in one set of elements and other sets?' Once the concept is thought of as a series of questions and an ordering system for the answers, then the analyst begins to move away from imposing limiting assumptions on the data collected. The analyst can then include the recognition that different parts of the entity being studied are only very loosely related.

The next point to be considered is that of the 'open system'.

Great emphasis is given by a number of practitioners to this aspect What do they mean? The answer is fortunately relatively simple. The emphasis upon 'open' is an instruction to the analyst of enterprise to examine the environment (e.g. markets, political intervention) and to relate this to the analysis of internal structure and functioning.

The systems concept was vigorously debated at the International Conference on Operational Research and the Social Sciences during 1964 (Lawrence 1966). Burns suggested that most users of the systems concept have tended to view industrial enterprises as consisting of a *single* system 'with all behaviour which cannot be contained within the definition of formally constituted roles being treated as fictional elements'. He cited the work of Emery, Trist, and Simon as being typical of this approach. Burns contended that there is tendency in such models to treat bargaining and learning processes within enterprises as residual or random aspects, adding that 'rationality models are both too simple and too complex for them to be other than dangerous instruments for research, or as a guide for consultative work, or for managerial practice itself'. The enterprise is better described as a plurality of systems of which politics, career and transport represent merely three examples. Burns emphasize that the analyst must take account of the ways in which individuals and groups pursue goals and adopt strategies for their realization that are quite distinct from the ideas inherent in the rationality models. In effect, the individual can and does determine the social significance of his behaviour 'in a way which presupposes a plurality of action systems available to him' (Burns 1966).

All this emphasizes the importance of noting *who* is defining the system. For example, Mumford and Banks (1967) suggested, quite specifically, that the systems analyst has only a partial view of the enterprise and does not take account of the social aspect. This neatly demonstrates that analysts with different starting-points and adopting different perspectives will have quite different understandings of the actual subject-matter of the system. The operational researcher will have one definition and the behavioural scientist another. This is an important and vital point which can be illustrated further.

Rivett (1969), an operational researcher, described the work he had undertaken for the firm of Petfoods as part of a consultancy project He suggests that one of the good results of the application of his recommendations was the smoothing out of peaks in production. He adds that this resulted in a lessening of 'conflict' in the firm. In fact what he says might be true of the firm as a whole or even of relations within a particular stratum (e.g. middle management). However, a behavioural scientist has some cause for scepticism at this un-documented claim. For example, there is considerable cumulative evidence to indicate that changes in the functional autonomy be-tween subunits in the enterprise lead to changes in the pattern of conflict, though not necessarily its intensity (Van Doorn 1966). Also Clark (1970) has argued, on the basis of comparative research on the 'peak period phenomenon' in enterprises, that the whole aspect of bargaining and involvement in peaks is more complex than many current levels of analysis have recognized. Boguslaw (1966), in one of the most critical attacks on systems design, provides considerable and extensive evidence of the neglect of the human and organiza-tional aspects by systems analysts.

This example illustrates the importance of identifying who is defining the elements that are being examined within particular applications of the systems concept (Bennis 1967). It raises the crucial problem of inter-system boundaries (Chin 1969). There is an assumption, particularly by operational researchers, that the activi-ties of the behavioural scientist will complement their own. Indeed, this illustrates the crucial message of this book that the behavioural scientist has been excluded from the design of organization and pri-marily used to invent ways of installing predesigned innovations – planned change rather than 'organizational design *and* planned change'. In fact, the advice of the behavioural scientist could indicate that, for example, 'management information systems' are in the long term debilitating to the enterprise.

The difference between systems analysis carried out by behavioural scientists and others leads neatly on to one of the great pieces of fudging that has occurred in this field. Though the emphasis upon systems has focused attention on the organizational aspect, the models that have been applied in analysis tend to be derived from either machine theory (Ashby 1955) or biology (Katz & Kahn 1966). Neither of these satisfactorily recognizes the distinctive characteristics of organization in sociocultural systems. This is a crucial issue in the teaching and practice of systems thinking, but since it has been so adequately dealt with by Buckley (1966) it may be seen as lying outside the field of this particular book.

POLICY ANALYSIS FOR THE ENTERPRISE

Katz and Kahn (1966) argue that the extent and nature of changes involving enterprises of all kinds are so great that there is a premium on the anticipation and direction of future changes and the following-through of policy decisions to the 'structural implications for the organization'. Much of the work at CCE Ltd may be seen as being directed towards this objective. In this section we examine the ideas of Dror (1967) because they have a double relevance. First, he is concerned to evaluate the contribution made by systems approaches to policy analysis and, second, he is concerned to promote policy analysis as an activity. Dror argues that systems analysis is of only limited utility because it cannot deal with qualitative and political phenomena.

Dror argues that systems analysis has made an important though limited contribution to decision-making and he suggests that much of the contribution may have been due more to the wisdom, sophistication, and open-mindedness of the leading practitioners than to defined professional tools. This is a crucial point because it affects the utility of systems analysis for second-generation men. For example, Miller and Rice have structured the introduction to their recent book (1967) in a systems format, but it is hard to believe that this represents more than the tip of their collective experience at the time of writing. For second-generation system analysts there is a defined set of tools and procedures, but these men do not have the experience of the earlier practitioners so there is therefore a requirement to create within enterprises a policy analysis unit.

Systems analysis, according to Dror, has a number of endemic weaknesses, of which the most important are: the attachment to quantification; incapacity to handle conflicting noncommensurate values; requirement for clear-cut criteria; neglect of political feasibility; omission of adequate recognition for non-rational decision-making processes such as tacit knowledge, creativity, and judgement; inability to deal with large complex systems; lack of instruments for taking account of motivations. Because of these weaknesses, systems analysis is of very doubtful utility for dealing with political decisions and overall strategic policy. If this is so, why has systems analysis been so strongly advocated and supported in America? Dror suggests that the answer lies with the brilliance and experience of the early pioneers and the exaggerated claims for success.

Dror argues that the primary solution to the problem he has posed is the development of a more advanced type of *professional* knowledge in which political phenomena are recognized as one of the central features. He suggests 'policy analysis'. This is intended to be a synthesis of the rationality approaches already established with non-quantitative approaches. At CCE Ltd, and in Chapter 2, on organizational design, emphasis was given to the distinction between research as an activity and designing as an activity. The points made there parallel the argument of Dror.

Policy analysis has a number of features: the development of theories and construction of models that typify the behaviour of the enterprise as it is; emphasis upon creating alternatives and the explicit encouragement of innovative thinking; greater reliance upon tacit knowledge and understanding; systematic integration of trained intuition through scenarios and similar devices; emphasis upon future-oriented thinking; recognition of the multiplicity of criteria to be considered in reaching a policy decision. It may be seen that Dror's proposals do much to take account of Burns's (1966) emphasis upon the enterprise as a plurality of systems. They also include Nadler's stress on design as a process and the usage of scenarios. His suggestions answer the tendency of systems analysis to ignore organizational behaviour, particularly the structural aspects.

For Dror, policy analysis is systems analysis plus. The plus includes inputs from the whole range of behavioural sciences, an emphasis upon qualitative analysis and innovative thinking, and the use of tacit knowledge and multiple criteria. He recognizes some of the difficulties of implementing his thinking, but tends to stress the absence of trained professional policy analysts and the role of universities in producing them. We would give an equal and perhaps primary stress to the changing of the decision-making infrastructure of enterprises so that there is greater emphasis upon innovative policy-making and a greater awareness of the implications of policy decisions for the future structure and behaviour of the enterprise. The establishment and securing of policy analysis as a function within an enterprise cannot be dealt with only by the production of university graduates; it requires a radical transformation of the policy-making structure of enterprises.

DIAGNOSIS OF PROBLEMS IN THE ENTERPRISE

The central themes of this book have included the assertion that organizational design must develop separate from, but complementary to, the planning of change. If we are to meaningfully relate the findings of research and practice in the behavioural sciences with the inadequacies of current methods of designing organizations then we must give primacy to the definition and tackling of problems in organization. This requires the diagnostic approach.

Too much emphasis in research and practice by behavioural scientists has been given to the process of change and too little to the diagnosis of problems. There is a paucity of diagnostic frameworks. What are the steps in a diagnostic approach? This question may be dealt with in two parts: first, what data are gathered and, second, what is presented to the client?

Lawrence and Lorsch (1969) suggest that the collection of data is typically done by interviewing a small number of senior managers and occasionally by use of a survey. These approaches tend to be somewhat cursory and, according to Lawrence and Lorsch, tend to be conducted in spite of the fact that the action programme has already been planned in advance. The cursory nature of the diagnosis is exacerbated by the concern of the practitioner with improving his relationship to the client.

The presentation of material to the client by the consultant is typically done either by offering raw data and asking for interpretation, or by compiling a report containing the practitioner's implicit analytical frameworks. The problem of the first approach is that managements apply their own frameworks and are likely to fail in comprehending the problems involved, while the second approach introduces problems of communication for the practitioner in securing commitment to the proposed plans. The problem is that the diagnostic stage and the action stage are closely interwoven. It will be difficult to achieve the objectives of policy analysis as outlined in the previous section. The great danger is that insufficient attention will be given to diagnosis and to the need for designing proposals and action plans that fit the unique requirement of the client.

At CCE Ltd we attempted to emphasize the importance of the diagnostic stage and its mutual nature in the notion of the 'dialogue', which we suggested in the first meetings of mid 1967. In practice we collected and analysed data both separately from CCE

Ltd and in collaboration with them, and also attempted to introduce management to the kinds of framework that would help them to interpret and understand the data. This has been central to our ideas about building a behavioural-science-utilizing capability into the enterprise. The real decisions have been taken by the Azimuth Group, and our relationship is best described as one of intermittent influence.

The diagnostic frameworks utilized stress the structural features of the enterprise and the varied definitions of the situation adopted by individuals, associations, and groups. There was little emphasis upon interpersonal relations. CCE Ltd was examined as a differentiated whole in which relations between subunits were in part influenced by external characteristics such as the differential environments faced by the segments (Dill 1958). Thus the diagnostic scheme, which first examined the enterprise-to-environment relationship (Chapter 2), treated subunits both separately and in relation to others. In this way it was possible to identify the particular characteristics of each department and note the similarities and differences between departments. Inevitably the exploration of boundaries between subunits followed. In this our focus had elements of the type of analysis of task and sentient boundaries suggested by Miller and Rice (1967). The importance of this aspect will emerge more sharply in the following chapters dealing with the Making and Packing Departments.

CONCLUSION

In this chapter some of the principal analytical frameworks used at CCE Ltd in the first part of the consultancy have been outlined. A distinction must be drawn between the cognitive mapping by Azimuth of the human-organizational aspect made prior to our entry and that which was subsequently adopted. Further distinctions must be drawn between the repertoire of ideas and experiences that influenced us in carrying out investigations and the framework we felt to be essential for the understanding of our ideas and data. Furthermore, we found it necessary to modify ideas as time progressed.

PART FOUR

Case study II

CHAPTER EIGHT

The Making and Packing Departments: The design focus

INTRODUCTION: PHASE IV

During the first year of the consultancy we had started by taking the preferences of some members of the Azimuth Group for 'participative management' and dealing with them in two complementary ways. First, we had demonstrated that there were features of the existing situation that actually closely approximated to the desired form of participative management, yet these areas *could* be radically altered if the proposed technological and manning plans were implemented. Second, we had demonstrated that there were features of the technology and the environment of CCE Ltd that exerted a crucial influence on the range of possible sociotechnical designs. To achieve an impact we had explored a variety of approaches which we came to call the Alternatives and Differences Approach to organizational design. Following what we felt was a useful trial of a joint method of working in the Processing Department, we now planned to apply this approach to the Making and Packing Departments.

In this chapter we deal with the first eight months of a sociotechnical design project for the joint departments. Additionally we examine two important meetings with Azimuth. One was taken up with the appraisal of the Amenities Report and Annual Report, a document of some 15,000 words; and the other was based upon the discussion of a paper on 'management ideologies' with particular reference to CCE Ltd.

During this part of the organizational design of Making and Packing we became increasingly aware of the necessity for a systematic study of the existing social structure in greater detail than in earlier investigations. This began in May 1969 and was not completed until May 1970. All this may seem like a great deal of time to be spent on the design of a new factory. In fact, of course, it emphasizes the great length of time involved in the technical design of plant and buildings also. There were also important changes during this period in the conception of the technology for the new factory. Some of the earlier views had to be modified, but more of that later.

STARTING THE SOCIOTECHNICAL DESIGN

The changeover meeting from the Processing Department occurred at a time when we were committed to writing the first annual report. We therefore decided to familiarize ourselves with the technological aspects of the Making and Packing Departments while writing the report. In this way we hoped to establish a good start to the design stage.

Making and Packing employed, at the time of the investigation, a very high proportion of the direct labour force. The departments differ importantly in labour composition. In Packing there are a large number of females who heavily outnumber the men, whereas the imbalance in the Making Department is not so pronounced. The two departments had always been separated geographically by being situated on different floors and by a buffer stock of some 5–8 hours. This meant that there were areas of autonomy for management and operatives. In practice the two departments had developed distinctive customs and practices and orientations to work. These had emerged over a number of years and could be of significance for the designs of the new factory. The major planned technical change was the introduction of a mechanized linkage system between the Making and Packing machines. This meant that the new task boundary should be drawn round the two departments, but the existing sentient boundaries (Miller & Rice 1967) were significantly different from the implied task and sentient boundaries. It will be recalled that in our early statement of intentions to CCE Ltd we had emphasized the following-through of decisions to trace out the implied social structure.

On returning to Making and Packing we were fortunate to link up again with the R & D executive who had played such an important part in the first study of female packers. The fact that he had been in on the very first meetings in 1967 was almost certainly crucial since he was operating in an area in which there were more unknowns than firm decisions. The design of the technology was constantly subject to minor modifications which could quite suddenly cumulate and indicate that a new conception of the final design was required. Despite the fragmentary nature of the design process, we were able to proceed.

In July 1968 we began meeting and talking with the managers and specialists engaged on the technical aspects with the aim of familiarizing ourselves with the situation and the range of alternatives, and generally bringing ourselves up to date.

The original plans for the grouping and layout of the machines had not been altered. The aim of the designers was to have the two departments on one floor of the new two-storey factory. There were to be four sets of making machines and four sets of packing machines, each of the sets being placed at opposite ends of the floor. Each set of making and packing machines was to be linked by some form of mechanical linkage. CCE Ltd had experimented and were continuing with experiments on a variety of linkage systems. No firm decision had at that time been reached about the most favourable mechanical system, though one was strongly preferred. The only firm conclusion we could draw was that the advantage of mechanical systems over the existing 'manpowered' method was either self-evident or proved beyond reasonable doubt.

We set out to get answers to three main sets of questions in this familiarization phase. First, what decisions had been made about particular pieces of equipment and their location in relation to each other? In contrast to the Processing Department there were many possible combinations and it was difficult to evaluate their relative advantages in the absence of complete sets of equipment for comparative trials. Second, what decisions had been made about manning and what principles had guided them? Third, what were the main sources of variance which the new production system would create for the social system? The idea of variance neatly summarizes the central issues for organizational design, since it indicates the parameters to any choice and is central to the formality/flexibility dimension (Perrow 1967).

The key decision on equipment was the adoption of the mechanical linkage system and the general commitment to find some device that would work. The specific choice had not been made, though the range of likely models had been narrowed. An important feature of this design for our work was the implications it would have for the human tasks required to operate the new technology and the nature of task interdependencies. The linkage system would reduce the buffer of work-in-progress between the two departments from hours to minutes. This could have an enormous effect on the interdependencies between tasks and hence between roles and role-sets. For example, under the old system the senior female packer could stop her machine if she felt there was a fault in quality without any effect on the operation of the department or production line as a whole. Under the proposed technology a short stoppage on either a making or a packing machine could have almost immediate consequences for other machines, and would require some kind of adaptive behaviour to be initiated. In other words, the entire process of the allocation of work, its monitoring and continuance, could be drastically altered. If we were to follow through the technological decision in the way suggested by Katz and Kahn 'to the structural implications for the organization', then we would have to identify the ways in which the tasks and relationships required of operators and management differed from the existing situation. For this reason we decided to include a representative of the Training Department in the Project Group on sociotechnical design. An important feature of the proposed technology was the changed role of management and supervision. Under the old system in the Packing Department, for example, the supervision was primarily involved in ensuring that teams of operators were up to full strength and that they had sufficient supplies of work to keep going. Operators exercised a high degree of control over the situation. The proposed technology implied the existence of someone who would coordinate the complexes of the linked packing and making machines. The R & D executive believed that one answer to this problem was to apply a modified form of the autonomous group. However, the situation at CCE Ltd was markedly different from coalmining. At CCE Ltd the tradition was of separate operation of two departments and high interpersonal autonomy within a fairly structured situation. Furthermore, the roles concerned were occupied by males and females who were structurally separated in one department but not in the other. In addition the size of the group on the planned technology was very much larger than in the studies conducted by Trist (1963).

The manning figures for the plant were now available. Two constraints had been introduced. First, it had been decided to aim at keeping the machines running continuously through the shift. Second, persons would be allocated to specific machines. Apart from these constraints and the available statistics of numbers there were no data available on the coordinatory activities that would be required to keep the new plant in operation. The manning figures were a good and well-worked-through illustration of the 'aggregates' approach to manpower planning (Cherns, Clark, & Sinclair 1970).

The sources of variance the production system would have to handle included changes in the state of the raw material, availability of labour by day of the week, and stoppages. The variance arising from the raw materials was not great in relation to the high degree of understanding possessed by the operatives, but it might become more critical if the existing social organization was severely ruptured. For example, a new female packer is able to gain a high knowledge of the raw material in a short time, but a more fragmented form of organization might require either further basic training or a recentring of knowledge with the male mechanics. The variances arising from day-to-day changes in the availability of labour and from machine stoppages would become more critical in the new plant if the interdependencies between machines were increased.

The questioning of the variances inherent in the production system refocused attention on the assumption about the market environment that underlay the technological designs. Our observations suggested that the technology was being designed on the basis of high-volume throughput of a limited number of lines. In the light of the market situation in the early 1960s this seemed a reasonable assumption. However, the members of CCE Ltd we met had always stressed that the firm used to be production-oriented and was now becoming market-oriented. Also there were signs that market competition was becoming more intense as attempts were made to keep the overall level of consumer involvement in the product at a high level and still retain a good share of the market. To our unexperienced thinking there were signs of 'market fragmentation' arising from the consumers and also from the reorganization of a sector of the principal intermediary between CCE Ltd and the consumer, namely the retail outlets and, more particularly, the supermarkets.

Thus the question of the relation between the designs for mechanically linked technology and the state of the market were important. The critical question was this: if CCE Ltd created a high-volume factory was there sufficient flexibility in the technology to allow the firm to meet market innovation and retain a distinctive competence. Later we asked specific questions about this aspect.

In this section we have outlined some of the ways in which we familiarized ourselves with the technological aspects of the Making and Packing Departments. During this period we established the new project group to work on sociotechnical design. Then we disappeared from CCE Ltd for a period to write an account of the first year's work to be presented to the Azimuth Group. The aim of this account was to ensure that all members of Azimuth were familiar with our aims and activities.

ANNUAL REPORT: ITS RECEPTION

At the end of the first year we compiled a general report of some 15–20,000 words covering the aims and achievements of the joint project. The report, which was in a chronological form, outlined the origins of the consultancy and the nature of the relationship between Azimuth and ourselves, dealt with various studies completed, and set out the main themes and conceptual aspects. Emphasis was given to the continuous clarification of objectives and to differences of opinion that had occurred. No attempt was made to gloss over these aspects. Though the report was designed to be an account of what happened it was highly selective and was in no way systematic and detached. Its orientation was political and not scientific.

For example, careful attention was given to the ways in which we had stated the objectives of the consultancy and the broad analytical framework used in the initial diagnosis. Also we carefully indicated the ways in which our work was related to interests of the individual members of Azimuth as well as to the group as a whole.

Writing the account occupied almost a whole month of full-time working for two members of the team and the result was in our opinion far from satisfactory. Its major defect was lack of clarity for those who were not behavioural scientists. Much of the argument we presented was heavily truncated and lacked the vitality or ordering expected by members of industrial enterprises. This problem is a real one for consultants whose premier audience is academic. It is perhaps worth noting Argyris's comment, at a seminar in London in mid 1970, that the most difficult articles he has to write are those for the *Harvard Business Review*. One solution to the problem of presentation is to write reports in collaboration with internal members of the client enterprise. We have experimented with this approach more recently on another project and found that it can provide an effective means of saying what you believe to be significant in a way that is meaningful to the client.

We anticipated that the report would not be easy reading. Apart from the reasons outlined above, there was one other important feature of the situation: we had rarely met with the whole Azimuth Group. Our activities had been reported upwards by representatives and we had discussed only with the senior members of the Group. Consequently the report dealt with certain aspects that were unknown to some members. In the report we attempted to show how the activities we had undertaken were interrelated and in some cases linked with groups or representatives not in Azimuth. Marketing is a good example. We were able to link these parts together, showing the connections between the initial questions asked of the adviser on production scheduling and our current activities. The meeting with Azimuth to discuss the report was our first opportunity to discover how successful this linking had been.

Following the printing and distribution of the report to the members of Azimuth, we visited a selection of members on an individual basis to work through the material. From these discussions, particularly with the assistance of the Industrial Relations adviser, we prepared a short note setting out the crucial points. This was circulated to all members prior to the main meeting.

At the meeting in September 1968, the agenda consisted of the Annual Report and another report we had helped to prepare on amenities. This had been undertaken with our supervision by an outside agency. It will be recalled that the report had arisen from the request from one member for a wider basis of information on the general practice of firms in the United Kingdom with regard to the provision of amenities. We shall examine this report in the following section.

At the opening of the meeting the Chairman asked how CCE Ltd could benefit most from the report, and how its lessons could be used to aid progress. In replying we stated that the report both summarized the dialogue to date and formed part of it. Its aim was not to offer concrete proposals, since decisions should be taken either jointly or by Azimuth in the light of the evidence and opinion they had heard. We added that, in looking back over the previous twelve months, we felt that more frequent meetings with the whole Azimuth Group would have been desirable.

Turning to the Processing Department and the various proposals for organization, one member of our team argued that the most appropriate form of organization was one embodying the principles of 'delegated autonomy'. That is to say, autonomous group working. He argued that if a conservative approach to planning was adopted then too many jobs would be 'built in' and there would be a danger of overmanning, which in time would lead to frustration. In his opinion the autonomous group facilitated flexibility with maximum interchangeability. This proposal was directly contrary to the preferred solution of the R & D executive for the Processing Department. It will be recalled that some limited form of interchangeability had been suggested in the R & D executive's final draft to the project group.

As a team we were not agreed on the autonomous group as the preferred solution. First, there was no previous tradition of autonomous group working. The department was essentially a hierarchy in which men worked their way through towards the top jobs of the operator/craftsman on the seventh stage. Also there were sharp skill differences between the clerical and leading jobs and the one of 'controller' and maintenance, which we felt would pose problems. However, we were agreed that high mutual knowledge of the operation of the whole process was crucial.

The proposal for the autonomous group provoked four further questions. First, what problems would the new form create for negotiations with the trade union representatives? Second, how would the proposal affect the payment system for the industry and the firm? Third, if this principle was widely adopted, how would it affect the lines of negotiation and responsibility between departments? Fourth, what were the implications for the management structure of the whole factory?

In addition to these four questions, the Chairman indicated that if the principle of responsible autonomy was to be adopted then it would be necessary to construct a special paper for the Board; however, before this decision was taken he would like to know our opinions on the questions raised.

In referring to the negotiation of new forms of organization with the unions we made two points. First, the project group which had undertaken the study of the Processing Department had included the senior adviser on industrial relations. He had indicated, from time to time, that some aspects of this proposal for group autonomy might create intractable problems at the negotiating stage. Second, that the objective and exercise had been for the project group to scrutinize the department as a sociotechnical system and to outline the form of organization that most closely approximated to the objectives of the management philosophy and the situational demands of that production system. This we had done. We recognized that this would introduce certain new features, which would represent departures from the current practice in CCE Ltd, but then that was why external advisers had been employed. All this meant that the Company would have either to revise or modify its ideas about management philosophy or to seek some means of making this philosophy more apparent than imaginary.

It may be seen from the above points that our role was closely concerned with the interplaying of a loosely defined set of goals against the realities of the actual decisions being made.

With regard to payment systems, it was noted that there had been a tendency to underplay the significance of the size and form of payments methods in recent researches conducted outside Britain. For example, Carey (1967) had shown that the significance of the part played by incentives in the famous (notorious) Hawthorne studies has been systematically neglected by both the original investigators and subsequent exponents and critics of the 'human relations' school. Within the autonomous group the people doing the less skilled jobs are trained to do more skilled ones though not necessarily to do every job. Further, it is expected that the persons most closely linked with the more skilled tasks would both have the capability to undertake less skilled ones and would do so. In practice this does mean paying premium rates of pay – that is, compared with the present form of organization and payment – but it does provide benefits both for the management and for the members of the group. Whether these potential benefits for members would be the ones they preferred would be a matter for negotiation. From the evidence we had to hand on the Primary Department, we had no good reason for believing that the autonomous group would be either unworkable or unacceptable. However, it was noted that these people, unlike the female packing crews, had no previous tradition of working that contained elements facilitating a less-well-structured form of relationships. In fact, the existing situation was characterized much more by a 'career hierarchy'. That is to say, persons started on labouring and transporting tasks and 'graduated' to the more skilled operations.

The third and fourth questions both referred to the form of coordination and control for the factory as a whole. These aspects had been accounted for in the design of the consultancy and were in fact specifically tackled in the Annual Report.

At first we wondered why the questions had been asked. Then

we realized that the linkages between the studies done at different levels of the organization and in different departments were easier for us to retain and *imagine* than they were for members of CCE Ltd. While they had a language for describing the organization, and were continuously attempting to extend and update it, they clearly found difficulties both in relating what they read to their own situation and in adequately describing their own situation in a non-ideological language. In fact, we should have realized that this would be the case from the results of the scan – when specific questions in this area had been asked and satisfactorily answered by only three respondents – and also from the study of the female packing crews.

We then perceived that, though members of Azimuth had adopted some of the current jargon used by ourselves and in the literature for managers, we could not assume that it was being utilized in the manner intended by ourselves or other writers on organization. This 'discovery' became one of the factors we had to take account of in Phase Four. Two examples of how we did so are set out later. One concerns a specific study of management coordination as it existed and was perceived. This was compared with the *new* organizational chart to produce some interesting results. Another approach was to write a special paper on the topic. This was the focal point of the very successful December meeting.

The discussion then moved on and we were asked about the stages we envisaged for the future. This question enabled the new project group concerned with the Making and Packing Department to report on progress to date. We stated that the method of operating that had been successful in the Primary Department was being extended to other departments. In this way we hoped to identify the organizational structures for each department and relate them to one another.

The first half of the meeting closed with a request from the Chairman for a series of questions that CCE Ltd should be considering. This request may seem a somewhat strange one to put to external consultants, but it is perhaps better seen as indicating both the role that Azimuth was playing within CCE Ltd in guiding the design of the new factory, and the special problems that arise in the early days of relationships between enterprises and behavioural science practitioners.

AMENITIES STUDY: ITS RECEPTION

In designing the new factory, Azimuth were concerned to deal effectively with the provision of amenities, particularly since the new factory represented an important innovation for the Company in the form of double-shift working. The discussion had been based on a general agreement about the extent of the basic onsite amenities, but their distribution had not been settled. For example, one issue which was carefully discussed was the provision of eating facilities. Azimuth had noted the current preference for integrated dining facilities (in 1967 CCE Ltd had seven different levels of dining and self-catering). Some managers felt that the creation of a new factory was a good time to introduce the idea of one dining area for every group of employees on the site, whereas others noted that some groups preferred segregated eating facilities. In addition to the basic provision of amenities, there were decisions to be made about general amenities such as those for recreation, bearing in mind the requirements of shift workers.

CCE Ltd had a long-established system of joint consultation and had additionally, since the mid-1960s, experimented with small discussion groups for dealing with the internal décor and amenities at the existing factory. These groups, composed of a variety of representatives based on the age, sex, and job composition of particular departments, had examined and reported on a number of topics including certain of the environmental features of the new factory. Members of Azimuth felt that they had a firm link with opinion within the firm, but were aware that their own experience and that of the groups had not typically included the provision of amenities for shift workers. Therefore they were anxious to draw on the experiences of other firms and to be cognizant of the published literature. They were particularly interested to identify some of the current trends and to know the reasons for them.

During the first meetings with Azimuth in mid-1967 and later, in early 1968, the topic of amenities was presented by Azimuth as one for our investigation. Since a literature search was involved it was agreed that the project could be profitably undertaken by a research services agency. The report, which took some three months to prepare, was based on the available literature, discussions and interviews with interested parties, and interviews with a small selection of firms. In its final form the report covered the changing emphasis by firms on the provision of amenities and related this to changes in the experience of the workforce, class mobility, in stratification and family life. It then examined a number of individual topics such as the special needs of shift workers and recreation facilities. At the September meeting the Chairman observed that the report had been received and read and had been very useful to Azimuth.

It will be noted that the nature of the relationship between the agency and the client, CCE Ltd, was one in which the client had specified the request and the agency had supplied the completed article. No direct exchanges had taken place, though members of our team had played a small part in the ongoing literature search and the final report.

ESTABLISHING THE PROJECT GROUP

We knew from our preliminary studies in 1967 that the anticipated technological changes would considerably alter the internal boundary between Making and Packing and that this in turn would affect the management structure, occupational identities and boundaries, power relations, status differentials, and certain of the traditional ways of operating. We felt, on the basis of experience with the project group in the Processing Department, that we would adopt a similar method of working through the sociotechnical design. We planned to hold a first meeting in July (1968) before some members went on holiday and then to continue the meetings after we had written the Annual Report and had our vacations.

Our first move was to convene the project group, obtain presentations from them of the technological and manning proposals, and then analyse these. The composition of the group was similar in the kinds of representative to those present at the meetings for the Processing Department, though, of course, the personalities were different. The earlier studies of the packing crews indicated major changes in organization were likely and so we requested that a representative from the Training Department should join us. We hoped that he would be able to see how detailed changes in tasks and technology would affect the existing social system and the steps which would be required in training to deal with these changes. For example, we expected that the relative status and identities of some groups would be changed. If this was to happen, then it would be necessary to consider how far the 'hidden' aspect of the training programme required modification. Under the heading of 'hidden' we include the many cues given to the female operatives about the relative status and significance of their jobs. Also we had in mind the possibility that the final proposals from the project group could include some suggestions for new forms of group autonomy. Thus we felt it important for the training personnel to know the reason why the proposals had been made and the role they might play at the stage of 'organization-building'.

The project group met first in July to examine the technological aspects, then in September to examine manning, and twice in October. As before, the periods in between meetings were occupied with particular studies. The initial meetings were straightforward, but by October some members of the group were showing concern at the enormity of the implications of the proposals being considered. We therefore summarized our ideas and presented them to Azimuth for opinion, questioning, and advice. At their suggestion a small project group consisting of three persons, including one of the social scientists, was established to study and report on the alternative technical designs that seemed most feasible. This new group began work late in November and reported in early 1969.

From these comments it may be seen that the project group as first established did not follow a similar pattern to that for the Processing Department. Why was this? The answer must partly lie in the personalities and the social milieux of those involved, but there were other problems that had not initially been foreseen. These include the technological options available. In the Processing Department the technology had an unalterable sequence of linked machines. The major areas of choice lay in the forms of linkage and in the shape of the sequence. That is to say, whether it was a straight line, a circle, and so on. Also the equipment for the Processing Department was, or appeared to be, largely known. By way of contrast the equipment for Making and Packing appeared to be largely unknown.

The Making and Packing Departments contained four basic pieces of equipment that had to be arranged in a sequential order as follows: making, packing, parcelling, and collating. In this case many machines were involved and though the sequence was rigid the forms of combination were wide open. The major concept that influenced the thinking of our R & D adviser was that of mechanical linkages between all the machines providing a continuous flow line. The Azimuth Group seemed to believe that this concept was feasible. Though there was general agreement of the choice of machinery there was little consensus on either the choice of devices to be fitted as modifications to these machines or the kinds of linkage systems that were appropriate. At this stage we did have a fair idea of the relative balance of the proportions of each of the four main machines, but their linkages and grouping were open to speculation and uncertainty. Consequently, there was considerable difficulty in obtaining usable data on the human tasks – and their interdependencies – required for the new technology.

With the assistance of the R & D executive and the linkman we began our first meeting and progressed through a careful recording and examination of the main technological aspects. This followed a similar pattern to the first meeting of the project group for the Processing Department. During the discussion following the first meeting and subsequently, the problem of coordinating the flow of made goods to the packaging machines reached central importance. There were several aspects to this problem, including the devising of a system to take account of breakdowns, tea breaks, and variations in the availability of labour. The key fact required to determine the exact nature of the problem was the size of the buffer stock between the various parts of the process. For example, the buffer stock between the making and packing machines would, on one of the plans we examined, be reduced from hours to a matter of minutes. Further, the state of the buffer stock was immediately sensitive to any variations in the running of the machines. According to the calculations we carried out and submitted to the October meeting, a failure by 2 per cent of the equipment could either exhaust or saturate the buffer stock.

The problem of coordination and buffer stocks highlights one of the major significant facts about the differences between the existing factories and the new factory. The reduction in throughput time means that the 'functional autonomy' of the various production departments is dramatically altered. It has been suggested, in previous studies summarized by Van Doorn (1966), that changes in functional autonomy between subunits affects both interpersonal relations and the patterns of conflict which an organization experiences. This difference in turn highlights another important fact about the new social system, which is the transferring of populations who have not experienced the kind of relations implied by the technical designs. It is important to remember that an important feature of the new plant is that it is being built for a labour force who have experienced a quite different production system. CCE Ltd started with established customs and practices that had emerged over a number of years.

One feature of the discussion of the linkage systems was the problem of the connection between market changes and the production system. Given that one requirement of the new factory was flexibility, how could a link system be devised that could absorb changes such as market fragmentation? This was an area of critical decisions. The choices made would influence the role played by management. For example, if the technical designs first discussed in 1968 were implemented then it would imply a need for either a more complicated form of coordination between female operators, mechanics, and supervision than had previously existed, or the building of small balanced sections of making/packing complexes.

At this point (October) in the investigation we moved from a focus upon the technology to an even closer examination of various proposals for manning the new departments. The industrial engineers had given an estimate of the amount of work of particular kinds that would be required. This was useful as data, particularly in view of problems in profiling the task requirements, but it was all presented within the framework of existing ideas about the jobs. That is to say, an estimate had been made of how the existing categories of job would be affected by the changes and how many would be needed in the future. In addition a calculation had been made of where 'new' roles would be required to handle aspects that had not existed before. The discussion of manning raised the central question of the principles of organizing that were being adopted in the social design of the new plant. In general terms it is fair to argue that the initial proposals from the work study specialists were in the form of the ideas of 'scientific management'. By way of contrast, the R & D executive made a number of suggestions incorporating the ideas of autonomous group working.

At approximately the same time we were asked in the Azimuth meeting that discussed the first technical report whether we considered that the autonomous group principle should be applied in all departments. Our response had been that it represented one means of making the delegation aspect of the participation theme operational. We had indicated that it was possible to think in terms of the autonomous group for the Primary Department. Was this a good principle for the Making and Packing Departments?

This is an appropriate point to re-emphasize that we were not unanimous amongst ourselves on the advisability of autonomous groups. In fact, two members had considerable reservations. Now we were faced with the same problem but on a very much larger scale. The doubts arose because of the awareness that we were involved in the design of an entirely new production system rather than the modification of a subunit within an existing technical system. For example, we suggested earlier that there were three kinds of organizational design, one of which was the redesigning of existing production systems. In fact many of the 'work structuring' and 'job enrichment' applications have been in this form. This has meant that the redesign has taken place in contexts where there were already stabilized 'meaning systems' for operating the technology, including its social coordination. By stabilized 'meaning systems' is implied an existing shared knowledge of the ways of operating a particular technology and of the kinds of problem it presents. By contrast, in a new technology the relevant 'meaning systems' have to emerge and be experienced. Consequently there are no known forms of social organization. A further point about many of the 'job enrichment' examples is that they have been applied to small groups rather than the whole organization.

In the initial literature searches this focus upon the small group had been apparent. It is perhaps easier to imagine the application of the autonomous group in situations where no account has to be taken of the overall requirements for coordination and control.

At the meetings in late October and November a number of possible sociotechnical designs had been identified for later evaluation. By this stage the main assumptions underpinning the initial manning proposals had been thoroughly scrutinized, but the project group could not agree on a set of guiding principles or select a particular example of what would be generally acceptable as an appropriate organizational system.

The difficulties of obtaining agreement hinged on the feasible solutions to the coordination of the making and packing machines. For technical and financial reasons the most appropriate designs were ones that linked a large group of making machines in one part of the room with a similar number of packing machines in the other part of the same floor. In this design the labour component was the flexible element that would in the case of direct workers have to be almost continually redeployed to counter difficulties arising from the sensitivity of the production system to the effects of breakdowns.

This form of organization was one that centralized the allocation of work by the manager or supervisor responsible for coordination. Some members of the project group liked this form of organization whereas others felt we should search for forms that ensured the delegation of responsibility downwards.

During these discussions we collected a number of assumptions that were being made about the preferences of members of the departments for different forms of organization. However, these assumptions and their illustrative support were frequently contradictory. Therefore we proposed that an extensive study of the existing social structure, aspirations, and orientations of the members of the two departments should be undertaken. This plan was formally presented at the December meeting and after a great deal of discussion the pilot studies commenced in April 1969. In the meantime, we had also proposed (October 1968) that a very small group should evaluate the sociotechnical designs to detail their respective technical and financial advantages and to indicate where possible their estimated social consequences and benefits. This group began work in November and reported the following February. During that period we also undertook a short study of the existing management system. We now turn to examine two important meetings with the Azimuth Group as a whole.

NOVEMBER MEETING: QUESTIONS

From the very start of the consultancy we had been comparing the intended aims of Azimuth, as expressed in the participative management philosophy of delegated decision-making, and the kinds of organizational system that were actually being created by the various teams of design engineers. On our return to the Making and Packing Departments we had attempted to apply the method of working found to be successful in the Processing Department. In the new subgroup we had made some progress, but found, by the time of the September meetings, that we needed to discuss our progress in some detail with Azimuth. As this needed to be clearer we planned a special meeting, which took place in November. That meeting raised a number of points affecting the direction of the consultancy and so we formulated these in a paper presented and closely discussed at the December meeting.

The central part of the agenda for the November meeting with Azimuth was a series of questions covering the areas of management philosophy, future developments in the market and distribution networks, the role of the trade unions, and the intentions for experimenting prior to the move. Two sets of factors influenced the selection of questions. First, the response to the first annual report and, second, the situation in the subgroup. We felt that there was a general requirement for further discussion of the actual principles underlying the design of the new factory, both in terms of the principle of delegated responsibility and in terms of the most appropriate system of organization for that situation. With regard to the latter point, we were not convinced that the design for the technology was adequately related to the changes we had noted in the composition of the market and in the rules governing its operation. We decided to feed back our concerns and doubts in the form of questions.

The first set of questions concerned the management philosophy. We had been asked to outline the problems arising from and associated with a participative approach and had shown how this approach could be adopted by applying a modification of the autonomous group concept in the Processing Department. In the case of the Making and Packing Departments the application – of the same set of human resources principles – would imply considerable alterations in the existing relationships and in the skill hierarchy of the work force. Given these problems and the fact that their existence was having an inhibiting effect on some members of the subgroup, we decided to ask for further clarification of objectives of Azimuth, and the Board. Their opinion was critical because of the potential consequences of any decision based on the human resources principles. In fact, we had been asked in an earlier phase to comment on the management philosophy, and though we had not done so directly there were a number of points in the Annual Report that might conceivably have led Azimuth to modify its original brief.

After pointing out the organizational problems of designing a system for coping with the coordination of workflow, breakdowns, and tea breaks, we asked Azimuth five questions relating to management philosophy:

— What do you mean by 'management philosophy'?
— How would you describe your present management philosophy?
— How would you describe your future management philosophy?
— What do you mean by participation?

— What effect do you see your management philosophy having on your organizational structure?

For the discussion of these questions we were joined by a member of the Board who had been given the additional responsibility of appraising management philosophy and related topics (at the time there was no Director of Personnel). We were told that the company was in the process of identifying a management philosophy and that CCE Ltd had previously been typified by a benevolent and auto-cratic regime. The current situation was one in which middle manage-ment had been exposed for some two to three years to 'new thinking' through the media of courses, articles in management journals, and visits by specialist lecturers. This 'new thinking' had started in middle management and was filtering upwards. The first reactions to this were that there was nothing 'new', but gradually the senior people, including himself, had become active.

He then turned to tackle the future directions and emphasized that this (1968) was a period of self-education. CCE Ltd had looked at the interests of other large companies and was currently exploring a number of possibilities including the 'Managerial Grid', the work of Herzberg, and also Reddin. He added that his comments did not specifically answer the questions, but did, he hoped, indicate the directions in which thinking was being channelled.

On the topic of participation, he suggested that everyone was conscious that change was desirable, that there should be more participation, and that developments should proceed from the top. At this point it was suggested by one member of the behavioural sciences team that the actual approach to the review of management philosophy, as just outlined, did not suggest that CCE Ltd was 'changing very much'. Members of Azimuth then pointed to a number of changes in recent times including the extensive use of special short-life groups of representatives working on specified problems, changes in payment systems, alterations in the allocation of privileges, and the current interest in the Managerial Grid and styles of management.

Drawing these points together, the Director said that he believed that CCE Ltd would move towards a more participative system at the shop-floor level, but the ease of moving might be hampered by the *ad hoc* use of consultants and packages. This was not intended as a criticism of either consultants or packages, but of the ways in

which managements utilized their services. Finally, the Director outlined some of the major constraints on management philosophy, and
then the meeting moved on to another topic.

Among the questions on the agenda paper were ones on the market
and the relationship with distributors. These questions were introduced by referring to the decisions made that would affect the
flexibility of the technology to cope with small-batch production and
a higher rate of product innovation than had previously been experienced. The answers to the questions we asked were in this instance
given by senior members of Azimuth. It will be recalled that the
marketing function was not directly represented. In practice several
members of the group worked in close liaison with Marketing on
product innovation. We learned that some fragmentation was expected and would be coped with by special production facilities,
otherwise the current trends had been taken as a basis.

Our questions on the changing composition and organization of
the distribution outlets was discussed, but it was not possible to
answer them fully at the November meeting.

The final set of questions referred to the plans for the transfer of
personnel to the new plant, the intentions with regard to experimenting with simulations of layout and manning, and the involvement
of groups outside Azimuth, including elected representatives within
the firm and at the local level. All these questions were about implementation. Our intention in asking these was to anticipate the change-
over from the organizational design to the planning of the change.

The responses to these questions indicated that a great deal of
thought had been given to the implementation of the selected designs,
but it was not possible at that time to do much more than introduce
the questions. After the meeting we followed up various aspects,
including payment systems, with the linkman. He outlined the current ideas on the stages of implementation of the new factory and the
detailed consideration that had been given to the presentation and
discussion of Azimuth's suggestions with other members of CCE
Ltd. It is important to re-emphasize that the social science consultancy was only one of a large number of ongoing activities within
CCE Ltd at that time.

DECEMBER MEETING: OUR PROPOSALS

The major part of the December meeting with Azimuth consisted of
our presentation of a paper drawing together the activities we had

jointly been engaged in during the previous fifteen months and suggesting directions for the future. In this section the main points of the paper will be paraphrased and then the response of Azimuth will be examined.

The paper was in four sections. The first three dealt with management philosophy and organizational design, employee orientations, and the relation between the production side and the advisory services for the new factory. The main argument in this was that CCE Ltd were investigating the idea of a new management philosophy in which the idea of participation seemed to be central. However, there were no constructive and positive plans for designing the factory to achieve these objectives and neither were there indications of how the transitions from the present to the future would occur. In practice a good deal of the thinking was in terms of scientific management and Theory X and this was influencing the planning of the factory. Though thinking about management philosophy had taken place, little consideration had been given to the forms of participation which the members of CCE Ltd would regard as essential and desirable. It therefore seemed sensible to investigate this aspect in greater detail. The paper contained a proposal for pilot study of orientations to work, the firm, and colleagues. The final section of the report dealt with four alternative sociotechnical designs for the Making and Packing Departments.

Management philosophy and organizational design

Under this heading we gathered together the responses to the questions asked at the previous meeting and related them to the slight impasse reached in the design subgroup over the relevance of the human resources principles to the structuring of the organizational system for the Making and Packing Departments. Feeding these observations back to Azimuth, we asked the question: 'How can the relationship between Azimuth and the behavioural scientists be most satisfactorily typified?' We suggested that the joint activities were best thought of as 'Azimuth clarifying its own ideas' about the organizational and attitudinal aspects of the new factory prior to more extended discussions and consultations with other groups within CCE Ltd. We, for our part, had attempted to identify some of the important problems created by the technical design and to show the ways in which the activities of apparently disconnected groups of experts working on aspects of the new factory are structuring the social relationships that are likely to emerge. (This was a reference to our initial terms of reference, as set out in June 1967.)

We observed that, while some members of Azimuth expressed a keen interest in the topic of management styles at the new factory, at the moment these were essentially ideas. There was no strategy for implementing them. In practice, the ground rules and criteria that were being implicitly applied to the design of jobs and the organizational system were not facilitating the introduction and implementation of the 'new thinking'.

We then moved our focus to examine the context in which Azimuth were attempting to formulate the 'new thinking'. CCE Ltd was, like many large enterprises in the postwar period, moving towards a more professional concept of management. This point was constantly emphasized to us by the managers we met. The younger men propounded this concept vigorously. In general terms there was a move away from benevolent paternalism and there was ample evidence to indicate that 'industrial discipline' was no longer a matter of personal whim, but was the application of standardized and agreed rules. This reflected a change in the relationship between management and other members of the firm, and was made manifest in the application of administrative practices such as Management by Objectives. These were an attempt to make a close calculation of the precise exchange between the firm and the employee. The new psychological contract (Schein 1965) which the professional managers were proposing was one in which there was a finely calculated balance of inducement (payment) in return for specified effort and thought. An important aspect of the new psychological contract was the extension of rationalization to the activities of staff members. Moving outside CCE Ltd, there were changes in social stratification that might be of importance. The role of the family had changed in significant respects since CCE Ltd had been founded in the nineteenth century. Certain trends, particularly in the case of the traditional working class, had been noted and documented (Goldthorpe *et al.* 1967). Though these changes may seem a 'far cry' from the problem of Azimuth because they were outside its immediate influence, they were, nevertheless, important to the future factory.

They were important because of their relevance to the kinds of legitimacy that the new professional manager attempted to invoke in support of his claim to have the right to manage. The new men had convinced themselves that the old-style authoritarian boss was not appropriate when the owner/entrepreneur had disappeared. In some senses the attack on the stereotype of the authoritarian boss had been successful. At least they had convinced themselves, but what was to be the basis of the prerogatives to manage for the professional manager in CCE Ltd? What principle of legitimacy underpins the authority of the new men? Is it to be participative management *à la* McGregor?

The paper emphasized the significance of developing and institutionalizing a new approach in defence of managerial prerogatives to Azimuth, but pointed out the ambiguity of the notion of participation. After all, how was it that students, management, and government ministers all seemed to be agreed, yet were in conflict?

How, then, was participation being applied in CCE Ltd? We reported that there was agreement that people should be free from close supervision, but little agreement on what people should be free to participate in. We then emphasized the cool responses to examples of job and organizational design that were based on the notions of responsible autonomy.

Drawing the points together we observed that the thinking by Azimuth on participation was somewhat vague and that in practice there was a preference for thinking in terms of Theory X.

All the comments paraphrased above were presented as feedback in an attempt to clarify the emphasis that Azimuth now considered crucial to the final stages of the organizational design. The paper did not suggest that Theory X thinking was wrong or inappropriate. Rather, it asked 'how in the light of some fifteen months' dialogue do you now see your management philosophy developing?'

The response to this part of the paper was interesting. It was generally agreed that the points raised were stimulating and important. We shall return to examine this response when we look back on the first six phases in the later chapters.

The second part of the paper contained the proposal for a systematic study of orientations to work of the members of two departments. It was argued that in instances where major changes of the kinds envisaged by Azimuth are planned there is a requirement to obtain more extensive specialized kinds of data than is normally the case. Thus, while the existing channels of opinion formation may be adequate for the continuing operation of the factories on the present site, we could not assume this would be the case for the change-over. Additionally, we required to know the aspirations of members of the two departments and their orientations to work, colleagues, and the firm. This specialized knowledge was, we felt, crucial to making decisions about job and organizational design, since it seemed unwise to assume that the members of the factory would have the same interest in, and feelings about, the ideas of McGregor as, for example, were held by management. Thus we proposed that the study of orientations should start in the new year and should complement another of our proposals concerning the activities of the subgroup. Here we suggested that a small group of three persons should evaluate the technical and financial aspects of the available sociotechnical designs. The second proposal was accepted, and had in a practical sense already been started. The first proposal was deferred for further consideration.

The third part of the paper raised the problems that might arise in relating the new factory to the existing advisory services. It attempted to use the ideas of Perrow (1967) with regard to the form taken by relations between production systems in the remainder of the enterprise under differing conditions. We introduced it in order to refocus our interests on the area of internal coordination and control. At the time we planned to follow this through and did in fact carry out a study of the existing system, but the development of the study on orientations in 1969 moved attention from this area and we did not return to it systematically until mid-1970.

The final part of the paper presented four sociotechnical designs for the Making and Packing Departments. Three of the designs assumed some form of mechanical linkage system between the making and packing machines, but differed in layout, manning, and deployment of people. The fourth alternative was a modification of the system actually in operation and did not include a mechanical linkage.

The four designs neatly illustrated the range of alternatives in both technical and social terms. The major problems were to evaluate their relative financial and organizational advantages and disadvantages. Calculating the financial aspects was delegated by Azimuth, but special provision was made for examining the relevance of existing and alternative sets of criteria for allocating people to roles. Basically, at that time, Azimuth felt that the preferable technological solution was one that included mechanical linkages in some form or another. Given the available data on the market, machine trials, and similar calculations, this decision appeared sensible and completely rational. The Chairman felt that, even though the options on alternative layouts were being finalized for the architect's brief, it would be valuable to consider all four designs. He and Azimuth were particularly interested in the different forms of 'group' organization suggested and wanted to know more about the problems to which this might give rise.

The paper as a whole may be summarized briefly: Azimuth expressed interest in examining designs of a factory embodying the principles of delegated autonomy; we argued that if they wished to implement these principles they would need to alter the criteria which were currently being applied and we provided examples to illustrate our arguments and the main problems involved.

How did Azimuth respond to the paper? In general terms the meeting was stimulating and constructive. Later we learned that members of Azimuth felt the discussion had been useful and relevant to their interests and problems. At that time CCE Ltd were facing some problems of adaptation in the factories and the comments on the nature of participation as actually practised were pertinent. One of our intentions had been to point to the aspirations of the members of CCE Ltd as an important factor to be accounted for in the final choice of a design and the planning of change. The paper emphasized that a change in the psychological contract between the firm and its employees was already taking place. This was an aspect which was to be of increasing importance in the next phase.

In the last sections of this chapter we briefly report the conclusions of the group set up to evaluate the technological designs and also describe a short study of the management communication system.

THE MANAGEMENT SYSTEM

A great deal of our work during the first fifteen months or so had been focused at the shop-floor level, yet the areas of coordination and control were becoming increasingly important. This was particularly the case in the work done in the Making and Packing Departments. Clearly, even with the principle of delegated responsibility there had to be coordination between activity groups and so we set out to make some initial inputs into the area of the management system as a whole.

We had learned from our previous experiences that the definition of problems is not a topic on which consultant and client necessarily agree. The onus is on the consultant to find means of demonstrating how certain decisions can have ramifications affecting the options available later. With these thoughts in mind we started a simple piece of fieldwork with the objective of discovering how the supervisors and managers perceived the management system of which they were a part. Our intention was to collect the data, analyse it, and then feed it back (Hesseling 1968).

We had, in the December paper, pointed to the actual practice of management by the newly emerging professional manager. An aspect of their belief system that we noted was the desire for clear and orderly job descriptions specifying both the content of the job and performance criteria for evaluating the incumbent. CCE Ltd had, following the application of a systematic method of appraising jobs and recording job content and objectives, implemented a number of organizational changes. These had taken the form of promoting the senior mechanics in the Making and Packing Departments to section leader and giving them responsibility for certain administrative tasks. This move was of considerable importance to the new factory because the section leaders might play a crucial role if the concept of responsible autonomy was applied. We therefore decided, as a first stage, to investigate the management system in one of the factories in which these changes had taken place. Our intention was to compare the new organization chart with the way in which the supervisors, section leaders, and managers actually perceived their role in relation to others and that of others in relation to themselves.

In order to achieve this objective we adopted a technique which we may call 'Scott's Diagram' (Scott 1956). The technique is relatively simple to apply but the analysis is best carried out in the light of knowledge of the particular situation. Each member of the management system in one factory was asked to place his own name in the centre of a blank sheet of paper and then to place the name of the person he reports to directly above his own name and the names of those reporting to him directly below. He is then asked to add selected diagonal relationships indicating their relative position in relation to the basic network.

This technique has been used by, for example, Sadler and Barry (1970) in their study of firms in the printing industry. At this stage of analysis the perceived networks are collated to reveal internal 'discrepancies' between respondents and to compare the collated network with the 'official' organization chart. As Sadler demonstrates, this can result in some surprises. In our case this was simply the first step in a larger exercise of examining the coordination and control aspects of the management system at the stage when the 'grass-roots' sociotechnical designs from the various parts of the new production system are reconciled. Having gained experience in using this technique and having established a bench mark of the perceived organizational structure in early 1969, we then moved on to carrying out the study of the orientations.

EVALUATION OF THE DESIGNS

This exercise was given to one member of our team, a representative from Work Study, and one from Research. The major problem they had to contend with was the continuing uncertainty about particular pieces of equipment. This meant that the concept of technical design was constantly subject to revision in parts and occasionally more widely. The final report demonstrated that, on the basis of existing knowledge, the design with the strongest technical and financial advantages was one which included the mechanical linkage system and kept the two different types of machine together, but separated from one another. The major objections to various designs that were more obviously technically integrated centred upon problems of maintenance.

The report was largely accepted by Azimuth, despite a plea that we had not yet conducted the study of orientations and could not therefore fully evaluate the designs. Azimuth decided that because of the time constraints it was necessary to make a decision in favour of one design. It was recognized that this considerably reduced the options remaining open since certain aspects of layout and configuration were being finalized. The orientations study was directed more to discovering the most appropriate form of organization, given that large areas of the technology were now decided. The study was also, of course, of value in the planning of change.

SUMMARY AND REVIEW

This chapter has largely discussed the problems raised in attempting to apply the method of sociotechnical design that seemed to have been successful in the Processing Department to Making and Packing. It has also been about the ways in which Azimuth's thinking about management philosophy was undergoing a transformation. This aspect emerges more sharply in the following chapter.

Despite the great difficulties posed by the uncertainties about which pieces of equipment should be included in the generation of sociotechnical designs, we had eventually succeeded in putting forward three alternative sociotechnical designs. One of those that was felt to have favourable social and organizational characteristics had to be abandoned.

From our point of view a major problem had been the lack of systematic knowledge about the existing social situation, particularly about the differences in expectations and aspirations between various categories of worker, and especially of their experiences of working in situations requiring the close interdependence of a large number of people.

From this phase of the project we began a study of social relations and orientations in the three existing factories. This forms the core of the following chapter and covers the period from March to December 1969. In the first part of 1970 the study of orientations was extended to the 'indirect' workers, and in mid-1970 the various aspects were drawn together in refocusing attention upon the management system. This last aspect necessitated a further study of 'control systems' for scheduling.

CHAPTER NINE

The Making and Packing Departments: The research focus

INTRODUCTION: PHASES V AND VI

This chapter contains two connected studies of (1) the direct, and (2) the indirect, workers, which were carried out between March 1969 and May 1970. The chapter takes the story through to the imposed cut-off point of mid-1970. The following chapter, which reviews the use of the Alternatives and Differences Approach to organizational design, also includes a brief postscript on the direction taken by the consultancy in 1970.

The main emphasis of the previous chapter was upon the design aspect – the generation of alternative sociotechnical designs. This process had been more fragmentary than had been the case in the joint study of the Processing Department. The range of alternative designs presented at the December meeting contained several aspects of interest and concern to both Azimuth and ourselves. In the main, the emphasis had been upon an analysis of the tasks the two departments had to undertake and the possible ways in which these tasks might be allocated to role systems. Here we are referring to the process of designing the organization and the application of some system of rules for matching tasks and roles. At the December meeting we had argued that the initial terms of reference for the project required us to give prime consideration to the ways in which the ideas of participative management might be built into the design of new organizations. However, we noted at that meeting that our attempts to achieve this objective were being continually frustrated at the various levels we were working at (e.g. Azimuth, cf. the project groups).

A major part of the discussion prior to the December meeting and during it had focused upon the advisability of adopting a form of organization that would resemble the autonomous groups described by Trist (1963). In the case of the Making and Packing Departments the actual experience of cooperative working situations was sharply different from that in coalmining. The existing situation was one in which there were several distinct occupational categories involving both sexes. In the Making Department all the evidence we had to hand suggested that the division of tasks and their allocation to roles brought males of relatively low status into a position of being responsible for the performance of females who were dependent upon them. By contrast, in the Packing Department, the machine crews were entirely female and the boundary between the crew and the mechanics was less fraught with tensions. One question we all asked was: Can the autonomous group concept be modified to fit the plans for joint Making/Packing Departments, and if so is there a 'fit' between the established traditions and autonomous group working?

We had argued that many of the important topics could be more adequately explored and clarified by an investigation of the existing social structure. This was initially planned as a 5 per cent sample of the 'direct' workers in the two departments, and it was intended that the findings from this study should inform the design process and might lead to further investigations. In practice, the study of direct workers was followed by a comparable study of the maintenance workers and both studies were completed by May 1970. During this period there were phases of feedback to Azimuth and discussion of the findings. Unlike the earlier phases, in this phase our relationship became less continuous and more intermittent as our attention became more and more concentrated upon completing the studies. Though we were aware of this change in relationship, we judged that sufficient collaboration had occurred in the earlier phases to ensure that the influence of our work on decision-taking was not reduced.

The specific proposal for the comparative investigation of the social systems of the Making and Packing Departments in the three existing factories was made at the December meeting. The actual pilot studies did not commence until late March of the following year. The main reasons for this gap in time were the need to complete the studies of the management system and the evaluation of alternative technical designs. Additionally there was a good deal of discussion and negotiation, both within management and with representatives of the groups in the departments to be studied. Meeting the Board of CCE Ltd, the union officials, members of management, and the elected representatives occupied a great deal of time.

Azimuth was sympathetic to the proposal, but was anxious to

ensure that the study did not clash with two other studies, one of which was being completed, the other being in a planning stage. The first study concerned the general responses of members of the company to changes in the existing factories arising out of an increased demand for CCE's products. This was undertaken by an outside independent body who collected opinion, formulated a report, and provided a basis for the extensive discussions that took place in the special advisory groups the firm had created. The second study was to be an extensive investigation covering the whole company. This did include some aspects which were of direct relevance to the design activities, but the aims of that investigation were essentially complementary to our proposals. When presenting our proposals to the Board and to Azimuth, we decided to make a brief statement of our objectives in the following way:

> We propose to undertake further and more detailed studies of the dynamic aspects of both the existing (and changed) 'social structure' and 'culture' in the Making and Packing Departments. Our proposal is based on the knowledge that there already exists a 'structured relationship' into which new people enter and learn their roles. This structured aspect cannot satisfactorily be revealed by methods of investigation which regard the working population of CCE Ltd as an aggregate of unconnected individuals. The most suitable approach for investigating the structural aspect is one which is best described as social anthropological.

The statement continued by outlining the details of resources and timing for the investigation and feedback to Azimuth.

The statement as set out above would almost certainly provoke a strong and unsympathetic response from some managers. However we had been involved in a collaborative relationship with Azimuth for some time and so we had a good expectation that the meaning of the statement would be taken as part of the dialogue. The more important aspect was our reason for wanting to do a study of the kind we were suggesting and the necessity to define fairly closely the technical reasons for this. In the paragraphs which followed the statement the main terms were defined more thoroughly.

We argued that more detailed studies were required to provide the basic valid knowledge needed to make a choice between the alternative sociotechnical designs and also to guide the planning of the change to the new factory.

— *Social structure* was defined as including the identification and delineation of the main groupings of employees, the salience of boundaries between groups, and authority relations within and between them.

— *Culture* was defined as including the orientations of individuals and groups to their work, their colleagues, and the firm. It also included such aspects as differential status, prestige, power, and notions of justice (Zaleznik 1957; Paterson 1957), and finally the linkages between life inside the firm and outside.

We suggested that detailed knowledge of these aspects would assist the definition of the responses of members of CCE Ltd to technical change (Touraine 1965). But how was this kind of operable knowledge to be obtained? Though we had some twenty months' experience in different parts of the Company we did not feel satisfied that we appreciated either the distinctive features of the social structure or the differences between the three existing factories. The advantage of adopting an approach that tends more to that of the social anthropologist is that it involves the use of a number of complementary and interlocking methods rather than the total reliance on one (e.g. an attitude survey). It thus permits a degree of cross-checking and familiarization for the analyst as well as revealing the subtleties of groupings within the enterprise. The 'map' which the analyst obtains should reflect the dynamic interplay of conflicts and cooperation between individuals and groups as well as providing clues about the factors that influence this interplay (Buckley 1966).

This approach was appropriate to a situation of collaborative problem definition and investigation because the analyst in that situation has to obtain a degree of operable knowledge about the context over and above that obtained in the attitude survey. The latter is more appropriate when the behavioural scientist is providing data to be used by other persons and does not take part in the decision-making process.

The general perspective we were adopting was one that combines a recognition of occupational features with a consideration of the organizational aspect. This decision was made because CCE Ltd corresponded in a number of important respects with the organizational theorist's definition of a bureaucratic organization (e.g. Crozier). It was therefore important to build a recognition of the fact into analytical frameworks adopted in the investigation of the social structure. The bureaucratic nature of the firm was also a critical point for the choice of change strategy.

In the sections immediately following, we outline the main theoretical elements of our approach and then report the findings from the investigations and the feedback of these.

PLANNING AND INVESTIGATION

Though there is a very considerable literature on the social and organizational aspects of technical change, there are remarkably few examples of collaborative projects involving behavioural scientists and technologists. There are some notable exceptions, including the work of Emery, Marek, Thorsrud, and their colleagues in Norway[1] and the fascinating account by Marrow and his colleagues (1967) of the way in which they 'modernized' a garment factory which had been acquired by a merger. One of the most difficult features of this literature is to make use of it when planning an investigation of the social structure and culture of an enterprise about to be changed. What should the behavioural scientist focus upon and how can he relate this kind of information and perspective to the problems faced by the members of a particular enterprise?

In recent times an increasing number of behavioural scientists have made recommendations to managements and unions on how the planning of investigations should proceed. We shall briefly look at one suggestion and then indicate the possible limitations of plans proposed by the authors. Mumford and Banks (1967) compared the experiences of two firms who were installing computers. Their observations on consequences of the change contain many interesting and a number of important points. For example, they point to the emergence of new categories in the occupational structure following the introduction of the computers. Towards the end of the account they draw together several mildly critical observations to suggest how managements should take account of the human and social aspects by meticulous planning. The suggestions are rational and apparently practical, except they do not seem to bear a strong relationship to the complex and dynamic aspects of technical change.

The complexity of change situations has been admirably demonstrated in Alan Flanders's (1964) account of the management of the productivity bargain at the Fawley refinery. He gives considerable

---

[1] For a full account of the Norwegian studies, see Thorsrud (1970).

emphasis and ample illustrative material to show how the internal management, the elected and official representatives of the maintenance workers, and the consultants 'worked through' the consequences of change in a peak of political bargaining, discussion, and persuasion. The utility of an attitude survey of the conventional kind in such a situation is a matter of conjecture, but it is hard to imagine how the social scientists' scientific models would have been of utility to those involved in the situation.

Many of the suggestions for attitude surveys as a necessary accompaniment to technical change neglect both practical and theoretical issues. At the practical level, for instance, there are in many middle-sized and large enterprises specialists experienced in negotiating and dealing with industrial relations. Such men frequently possess a highly selective and useful – to those involved – map of the patterns of conflict and association in an enterprise. The principal role of the external behavioural science adviser engaged on technical change in relation to technically oriented design groups is frequently to provide supplementary support to the internal experts. This aspect is all too frequently ignored in the popular criticisms of the lack of diagnostic skills among personnel specialists. Given that such people exist, it seems sensible to consider the kinds of valid knowledge they possess when deciding on an investigation.

Another frequently neglected aspect is the availability in many enterprises of extensive and detailed records of strikes, agreements, and similar incidents which can be analysed to reveal crucial features of the social structure and its emergence over time (Wilson, B. R., 1961). In the study at CCE Ltd an analysis was made of a wide variety of documentary evidence of this kind.

A theoretical objection to some of the literature on planning investigations in preparation for change is that much of this has been undertaken solely by social psychologists and mainly in America. Clark and Ford (1970) have set out a number of important objections to these accounts, particularly for their neglect of structural features of the enterprise. In the instance of CCE Ltd structural features were of importance. Another facet that has been wrongly neglected is the significance of established customs and practice for organizational design and planned change. Trist (1963) demonstrated the importance of this dimension and gave considerable stress to 'the loss, rediscovery, and transformation of a work tradition'.

Given these preliminary considerations, our role in relation to

Azimuth and the problems envisaged for the future, it was decided to concentrate on two kinds of data – orientations to work and the social structure. In each case we angled the investigation to take account of the difficulties of feeding back our data and interpretation. Thus the focus upon orientations was tackled within the perspective adopted by Goldthorpe (1967) in the study of the 'Affluent Worker' at Luton. This perspective had several advantages. For example, in our seminar explaining the perspective adopted by Goldthorpe and the typologies he produced, we were able to include Azimuth's current interest in the work of the various organizational psychologists and show the importance of knowing about orientations before adopting particular criteria for organizational design. Also the Luton studies provided a comparative framework. Provincial City was characterized by a locally born labour force and CCE Ltd was a long-established firm (cf. of the mixed situation in Luton). The focus upon structure was largely taken within the analytical framework of the French sociologist Crozier, whose work was summarized and circulated.

Crozier emphasized four features of the French bureaucracies he investigated, as follows: the extent and development of impersonal rules governing job specifications and the allocation of work; the centralization of decision-taking; the social isolation of different strata and the group pressures exerted on newcomers to adapt to the prevailing norms; and the development of crucial power relationships around those areas of the operation of the bureaucracies which could not be specified, or were the least specifiable.

The choice of these two writers was influenced by the necessity for emphasizing both the existing and the future structural features that were concomitants of the present traditions and the new technologies. From the point of view of the consultancy both perspectives were fruitful to our dialogue with Azimuth.

In the whole of the planning of this phase the linkman played an important role in advising about areas of the factories he considered important and in introducing the project to official union representatives at the meetings held with them prior to the field studies.

The full study began in May 1969, with the pilot studies in each of three factories. (At this stage it was necessary to supplement the basic team by adding Pauline Earnshaw and Janet Ford.) Once the main part of the study had been started we arranged for a meeting with Azimuth to re-examine the principles underlying the studies.

The main points had been introduced at earlier meetings, but we now felt it necessary to outline the ways in which the findings would be reported and also to raise the question of the rules to be applied in interpreting the findings and relating them more directly to decision-taking about organizational design and its implementation. It will be recalled that the members of Azimuth had different viewpoints on the importance of the human aspect in general, and on the relevance of the ideas of the human resources approach in particular. We emphasized our position in that debate and pointed to the ways in which the study would answer some of the implicit questions.

The meeting took place in July. The objective of the meeting was to re-appraise the various ideas involved in the participative Theory Y approaches to management styles. More specifically, to focus upon the assumptions about motivation that underpinned these approaches and to show how the study – which was ongoing – was designed to identify critical features of existing motivations and to locate the factors explaining them. It may be seen that the emphasis was placed upon the ways in which the members of CCE Ltd defined the 'rules of the game' and the kinds of involvement in the 'game'.

The paper caused some surprise and concern, particularly since it was expressed in terms of a series of propositions that were being tested. The surprise arose because some members of Azimuth anticipated that we would be advocating the human resources principles of organization (Chapter 2). The concern arose because the findings of the study might suggest that one set of principles (e.g., scientific management) was more appropriate in this context, and nobody knew what would emerge. The fact that we were able to test out a proposition about motivations in this way owes much to the skill of the Chairman, who was able to create an atmosphere in which differences of opinion within Azimuth were explored by carrying out investigations of the human aspects.

A KEY PROBLEM: THE ROLE OF RESEARCH IN DESIGN

In Chapter 2 the activities of research and of design were distinguished. The question arises of what part researchers should play in the design activities of behavioural science practitioners. This question introduces an issue which is currently dividing academics from practitioners and bringing each into conflict with administrators. There can be no doubt that the kinds of evidence which each of these three sets of persons would regard as adequate for taking decisions are quite different. The academic is principally concerned with accurate exploration and delineation of the phenomena within a field of inquiry which is defined by the division of disciplines within the institutions of learning. The academic social scientist is concerned to understand and explain, not to change. By way of contrast the administrator is concerned to make decisions that take into account what is known and relate that to a repertoire of performance programmes possessed by the enterprise. The decision-taking administrator works within a value system possessing a kind of rationality, but of a dissimilar kind to that of the academic. The behavioural science practitioner is the specialist on the human aspect whose activities are bounded by the values of the client system (Churchman & Emery 1967; Jones 1969).

The behavioural science practitioner may carry out pieces of investigation that are termed by members of enterprises as 'research', but it is quite likely that academics would reject this definition and limit the term 'research' to any activity that advances the state of understanding (Kuhn 1962) and knowledge of a particular discipline. The academic would almost certainly describe the practitioner's activities as short 'investigations', which are designed to add to the knowledge of the administrator and occasionally to increase his understanding. The distinction between knowledge and understanding is an important one.

Typically, the behavioural science practitioner has been used by the administrator on counting exercises. The prime example is the attitude survey. Counting is carried out within a prescribed framework and the results are presented to the administrator and may add to the stock of knowledge and administrators. It is not likely to influence either the practitioner's or the administrator's understanding. In contrast our activities at CCE Ltd described so far have been directed at changing the understanding of the Azimuth Group and of associated individuals and groups.

The work at CCE Ltd has been primarily concerned with understanding and changing the ways in which technologists and engineers look at the social system. The method adopted to achieve this objective has essentially taken two forms – naming and propositioning.[1] The naming has consisted of interpreting the existing social system and presenting this interpretation to Azimuth and asking them to

[1] See Chapter 10 for a more extensive discussion of the topic.

compare it with their perceptions. The study of the packing crews is an excellent example. The propositioning has taken the form of selecting hypotheses from the literature on organizational studies and comparing these hypotheses with the assumptions of Azimuth. Examples include the work of Woodward, Burns and Stalker, and Perrow.

Thus we were able to go beyond the usual activity of counting. The question which the administrator will ask is: how much research (cf. investigation) is required?

The response to this question must necessarily depend on the nature of the problem involved. At CCE Ltd, in the case of organizational design, we judged it necessary to carry out a short piece of research in the Making and Packing Departments. The objective of this work was to highlight the actual orientations that members of these departments had to work, colleagues, the Company, and the union, and compare these with the expectations of Azimuth. We found it useful to adapt the perspective developed by Goldthorpe and his colleagues. This was because of the emphasis given to the variety of ways in which people define their own situation in the enterprise and the stress on the role of factors external to the place of work in influencing orientations. We felt that the influence of external factors, though important, had been exaggerated. Our earlier researches had suggested that the role of internal factors was important, and so we formulated the following question: 'How far does the situation within the company influence the formation of orientations to work?'

We considered that an approximate answer to this question was relevant to the design problems at CCE Ltd. Its relevance lay in the identification of the factors that most influenced the ways in which the 'rules of the game' played by individuals and groups within CCE Ltd would be affected by the technological and administrative modifications and innovations.

The crucial question here is the extent to which orientations are formed inside CCE Ltd at present and will be in the future, the factors influencing this process, and the relevance of understanding them to the decision-takers within Azimuth. Typically, practitioners do not give much recognition to events occurring outside the enterprise. They tend to focus upon dimensions that are within and open to some alteration by managerial strategies. For this reason they frequently omit reference to the kinds of variable an academic researcher would consider important. The practitioner justifies this selection of variables by arguing that he is only interested in identifying critical points of leverage in the social system and showing how administrative strategies can be applied to alter the existing situation in a desired direction (Bennis *et al.* 1969). In the case of CCE Ltd, however, there was a good case for including a wider range of variables than has typically been the case in the work of practitioners.

We now briefly note and examine Goldthorpe's specific contention that orientations are largely formed outside the enterprise. This conclusion is presented as an 'overriding impression' from the data and is at a high level of generality in comparison with many studies of enterprises. It is not an unusual conclusion, but it is a controversial one for those who believe strongly in the human relations approach.[1] Goldthorpe is essentially arguing against those writers like Mayo (1949) who have suggested that society is in a state of disorganization (cf. Goldthorpe 1969) that can only be remedied by making the enterprise the stable social unit.

It may be asked: if the orientations are formed outside the enterprise how are we to explain the 'overriding impression' that the workers in the Luton sample had a similar orientation to work? Goldthorpe argues that this arises because individuals with a similar orientation have elected, and been selected, to join the same organization. This assertion would clearly make nonsense of our analysis of the position of the packing crews as described in Chapter 5. It would also make nonsense of a great deal of previous research and so it is pertinent to inquire about the basis for it. In its defence it may be argued that the Luton sample is an unusual one in so far as a large proportion of the population investigated did come from outside the town and specifically selected the industries there because of their known high wages. Thus the population differs greatly from that of CCE Ltd and of Provincial City as a whole. In the latter case the working populations were largely local. Some 70 per cent of the members of CCE Ltd were local to Provincial City and its environs.

At a theoretical level there is good evidence for assuming that the worker's definition of his work and its meaning for him may be

[1] The attack on the human relations school has largely succeeded by ignoring both the objectives of its exponents and the variety of approaches within that school of thought. Critics have frequently argued that the cognitive content neglects structural factors, but it is not so self-evident to certain writers (e.g. Weick 1970) that organization is as structured as this criticism would suggest. (Mouzelis, 1967, makes a sympathetic appraisal).

influenced by the social context in which he is working. For example, Crozier demonstrates that, even allowing for the factor of self-selection, the new members of the bureaucracies studied are pressured to accept the values of the particular groups they join. Similarly in studies of shipyard workers, Brown and Brannen (1969, 1970) have suggested that the complex division of labour characterizing the industry exerts an influence in forming the orientations of the members of particular craft groups.

Perhaps the most surprising aspect of Goldthorpe's argument is that it is based upon a survey approach that has neglected the processual aspects of interrelations between administrators and other groups (Blau 1964). Indeed, it may be argued against Goldthorpe that the major problem for industrial sociologists is actually to penetrate the enterprise and carry out meaningful researches within it. Much of Goldthorpe's criticism of industrial sociology is doubly misplaced. First, he mistakes practitioners for researchers. Second, he includes the work of practitioners within the basic framework of industrial sociology rather than regarding it as data (Bendix 1956).

To summarize: in this section we have argued that the practitioner carries out investigations rather than research in the sense meant by the academic. The investigations typically consist of counting and the results add to the knowledge of administrators, but not necessarily to their understanding. At CCE Ltd the focus was upon understanding and this involved pieces of investigation which approximate to research in so far as they include the testing of propositions and the imposition of the perspective of the behavioural scientist on the findings. Finally, we note that administrators are impatient with the academic's definition of adequate evidence and the academic is frequently irritated at the practitioner's definition of research.

FEEDBACK

The change in our activities from involvement in the design team to the carrying-out of a piece of investigation (research) also changed our relationship with Azimuth. This mainly took the form of a more prescribed and formalized pattern of presentation and discussion, though personal relationships were largely informal.

The problem of feeding back the findings was approached in two parts. The first was to establish the framework of interpretation to be applied to the findings. This was achieved at the July meeting described earlier. The second was to arrange for the feedback and discussion of the studies of the three factories and the connecting of the implications to the design proposals and plans for managing the change.

The actual feedback of the findings and their discussion occurred in two stages. Following the completion of the study of Factory A, the results were presented and circulated in case-study form and discussed at a feedback meeting in August. The findings from the two other factories were included in the second annual report and discussed at a meeting in November. At the meeting it was decided that the study should be extended to include the maintenance workers. This was undertaken in the first part of 1970 and fed back in May 1970. That study ended the period of investigation and forms the cut-off point for our case study.

THE THREE FACTORIES

The investigation of the orientations and the social structure of the Making and Packing Departments was planned on a comparative basis. The reasons for this were that many of the earlier studies had been undertaken in Factory C and we had been continually informed that each of the factories had quite different customs and practices. Among management Factory C was regarded as the most modern and Factory A the most traditional. If there were such differences then they might be of relevance to the plan for taking members from all three factories and transferring them to a new one. In some senses this plan may be seen as a mini-merger.

The three factories possessed certain features of similarity and comparison that may be quickly dealt with. First, there is the range of products manufactured. CCE Ltd made a single basic product which could take one of two major forms, which we shall refer to as the 'old' and the 'new'. Beyond these major differences there were minor variations designed to cater for particular markets. Factory A was mainly concerned with 'old' products and Factory C with 'new'. Second, the technology. The technology for packing was similar for both 'old' and 'new' products, while that for making was different, as shown in *Figure 9*. These differences had important consequences for the allocation of tasks and for manning. Third, there had been differences in relative status between the two departments, with Packing being traditionally regarded as having higher status. The introduction of 'new' products coupled with modifications in machines was complicating and blurring this distinction. Finally there are general differences in the sex composition of the two departments. In both departments the females outnumbered the males. In Packing, the ratio was 5 : 1 and in Making it was 3 : 1.

Figure 9   Making: technology and manning

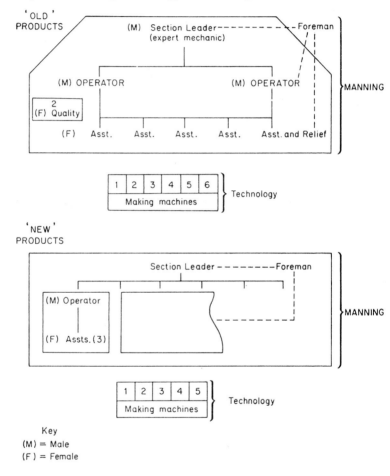

Key
(M) = Male
(F) = Female

The female roles are the ones which would be most immediately affected by the technological changes.

In the section following we note some of the findings from the study of Factory A and then examine the feedback meeting.

FACTORY A

Factory A (the smallest) was generally regarded as the most paternalistic and traditional of the three factories. It was located in part of the original set of buildings purchased by the founders of the firm in the last century. Almost the whole of its production consisted of the 'old' products which had been the basis of CCE Ltd's reputation until the 1960s.

The investigations had a slightly different emphasis in each of the three factories, but three topics were included in all the studies, as follows: orientations, group boundaries, and the role of the shop stewards and the trade union. From the report on Factory A we have extracted the data on orientations for illustrative purposes. In the section that follows, on Factory B, the emphasis of the extract will be upon group boundaries. The total findings from A and their interpretation were presented to a feedback meeting in August.

The main conclusions on orientations are set out in *Figure 10*. This shows considerable variations between the various occupational categories and also differences associated with age and length of service. In the main, the young female workers, particularly the part-timers, had an instrumental orientation. Their involvement in the job and the firm was neutral and they regarded work as a means of obtaining earnings. In almost direct contrast the females over the age of 45 and of long service involved in their work and the firm were typified by an expressed interest in the work.

Among the male workers there are also differences. The section leaders – the former senior mechanics – in both departments are typified by involvement in the job and with the firm. They see their work in the firm in terms of status and careers and possess a service orientation. Also both they and the packing mechanics experience strong linkages between activities at work and outside. The main difference between the two groups is that the packing mechanics see work as group activity and place emphasis upon the career and status aspects. The male operators in Making are typified by dissatisfaction with the firm and their work, which they define as a mere means to an end. Their work and outside activities are not directly related. Their overall orientation is highly individualistic, but motivation to work is more involved than in the case of the typical instrumentally oriented workforce.

The feedback of the report which collated the findings on all the topics investigated is of interest for two reasons. First, those members of Azimuth who were somewhat sceptical about the opportunitiesfor introducing a delegated form of decision-making were pleased to find many points they could interpret as supporting the view, while supporters of the autonomous group idea saw that the existing situation posed a number of problems that were not immediately surmountable. Second, the content of the meeting was largely in terms of questions asking for further clarification and there was little controversy. This surprised Pauline Earnshaw (1969), who had had primary responsibility for the investigation and the feedback. She noted

Figure 10   Factory A: Summary of orientations by occupational categories

Department		Orientations	
Making Packing		Work seen as	Involvement in job
Females under 21 years		Means to an end	Neutral
Females over 45 years		A source of interest	Positive
Male		Means to an end	Job a source of discontent
operators			
	Male mechanics	A group activity	High
Male Section Leader		Work seen as service to firm in return for status and career	High

the absence of controversy in her account of the meeting. Her expectation of controversy had been based on an earlier experience with feedback meetings when groups of employees were brought together and presentedwith the tabulated summaries of their perception of one another and asked to comment. In that situation there had frequently been a great deal of argument and controversy. We should not be so surprised at the difference in response of the Azimuth Group. They were a design team examining data about other groups who were not present.

FACTORY B

The principal focus of the investigations in Factory B was upon the identification of main sentient boundaries (Miller & Rice 1967). The concept of sentient boundaries and groups is an important one and requires some brief elaboration. It is widely recognized that individuals identify themselves with particular groups and these groupings may, or may not, coincide with task groupings created by the division of activities. The concept of sentient group refers to the group that receives and demands loyalties from its members. Some groups may have only a tenuous basis of mutual feeling and their sentient boundary may be weak. The importance of the sentient groups and boundaries is that they represent the points to which individuals direct their loyalties and seek support. The existing pattern of sentient groups and the nature of their boundaries have considerable implications for technical innovation and for the choice of a system of organization. The focus upon sentient groups and boundaries is based on the recognition that any enterprise has to ensure the commitment of its members to the main objectives.

We first of all examine the Making Department in terms of three main categories, as follows: section leaders, male operators, and female attendants. The section leaders had formerly been known as senior mechanics and had had their titles and job content altered in 1967 to include more administrative work. They were a definable group with departmental status but not a great deal of cohesion. In many ways they were in a transient state of movement from one set of duties to another and were subjected to a deal of ribaldry. Their feelings towards the male operators were of resentment, which was reciprocated, particularly by those operators who had not passed the newly introduced examination system. The section leaders were not – in 1969 – clear and sure about their position in relation to the female attendants and generally felt that management had not explained their role adequately to the attendants.

The male operators in this factory were both a job category and a sentient grouping with moderate cohesion. The group boundary was in one sense rather precarious. This was because there was a cleavage between the men manning the 'old' and the 'new' machines. The latter had been specially selected and tested whereas the former had not. The operators found difficulty in acting as a solidary group in presenting a front to other groups, especially management. Some members seemed to feel that they were men with a career orientation but had been unsuccessful. Their expectation of the union was limited to the job. The operators felt that the section leaders were unable to spend sufficient time in helping them with their work and that when they did they frequently had not got the technical knowledge

required. Their feelings towards the female attendants were ambivalent. They felt that the attendants were too vigorous in emphasizing
quality standards and that females were always changing their
decisions. This was said to be an inborn characteristic!

The female attendants' definition of a team included the other
females, but excluded the male operator. The attendants were responsible for quality and the operators for quantity and this difference in emphasis was perceived to be an important source of tension.
The attendants expressed a strong preference for stable and continuing membership of the same team (i.e., the crew on the machines).
Few of the females had interpersonal contacts at work and very few
had friends they had met in the department and visited outside. The
main topic of conversation was the job (Garfinkel 1969). They expected the union to be interested only in the job and were not
concerned about wider issues. The female attendants in this factory
were essentially a job category and they did not represent a cohesive
group with shared outlooks and definitions of the situation. They
had virtually no control at a social level and tensions were expressed
more in terms of individual than group strategies (Scott, W. H.,
1963).

In fact, the Making Department manufactured both the 'old' and
the 'new' products. These had two distinct forms of organization
which almost certainly increased the fragmentary nature of relationships.

The situation in the Packing Department may be contrasted with
that in Making. The section leaders form a cohesive group with an
identifiable sentient boundary. They had held a respected position
prior to the change in status and duties in 1967 and were not subjected to the same pressures as their equivalents in Making. The
change in title had not affected their favourable perceptions of the
mechanics. The section leader had little direct contact with the
packing crews.

The male mechanics were a sentient group with a strong and
identifiable boundary who had been strongly allied with the section
leaders until the alteration in duties of 1967. Though there was no
direct expression of antagonism from the mechanics they expressed
uncertainty about the long-term implications of the changes. So far
they had acted in alliance with the section leaders, particularly over
the differentials with the Making Department. The mechanics perceived their relationship with the senior member of the packing crew

as variable and important. They defined a small group including themselves and the senior girl, but excluding the remainder of the crew.

The female packers formed sentient groups at two levels: the machine crew and the occupational group. As an occupational group they attempted to exert concerted influence particularly over the role of the quality attendants in the department. They had very little contact with the section leader, who was still defined as a technologist rather than an administrator.

The Packing Department contains sentient groups with identifiable boundaries. In this case the job categories coincide with relative solidary and active groups. The bargaining position of these groups was recognized in the style of overall management adopted. This corresponded to Style 3 (Chapter 2). Historically, the groups in Packing have been active in union affairs.

It may be seen from these summarized observations that the social relationships and formations of sentient groupings in the two departments present a number of important contrasts.

Two further areas are of importance. The first concerns the boundaries between the Making and Packing Departments as defined by the members of those departments. Though there was good evidence that each group within one department noted the pay and privilege position of groups in the other department, there was little direct contact between them. This was especially the case for the female employees. An interesting finding in Factory B was that the general hypothesis that the females in Packing defined themselves as occupying a superior status was not supported. That indicates the importance of the earlier decision to compare the three factories and to view the future as having some of the characteristics of a mini-merger. The second main area concerned the expectations about the role of the unions and the elected representatives. The relevance of this topic is that management frequently assumes that it is actually talking to people who are representative when it discusses with shop stewards. In practice this is not always the case, and is least likely to be so in a change situation. An important finding was the sharp difference in the images of appropriate union activity as defined by the men and the women. The men expected (i.e. 80 per cent of those interviewed) that the unions and shop stewards should deal with collective matters, while a similar proportion of the females expected representation on personal matters. The greatest satisfaction with the union came from the Packing Department. There were considerable variations in awareness of the union, particularly among the women, some of whom were not sure to which union they belonged, even though they were wearing a union badge. One of the more important facts to emerge was a general concern with the problems of representation in the new factory and during the negotiations prior to the move. In general there was fairly heavy criticism of the shop stewards, a number of whom were felt to be closer to management than to the people who elected them.

The investigation of Factory B provided useful data for comparison with the previous studies in Factory C. The findings emphasized the general belief that the factories had developed distinctive customs and practices and indirectly indicated some of the problems that would have to be dealt with if persons with such diverse attachments to groupings were to work together in the new factory, particularly if the new situation demanded close dependencies.

FACTORY C

A large part of the earlier studies had been carried out in this factory. It was generally regarded by management as the 'most advanced' and was one of the main areas for carrying out machine trials and similar investigations. Our study mainly concentrated upon the attachments of the members to their job, their colleagues, and the firm. The findings differed in some respects from the other two.

THE THREE FACTORIES: FINDINGS

In looking at the findings of the investigations in the three factories we concluded that they could be thought of as three separate entities, each having a distinctive style and culture. Employees had different images of their own factory and the others. Members of Factory A defined A *as* CCE Ltd and viewed the other two as peripheral. While someone in Factory C would typically look on A as a 'bits and pieces' factory, and feel that the *real* production was done in C. Though attachment to the firm and factory varied, there were virtually no persons who wanted to work in another factory in preference to the one they were in.

Although the production systems of the three factories might seem similar to a visitor, the members of each factory felt that there were distinctive customs and habits for each. Factory A was seen as the small-batch factory and the other two as mass production. However, the picture must not be exaggerated. While those in A were extremely reluctant to think about moving to a new site or to another factory, there was no such strong aversion on the part of B and C. An interesting aspect here was that many employees had quite distinct and unitary images of the managements in the other factories. This finding and others influenced the analysis of the part played by management in the formation of images of the work situation.

ANALYSIS AND INTERPRETATION OF THE RESEARCH

In this section we shall concentrate upon the analysis of the orientations. Emphasis has been given in the earlier chapters to recognizing that orientations are not a simple function of a given profile of technological characteristics (see Turner & Lawrence 1965). The crucial point is that the definitions of technology and of its change are given by employees and that these definitions are in part formed outside the firm. Goldthorpe has considerably sharpened this point by arguing that orientations are almost entirely formed outside the (industrial) enterprise and that their formation is largely influenced by the individual's position in the life-cycle and his experiences of the class structure of society, particularly experiences of social mobility. This argument was useful to the consultancy in drawing attention to the way in which new employees were defining the firm as compared to the long-service members. In general new employees were neutral in their attachment to the firm and more calculative in their attitude to management. While not wishing to underemphasize the significance of this, we judged on the basis of extended examination of the literature, and on the basis of our own investigations, that the part played by management in providing and reciprocating definitions of the firm had been neglected.

Management is *not* taken as a given by employees. They are quick to note and point to any changes that are occurring in the 'managerial climate'. An individual joining the firm has a variety of expectations about the whole pattern of rights, privileges, and obligations between himself and the enterprise. This might include, for example, expectations about the general level of payment and the method of firing people. CCE Ltd had, during the depression of the 1930s, been a significant employer in Provincial City and had been noted for the high level of payment, the job content, and security. Also the authority pattern at the time was essentially paternal.

Many of the older employees, who formed a significant proportion of the total population, had joined in that period, or under its influence. We might call this bundle of expectations the CHARTER OF CCE LTD – a kind of social contract, entirely unwritten, involving all members of the firm.

Management play an important part in forming the rules that govern this charter, and as we have already noted, the younger managers were somewhat critical of the paternal form of authority and proposed to replace it with 'professional management' and 'more participative management'. A very interesting combination. Thus a number of changes in the 'rules of the game' had been introduced by management. There was still an atmosphere of security evidenced by the promises about redundancy. The new rules affected the autonomy of the separate factories and the differential between blue- and white-collar workers. The whole issue of the charter and the contract between the various individuals and groupings within an enterprise is one that becomes crucial in a period of major change.

Relationships within enterprises are essentially interactive and they unfold through mutual influence and bargaining to the establishment of a charter, which is in its turn replaced by another. This means that we must acknowledge the role management play in this context and show it in the analysis of the data. We did so by postulating changes in the expectations of new and older members over time. *Figure 11* sets out a time dimension along the horizontal axis indicating the date of joining the firm. The vertical axis holds the employees of the firm trichotomized into operators (male and female), supervisors, and management. (The intention of the diagram is entirely illustrative.) It may be seen that we are suggesting that persons joining in the prewar period had developed a 'service' orientation towards the firm. They regarded work there as having high status and as being a career in which a lad started by pushing trollies, worked his way up to becoming a machine attendant, or mate, and then possibly moved on to becoming a skilled mechanic or supervisor. Each department and factory was organized hierarchically in these terms. The basis of promotion was loyalty, reliability, a satisfactory level of competence, and length of service. Those people who joined in that period now occupy the skilled operators' and supervisors' jobs and in some cases are technical experts, or managers. Management were major agents in operating and sustaining the rules of this game. Such evidence as we were able to collect suggested that technical changes, even those involving major alterations in the numbers employed in a department or in the skill hierarchy, were either accepted or largely unopposed by strategic bargaining.

We suggest in the diagram that during the 1950s and into the 1960s the 'rules of the game' were altered by management. An increasing emphasis was placed upon measured competence (e.g. testing of abilities prior to promotion) and upon tighter control by

Figure 11   Changing management styles and employee orientations (1930–1970)

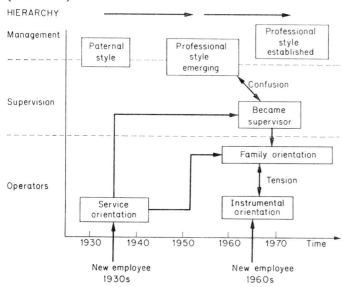

impersonal means. The locus of initiative for decisions about production gradually moved from the lower levels in the separate factories upwards to senior management and to the new functions such as production scheduling. These changes were heightened by the introduction of the 'new men' into marketing and the general changes in the role of the production function. Towards the end of the 1960s there was an increasing emphasis by production management on measures of performance and similar ideas. Management became, as its composition changed, less oriented towards paternalism, and more interested in the 'professional' image. One member of our team argued that in the 1930s there was a good 'fit' between paternalism and the service orientation, and that in the future there would be a good 'fit' between professionalism and an instrumental orientation, but that currently the situation was one of tension.

The analysis in its raw form and the findings were prepared as a report. Because of the demands of time and our increasing confidence that there was less necessity for restating the initial objectives of the work, we included the findings in the second annual report. The report was an improvement upon the first in some respects but not in others. The decision to avoid a recapitulation in diary form of the year's work meant that a number of ongoing activities tended to be neglected. The report was also rather lengthy, even though it was much easier to understand. It was decided that copies should go to Azimuth and the Board and that a separate shortened account should be made available for interested parties.

THE FEEDBACK MEETING

The feedback meeting did not take place until late 1969. By that stage the findings had in fact been circulated and Bernard Leach had started on the process of linking the findings into the ongoing work on design by R & D and other groups. At the meeting it was confirmed that a number of technical options had become closed for financial and developmental reasons. In practice the possible forms of sociotechnical design were still wide as compared with the Processing Department (Chapter 6).

The meeting crystallized a change in the relationship between Azimuth and ourselves. In the early stages we had given an almost equal emphasis to design/development and to research activities. Our focus upon research had left the developmental aspect to Azimuth and had weakened the strength of the input. There was a division of labour emerging in which the developmental aspect was undertaken by Azimuth.

Two consequences of the discussions were important to the next phase. First we began some design work in areas we had not yet covered. Second, the report raised a number of problems about the role of the maintenance workers in the new factory (e.g. electricians), and the ways in which Azimuth should consider taking it into account in the organizational arrangements. There were already differences between the role of maintenance in the Processing Departments as compared with the remainder of the factory, and the evidence we now had about the proposed technical innovations suggested that this difference would remain. It was proposed that the study of the existing social structure should be extended to these other groups. This was agreed.

SOCIOLOGICAL ASPECTS OF . . .

When we were able to return to the design aspect of the consultancy we discovered some interesting developments, which were exemplified in the title of a paper given by a member of R & D to a working party. The title was 'Sociological aspects of . . .' and the paper was concerned with the likely social consequences of several alternative technical designs. In this case the role of our team had changed and we were represented in an advisory capacity. That is to say, the working party were using Project Officer Bernard Leach as a resource to inform them. This indicates that members of the firm felt some competence at defining problems and using the behavioural scientist as a resource (cf. O'Connel 1968).

The author is something of a pessimist and feels that, though this development had some encouraging aspects for the behavioural scientist, in practice it is not possible for those who are not behavioural scientists to sustain a role of this kind for a great length of time. It would need backing up and supporting by provision for a post for a full-time behavioural scientist, but that argument takes the story back to the opening remarks in Chapter 1 and to an earlier contention: 'Since the activities of work study men, especially in the field of "broad method study", affect the individuals and groups concerned, every department of ten or more practitioners should include a sociologist' (Clark 1963).

THE STUDY OF MAINTENANCE MEN

CCE Ltd had approximately 1,000 men who came into this category, and that figure covered electricians, mechanics, engineers and their mates and assistants, as well as the less obvious functions such as the fire service. It was agreed that the study would follow very similar lines to the previous investigations, that is, observation, interviewing, discussion, and documents. One of the major objectives was to provide a characterization of the maintenance function, pointing to the distinctive features of its social organization and comparing it with the system among the production workers. An area of real concern was that of the relative images of each other held by maintenance and production workers and managers.

There were a variety of other reasons for Azimuth wanting to look more closely at this aspect. First, there was the changed importance of the maintenance function in the eyes of management. They felt that they had begun to gain some predictability in the operation of the production system, and, though considerable improvements in productive performance could be achieved, that the real area of uncertainty lay in maintenance activities. The emphasis was so strong because of the costs of 'machine downtime'. Second, no one was quite sure how maintenance could and should be related to changes in the organizational system envisaged for the production workers. For example, one member of Azimuth argued that he would prefer to see autonomous groups created in the areas he was designing, and that the maintenance men should be included within them. This leads on to a third point, that in the new factory it had been planned that the activities of production and maintenance workers would be more closely related. The problems involved include: the co-existence of groups with different values and the change thereby introduced into the overall power and bargaining structure; the question of differentials.

The investigation was designed to cover five main topics:

Job – orientations towards; the workload; selection and training; promotion.

Colleagues – orientations towards; preferences about groupings; supervision and management.

Production workers – definitions of them and beliefs about their definitions of the production worker.

Modernization and change – in the past and with reference to the new factory.

Trade unions – perception of the local and national levels; expectations of future role.

Additionally, the topics included aspects of the local community and the family. For example, the investigation demonstrated that for these workers individual hobbies (e.g. fishing) were important, and that the family is essentially thought of as two generations – parents and children, i.e., the nuclear family. The men were particularly concerned about the impact of shift work on their families. The inclusion of these aspects might seem idle and unimportant, since from the viewpoint of union officials and management they are largely 'givens' and cannot be altered. In practice, they were important in revealing expectations of the firm, and in guiding the provision of amenities. A great deal of organizational design by technologists and the planning of change by behavioural scientists (e.g. Bennis, Benne, & Chin 1969) has neglected the importance of the family and the local community, in terms of both social responsibilities and planning (Clark, Ford, & Eling 1969).

The main findings of this investigation were as follows (this is of necessity a truncated account): that the maintenance workers were typically in their middle 40s, of long service, and with working wives. They were typical of the census material in the sense that 80 per cent were local men and the corresponding census figures for 1961 were approximately 70 per cent. The most skilled men in each category (e.g., mechanic, cf. electrician) defined themselves as a group, and this was a horizontal formation. The assistants tended to define themselves as a group in hierarchical terms and were less cohesive. Generally speaking, the greater the skill level, as defined by the job evaluation data, the greater the attachment to the job. The greater the skill of the man, the more likely he is to regard CCE Ltd as one of several possible employers, even though there is no comparable production system in Provincial City. Management and the unions were regarded as distant. The management were defined as competent, but the remarks about the union were rather less complimentary. The general feeling towards production workers and their managers was ambivalent. The maintenance men expected to be disliked and unappreciated. They saw the new factory as a situation that would make life easier for the production worker and more difficult for themselves.

The actual report was set out to report the overall findings – from which the above observations represent some examples – and to focus upon the distinctive features of the 'craft' organization of work. As a report it was read by members of CCE Ltd for two reasons. First, it was presented in a more readable fashion than some previous reports. Second, the topic was central to a number of interests and this was a politically important zone of CCE Ltd at that time.

SUMMARY AND POSTSCRIPT

The presentation and discussion of the findings of the study of maintenance workers carries our story through to the imposed cut-off point in mid 1970 approximately three years after the first tentative discussions. The next stage of the project began with the first steps in pulling together the various pieces of work in which we had been engaged. The strategy of thinking about applications of the behavioural sciences in general, rather than specific, terms had had one important advantage in the situation of design. Given that the technological aspect of the design was always subject to change, as was the industrial relations climate, it had been useful to work through ideas with the various individuals and groups to whom our inputs had been linked. By mid 1970 it was possible to have a good picture of what the final form of the technology would, in practice, be like. Everyone was familiar with the way of working we had adopted and could see how it operated, though they did not all necessarily agree with it, or feel it to be relevant.

Our hope was that the kind of thinking we felt to be important would be diffused, and to varying extents, adopted and, also that a behavioural scientist would be appointed within CCE Ltd to continue the work. We cannot say yet whether this has been a successful proposal. The inclusion of new roles in enterprises results in alterations in the balance of prestige within and between functions and elites. The activities of behavioural scientists are as much bound up in the web of political alliance and intrigue as is any other aspect of the government of enterprises, so we shall not know for a little while whether behavioural science will become established.

The plans for the second half of 1970 are to tackle the areas of coordination between departments and functions and to focus more upon the planning of the change-over. The emphasis has increasingly swung from organizational design to planned change. At the start of this book we pointed to the need to look at the processes involved in utilizing the behavioural sciences just as closely as we look at results. We hope we have indicated some of the problems and possibilities, so that practitioners, managers, and designers can begin a more fruitful dialogue about what organizational design and behaviour can be, instead of regarding the human condition as inevitable and unalterable.

PART FIVE

Implications

CHAPTER TEN

A role for behavioural scientists in organizational design

The Alternatives and Differences Approach (ADA)

INTRODUCTION

In this chapter the key aspects of the case study are drawn together and discussed to show the relevance of the Alternatives and Differences Approach to organizational design. It is perhaps most helpful to begin by examining the title 'A role for the behavioural scientist in organizational design'.

Before we can adequately assess what the role should be, we must specify what the activity is and restate an earlier distinction between 'design' and 'research'. The behavioural scientist has had a long involvement in research studies, but only a short experience of design. Research may be narrowly defined as the activity that adds to existing knowledge and understanding about social phenomena at a general level. It is oriented towards the accurate categorization and delineation of phenomena, and to the development of general explanations of the discoveries made. These explanations are, in part, simply abstract ways of looking at reality, and in part take the form of theories. The major audience for explanations is to be found within the universities and similar institutions, not within enterprises. The activity of design is essentially concerned with the generation of a range of alternatives and their appraisal. The work at CCE Ltd illustrates the kind of activity involved and some of the problems it gives rise to. The term 'design' is preferred to 'research' because it highlights the difference between the interests of the academic and those of the practitioner and the manager. This distinction is crucial, because much confusion is unwittingly created when researchers and managers attempt to talk to each other. It thus seems more sensible to emphasize the difference in interests, since this is the area in which the behavioural science practitioner will be most active. A major problem in organizational design is to include behavioural scientists who can break away from the traditional research role.

The first question which we should be asking, and seeking to clarify and to answer, is this: what differences, if any, are there between the activities of behavioural science practitioners and those of the other specialist groups within enterprises such as operational researchers? The case study at CCE Ltd was one in which the members of Azimuth and the behavioural scientists involved began with the assumption that a useful contribution could be made. Now this assumption can be transformed into a hypothesis and the case study can be examined to see what happened in CCE Ltd.

In many ways the case study is exciting and stimulating. This is in part because there are some aspects which, though not unique, are rarely found, but the principal reason is that the study cannot easily be fitted into the convenient sets of categories available for talking about activities within enterprises. The case study has illustrated the fragmentary and unplanned nature of both organizational design and plant design. In the case of plant design, the whole of the work undertaken by Research and Development had many uncertainties and was subject to alteration because developments in one aspect of the modification of equipment did not fit the overall concept of the new technology. When this happened a new concept had to be generated and defined. None of this surprised or daunted the members of Research and Development, though it might well have appeared to be an untidy process to managers from the production side of the firm. Here we draw the distinction referred to earlier between the activity of design and that of managing an operating system. The Azimuth Group were largely concerned in the design of the new factory. They were constituted as a design group and not as an operating group. This is an important fact, which almost certainly affected the kind of work we carried out. For example, members of Azimuth were constantly asking themselves questions about an unknown situation which was five years away, while the production manager is more orientated towards the day-to-day occurrences. It was thus both relevant and possible to focus upon alternative sociotechnical designs when in a dialogue with Azimuth. Had Azimuth not existed the whole form of the consultancy would have been different (see Chapter 12). Our relationship was to a design team largely composed of men who were familiar with the design role. In that situation we had to see how we could link into their work.

We now turn to examine the first part of the title of this chapter: 'A role for . . . ' It may be noted that we were apparently diffident about aligning our activities with what is now being called 'the new thinking in management'. This new thinking is exemplified by the varied, and perhaps irreconcilable, notions of Management Information Systems, Job Enrichment, Management by Objectives, and Participative Management.

The adoption of any one of the ideas within the 'new management thinking' presupposes that certain minimum motivational conditions will be met in the way we alluded to in Chapter 2. When faced with the situation in which the client in considering a range of ideas – and this was the case in CCE Ltd – the behavioural science practitioner can fruitfully attack a number of connected problems, or he can help the client to install a preferred practice (e.g. System 4). We chose to focus upon the first approach, and this was accepted by Azimuth. Among the problems involved were the following: the charter[1] of the firm in relation to its members; the design of layouts and organizational systems; and problems of coordination in the new management system.

In the case of the charter, the behavioural scientist can provide a language for dealing with this, and can also stimulate useful discussion by raising questions that the 'bounded rationality' of those inside the firm precludes their mentioning publicly, or, perhaps even thinking about. Part of the behavioural scientist's competence is to map and schematize the existing situation, indicating the ways in which the social structure is differentiated and coordinated. This can be particularly valuable because managements typically differentiate their own level very carefully to reveal every small nuance in status, prestige, and competence, yet group together large numbers of other people into one homogeneous aggregate. This point was brought to our attention from one study in which members of the Board carefully distinguished three levels within ten people, and only four more categories for the remaining several thousand. Such thinking is not necessarily dysfunctional in most situations, but it is when the whole organization is being altered. The behavioural scientist can contribute by applying his language of concepts, and the perspective in which the concepts are embedded, to the analysis of a unique situation. This sometimes necessitates developing new concepts to

---

[1] The notion of 'charter' is adopted from Bakke (1950).

categorize the existing situation adequately. These concepts then become part of the new language.

We have given considerable emphasis to the development of a language for identifying and dealing with problems along the organizational dimension. This is an important aspect all too frequently neglected in management education. We have found this process of categorizing – or naming – to be enormously useful, and have adopted it on several projects undertaken from CUSSR. An aspect that is complementary to the careful description of the existing social structure and processes is the application of propositions taken from organizational studies. This point has already been illustrated in the case study, when propositions taken from the work of organizational analysts have been applied to the unique situation of CCE Ltd, and then fed into the dialogue.

Looking at the way in which the behavioural scientists can explore the charter of the firm with some of its members illustrates an important feature of the case study. That is the low emphasis upon measurements, and the preference for examining and comparing alternatives with the existing social structures (see Lazarsfeld & Reitz 1970). Also there was no commitment to the particular tenets of, for example, the human resources approach, but rather an emphasis upon identifying the ways in which the members of CCE Ltd perceived and defined the boundaries of groups. The importance of the consideration of this aspect is illustrated in the analysis by Miller and Rice of the distinction between systems of activities and the members' perceptions of and beliefs about the activities.

Diffidence about aligning ourselves with 'the new thinking in management' was a major factor in determining that our approach was essentially to generate alternatives and compare them with the existing situation. In many senses this procedure corresponds to an R & D approach applied to the human-organizational dimension. It is a mixture of investigations and designs, all of which contribute to the dialogue.

THE CASE STUDY

The case study covers a period of some three years, the greater part of which has been concerned with the design aspects of the new factory. We have imposed a cut-off point in mid 1970 when the focus of Azimuth's activities became more obviously directed towards the implementation of the designs. In the case study the focus has been upon the activities of the behavioural scientists in their relations with Azimuth and individuals and groups. Clearly, this is only a very partial and selective picture, but the objective has been to illustrate the activities that behavioural scientists can undertake and the problems that arise.

The case study commenced by reporting the stage that the designs had reached at the start of the consultancy. At that time Azimuth had an outline plan of the major features of the layout and of the shape of the proposed factory. In addition they had carefully calculated estimates of the manning requirements. These had been based upon the assumption that the initial expectations of designing a factory that would be 'the most modern of its kind' could be achieved within the time set aside for development and testing of equipment. Though these outline plans existed, they were regarded by Azimuth and other groups as the general framework for the design.

We began by pointing to some of the organizational complications of their proposed designs and by comparing the interest in forms of organizational design based on the applications of the human resources principles with both the existing situation and the one emerging from the technical designs. The consultancy had started with the suggestion that technical and organizational design should be a coordinated activity of joint optimization of the technical and organizational systems. It had been necessary to carry out an initial survey of the enterprise – the diagnosis – to decide whether a relationship with Azimuth was feasible. This had been followed by a short period of examining the technological impacts in one department with reference to one particular group of female workers – the packing crews. The difference in approach between the investigations of the behavioural scientists and the teams studying manning had resulted in a confrontation, which had in turn led to a demand that the behavioural scientists should explain what they meant by the concept of 'organization'. Members of the subgroup of Azimuth also required the behavioural scientists to produce a clearly defined time-table of activities indicating the exact dates on which data and decisions would be forthcoming. The definition of 'organization' that was presented and the examples selected from inside and outside CCE Ltd created sufficient interest within the subgroup for members to decide that a joint working party on sociotechnical design was worth while and feasible.

The subgroup eventually established worked for some months in jointly analysing the technology and the organization of the Processing Department before selecting two forms of organization for further evaluation in the light of the designs proposed for the remainder of the factory. One characteristic of this study group was its orderly and systematic progression through the prearranged schedule of topics. The investigations and discussions in between the formal meetings progressed at the planned pace. In contrast, when the behavioural scientists moved on to the next studies in other departments, the neat programme of activities had to be constantly changed. In time it became necessary to move away from the continuous association with the design teams and to carry out specific investigations of the existing social structure, and of the orientations of the members of the existing production departments. This study led in turn to the carrying out of a further investigation which focused upon the engineering and maintenance workers. The change in the activities of the behavioural scientists had the consequence of changing their relationship with Azimuth and other design groups from one of continuous association to one of intermittent and structured feedback of data. This activity was completed towards the end of the third year, when the focus of the consultancy shifted to the integration of the previous studies and the examination of the overall coordination of the factory. By that time some modifications had been made to the 'most advanced factory of its kind in the world'. These modifications had in part been necessitated by technological problems, and possibly also by slight indications of changes in the composition of the product market. The changes in the market centred on the emergence of some forms of organization within the distribution network and also the signs of market fragmentation.

Within the case study there are a number of aspects we wish to emphasize. The remainder of this chapter contains an examination of selected topics, starting with the terms of reference and their importance, and progressing through the following: meetings and feedback, reports and similar documents, our views on 'new thinking in management', relations with Azimuth, the feelings of Azimuth about the consultancy, the factors influencing the form of the consultancy. Each of these topics has been selected to illustrate and point to the kinds of problems faced by both clients and consultants in the process of organizational design.

TERMS OF REFERENCE

One of the most important features of the first stages of a client – consultant relationship is the formulation of the terms of reference. These should be understood to include both the formal prescriptions, as contained in the terms of the contract, and also the expectations each has of the other with regard to the kind of work undertaken and the sorts of relationship entered into. Many enterprises employ consultants to install pre-agreed administrative devices such as Management by Objectives. In such cases the client has some knowledge of the 'package' of ideas and procedures involved. There is no question of a joint relationship between the client and the consultant to define and deal with problems as was the case at CCE Ltd. A similar situation exists when a client utilizes the behavioural scientist to carry out attitude surveys. The relationship is one in which the client has defined the problem and selected a method which the consultant implements. Even in situations like these considerable difficulties can arise. For example, the particular method selected by the client may have features that make its application in the chosen context extremely difficult. The application of the plant-wide incentive scheme described in Chapter 2 illustrates this point.

Much of our thinking about the terms of reference was influenced by the awareness of the problems of misunderstanding that can arise when new ideas are brought into unfamiliar situations. Dalzeil and Klein (1960) have illustrated some of the problems involved in their study of the (mis)application of work study in a packaging firm in England in the mid 1950s. The management of that firm believed that they understood work study, but in practice they employed consultants who were specialists in payment by results schemes when they really intended to employ specialists in method design.

In anticipation of the problems that could arise, we spent considerable amounts of time in the first phase (the diagnosis) in both clarifying what we meant and in finding out what the client group expected, and how they themselves looked at the organizational aspect. Though we did not consciously seek to cause a confrontation as part of the consultancy, the strategy adopted to make the terms of reference 'alive' meant that this was inevitable. One of our colleagues described the strategy as one of 'discriminated confrontation'. This makes the strategy seem too rational and thought out, when in fact it arose out of an awareness of problems faced by consultants, and a desire to bring them into the open (see Beckhard 1969). In this case the strategy was successful in defining the particular perspective we considered to be relevant. It is not difficult to imagine that the same approach in another context could have had disastrous results. For example, it seems unlikely that it would be similarly successful in consultancy on organizational design in hospitals (see Revans 1967, and Chapter 12 below).

At CCE Ltd there was a considerable change in the topic of the consultancy as presented in mid 1967 and as reformulated in early 1968. This indicated the joint nature of the organizational aspect of Azimuth's activities. An important change was the inclusion of the originally suggested aspects of organizational design and the addition of the topic of management philosophy. The latter was dealt with more directly towards the end of 1968 when we presented the paper on managerial ideologies.

The idea of the consultancy as a 'dialogue' had been explained and agreed upon in the early meetings. However, the understanding of this and its implementation in the new joint group composed of Azimuth and ourselves created numerous problems, particularly since we were not able, or prepared, to occupy the role of the adviser who says 'do this'. The attempts of the client to impose formal controls illustrates the difficulties. We were requested to present a critical path network of our activities. In practice this is a fairly familiar approach by clients to behavioural scientists in projects as diffusely defined as that undertaken with CCE Ltd. The crucial point for the client and the consultant is the way in which each deals with the control strategy. Complete acceptance of the client's controls may remove the value of the consultancy while ensuring its continuance and vice versa.

The acceptance of the general terms of reference at CCE Ltd took some eight months to establish. By this time there were sufficient grounds of understanding to proceed. Accord was greatly strengthened by the orderly nature of the sociotechnical design of the Processing Department, which provided a general role-model for all of those involved. At later stages it was necessary to define specific terms of reference for particular studies, especially those involving investigation of the existing social structure. It may be seen from Chapters 8 and 9 that in each case the terms of reference were used as an opportunity to restate the general objectives of the consultancy and the particular kinds of work we were undertaking.

In many ways the defining of the terms of reference with CCE Ltd presents an extreme case for the behavioural scientist. The nature of the project was diffuse, the previous experience of the firm rarely included joint problem-solving, and we were the external input to an internal group. Clark and Cherns (1970) argue that this kind of situation makes the forming of the terms of reference most awkward, and the continuance of the consultancy demands their constant re-emphasis. In practice this was achieved by introducing each formal meeting with a statement of objectives. The practice of joint formulation of the terms of reference probably helped to ensure that all those involved had some recognition of what was expected of them.

An important feature of the terms of reference is the scope of the activities the behavioural scientists intend to undertake. These may be broadly summarized under three headings, as follows:

COUNTING Typically the behavioural scientist is expected to undertake some kind of counting or measurement. Attitude studies are obvious examples. Such studies are frequently based upon simple questions and tend to be evaluative in intention (i.e., to show that 'morale' is high/low). Their construction is frequently strongly influenced by the prevailing beliefs about what the firm is like, or should be. Counting in this form does not really require the special expertise of a behavioural scientist.

NAMING This is only rarely undertaken by the practitioner, but it is of considerable and increasing importance (Chapple & Sayles 1961). The focus of activity is upon providing a 'map' of the existing organization. This means the application of specialist concepts. For example, the concept of 'total institution' can be abstracted from Goffman's (1961) study of asylums and applied in the modified form of 'total community' to the induction stage of the entry of the civilian into the military (Cherns, Clark, & Parrott 1970). In practice it is frequently necessary to develop new names in order to make an accurate 'map'. Touraine (1965) cites the example of 'horizontally hierarchized cooperation' from one investigator's analysis of relationships in advanced technologies. The importance of naming as an activity is that names provide definitions of reality. It is noticeable that there are an increasing number of references to the requirement for developing a special language of names for the organizational aspects of enterprises.

PROPOSITIONING In the CCE Ltd case study we used a number of propositions from previous studies of enterprises to focus attention upon the linkage between key sets of variables. The work of Perrow illustrates this.

At CCE Ltd the consultancy started with a mixture of 'naming' and the application of 'propositions', and only included 'counting' activities when the behavioural science perspective was established. This meant that the counting was undertaken within the framework of names and propositions that had been established as useful in the previous stages of the work. The terms of reference did not specify the kind of activity we would undertake, but they did emphasize the need to leave the details of design work to be discovered by practice.

We have stressed the importance of terms of reference. The ideas gained from CCE Ltd have been developed and used in other contexts to give presentations of the approach that organizational design requires. Though in some ways it has been possible to explain organizational design more precisely in subsequent work, the main impression we have gained is that formulation of the terms of reference cannot be dealt with in smooth presentations to clients. Essentially it must be experienced, and neither the client nor the consultant should assume that he understands the other. Considerable uncertainty is thereby introduced into the situation, but this is inherent in design as an activity.

MEETINGS AND FEEDBACK

In general terms the case study may be summarized by stating that the design activities were undertaken on a joint basis and the investigations were carried out independently by ourselves. This meant that when, in the first half of the case study, the emphasis was upon design there was a relatively close association between ourselves, Azimuth, and other relevant groups. In the second half the emphasis was upon investigations and here the relationship tended to be more separated, the meetings assuming greater importance and becoming 'set pieces' of feedback and discussion. The impact of our activities upon the relationship with Azimuth is an important factor influencing the form the consultancy eventually took (Jones 1969).

The actual case study does tend to overstress the part played in the early days by formal meetings and it certainly underemphasizes the intervening activities. The various informal connections that arose, and the informal diffusion of our ideas by the main Project Officers, were of considerable relevance to the success of the meetings. Appreciable amounts of time were spent in talking to members of CCE Ltd. both before and after meetings. The case study also underplays the part of certain key individuals within CCE Ltd. Although we have undertaken researches to discover more about this, our knowledge is essentially limited. Clearly, the employment of consultants has considerable political implications for the internal status, career, and prestige systems of those within the enterprise, and this influences the content of the consultancy.

In the literature on planned change the topic of feedback occupies an important place, so it is relevant to clarify the normal usage of feedback in behavioural science studies and then to apply this idea to the case study. The typical feedback exercise is one in which the consultant applies some measurement instrument (e.g., an attitude study) to part or the whole of an enterprise. The findings are then tabulated to identify characteristic features of the situation. For example, an instrument applied in a hospital to doctors and nurses might indicate divergent beliefs about their own roles and importance. These data could be presented in feedback to representative groups including both nurses and doctors who would be asked to comment upon the validity – in their opinion – of the findings and to discuss areas that seemed to be problematic. They might be asked for suggestions for improving the existing situation.

Behavioural scientists who use the feedback method believe that it is an effective way of achieving changes in attitudes within and between groups. Floyd Mann (1961) has observed: 'Change processes organized around objective new social facts about one's own organizational situation have more force for change than those organized around general principles about human behaviour.' It will be noted that in this case the collected data were fed back to the groups who were surveyed.

At CCE Ltd the greater part of the data fed back to Azimuth was based upon studies of individuals and groups outside Azimuth. For example, the first pieces of feedback were the field notes on the packing crews and then the report produced in late 1967. In a similar way, the later studies concerned members of the Making and Packing Departments. The exception was the examination of the way in which Azimuth tended to favour the scientific management approach when designing the layouts and manning, but attempted to implement some aspects of the human resources approach. The paper we presented in late 1968 to Azimuth essentially said 'this is how you are carrying out organizational design'. Our presentation of this observation – based upon a good deal of evidence – was very similar to the approach described by Argyris (1964) when examining the 'risk-taking' of senior executives. Argyris makes various kinds of record of the actual behaviour of executives and presents the conclusions back to the subjects.

An important feature of the feedback in the case study was the use of the 'lay hypothesis'. The behavioural scientist is continually dealing with the practical problems presented by members of client enterprises, rather than the theoretical problems of interest to the academic social scientist. In dealing with 'practical problems' the behavioural scientist is confronting the kinds of question to which the layman often believes he has answers (Gouldner 1957). Typically, the layman, in this case the manager, has explanations which he favours and these explanations cannot easily be ignored. The practitioner 'must take some of the layman's favoured hypothesis into account if he is to establish or maintain a relationship with them' (Gouldner 1957). There are numerous examples in the case study of the adoption of this practice. For instance, in the early phases we tested the hypothesis that the technological designs for the new factory would facilitate an increased application of participative management by comparing the existing situation with the one that was being designed, and showed that the hypothesis was not supported. Again, in the study of the Processing Department, we tested a hypothesis from the design group about the social position and status of a group of machine operators. The willingness of the behavioural scientist to adopt a strategy that would seem nonsensical to pure scientists is crucial for the success of applied behavioural science. Again Gouldner has put this aspect succinctly when he argues 'that certain of the devices of applied social science, which seem sometimes scientifically senseless, are at least sociologically sensible' (Gouldner 1957). Thus the selection of hypotheses from the client's beliefs and their inclusion in the range of hypothesis to be tested by investigation is frequently crucial to the success of applications.

In the later half of the study there was an increasing emphasis upon feedback meetings and it is important to note the preparations which we made for them. For example, the study of the Making and Packing Departments arose to solve certain problems that could not be resolved within Azimuth or the study group specially established for sociotechnical design. Over time the origins of this part of the project became less salient, so we arranged special meetings to discuss appropriate ideas to apply to the findings when they became available. Here it was necessary to introduce some organizing ideas to serve that purpose, and we selected the general approach of Goldthorpe from his study of workers in Luton. Our presentation outlined the background of that study and then concentrated on the aspects of particular relevance. In this sense there were pre-feedback meetings that were crucial to the later feedback of the findings since they provided a good part of the context within which the findings were examined.

The change over time in our relation with Azimuth is reflected in the content of the main documents. Leaving aside the working papers, there were no major documents until the end of the first year when the annual report was produced. Similarly for the second year, but thereafter there were a number of documents containing the findings of particular studies. The first annual reports were essentially histories of the joint working relationship with Azimuth, showing how it had changed and for what reasons. These reports were intended to provide an overall picture showing how the various activities related to the functions represented on Azimuth (e.g. production-scheduling) and to the group as a whole. To summarize: during the early design phases of the project the relationship between ourselves and members of Azimuth and other groups was one of joint association and there was continual contact. During that phase there were few feedback sessions in the strict sense of that term. Later as we became more involved in particular investigations the emphasis switched (see Jones 1969). Our work became separated from that of Azimuth and we kept contact at an informal level and through planned meetings. This was appropriate to the nature of our investigations since it was essential that we should be able to maintain the anonymity of the general findings and avoid revealing where individuals were affected. In practice this switch in emphasis did alter the relationship with Azimuth.

In this section we have attempted to indicate how the relationship between the external behavioural scientist and the manager is influenced by the kinds of work undertaken. The relationship adopted in the second half of the design phase was more reminiscent of the relationship between the firm and its external consultants, and that of the earlier design phase less so. We regarded the early phase as crucial for presenting our perspective on the design process and organizational issues involved, and think that it strongly influenced the work at the later stages.

DESIGN AS A FRAGMENTARY PROCESS

In the early chapters we noted that a number of social scientists who had studied technological change had suggested, first, that the managers who introduced the change should have paid more attention to the sociological and organizational aspects and second, that sociologists and social psychologists should be increasingly involved as advisers in the planning of change.

In looking at these suggestions and comparing them with the experiences at CCE Ltd, we note that many of the suggestions for the detailed analysis of the sociological and organizational dimensions included attitude studies and similar techniques. Elsewhere (Clark & Cherns 1970) we have suggested that the social scientist may recommend methods of working that are more appropriate for scientific investigation rather than for applied work. The remarks made on the lay hypothesis emphasize this point. We also suggested in the earlier chapters that behavioural science practitioners should work on the design process and should regard it as separate from, and preliminary to, the planning of change.

In this section we look back at the case study to summarize our observations about being associated with the design stage, and we comment on the relevance of methods that are similar to those adopted by the pure scientist.

One of the overriding impressions from our involvement with those concerned in plant design is that design is a fragmentary process subject to a high degree of alteration. The Azimuth Group began with a slightly utopian intention of designing a factory that would, in technological terms, 'be as advanced as any in the world'. To this end they visited similar factories in other countries and examined a wide range of technical developments. The initial designs for the factory were based on the working assumption that many of the most advanced ideas could be implemented within the period set aside for machine testing and development. During the next three years some of the initial conceptions of the future factory had to be modified. In practice there were some areas of the factory where there were, at any one time, a number of competing possibilities.

Thus it may be seen that design is both fragmentary and subject to the idealism and optimism that characterize all areas of life.

Given that design is not a simple, well-controlled, unilinear development from first ideas to the application, is it possible for the behavioural scientist to operate away from the technical design experts? The answer is, clearly, yes. However, when this happens the opportunity is lost for dealing with the problems noted by Miller and Rice in their study of the 'green-fields' site.

Acceptance by the behavioural scientist of involvement with ongoing design teams does mean throwing away the conventional activities characteristic of social science research. This can be an uncomfortable feeling for the behavioural scientist and it is a feeling that managers would benefit from understanding rather than criticizing. For those who work within enterprises there are certain established rules for arriving at decisions about what shall be done. From the perspective of the scientist these decisions are frequently made with an inadequate understanding of the situation and appear to be based on political considerations rather than 'purely rational' ones. When the manager looks at the scientist his complaint is that the scientist is most proficient when he has the time to define the problem and carry out lengthy investigations. Until recently managers have mainly been talking directly to the researchers and have found the experience to be puzzling and sometimes frustrating. In the future there will be an increasing number of persons who have been trained in the basic disciplines of sociology and psychology, but have opted for problem-solving work rather than academic work. This is already happening. These people face exactly the same problem as Azimuth when they decided to look at the behavioural sciences – there is an absence of role-models illustrating how the various parties can actually operate collectively. This is particularly problematic for the young behavioural science practitioner who will have little prior knowledge of the difficulties that arise in design and planning.

We have argued that design is a fragmentary process for both the technologist and the behavioural scientist. This means that the latter has to develop competences that parallel the ways of operating of the R & D experts on the technical side. In this kind of work the academic models of research are rarely valuable because they inhibit the behavioural scientist.

In our involvement with experienced R & D experts, we developed an approach that does in some ways parallel theirs. First we focused upon the development of alternative designs by indicating how particular ideas about the desired future organization could be translated into a new organizational structure. Also we carried out investigations to test particular ideas about the most appropriate forms of organization. For example, when faced with the proposition that the human resources philosophy should be applied we attempted to appraise – in conjunction with others – what would happen if it was adopted. The approach adopted eventually became formalized by ourselves into the Alternatives and Differences Approach. We found this helpful, and believe it to be useful because it highlights the importance of the major sociological features.

In looking at the case study it may be noted that our approach was felt by Azimuth to be comprehensible and relevant. We would hypothesize that the orientations to problem-solving typical of R & D experts enable them to have a higher toleration for the kinds of uncertainties that our association introduced into the design teams. We would expect to find quite different problems in applying the same approach when dealing directly with managers who are operating the day-to-day system.

We hypothesize that because design is a fragmentary process it requires particular outlooks. A willingness to experiment, for example, and also a long time-perspective. Our suggestion is that the Alternatives and Differences Approach was dependent upon the outlooks of the members of Azimuth and other similar groups within CCE Ltd. Hence we would not be certain that the same kinds of consultancy could exist where there was no design team within the client system. There are tentative pieces of evidence from published researches to support this point (e.g., Lawrence & Lorsch 1968), and we shall note in another instance of organizational design (Chapter 12) that the absence of a similar group to Azimuth created considerable difficulties.

In this section we have looked at the case study and suggested that its continuance was dependent upon certain characteristics of the client system (e.g. Azimuth). This is an important practical point for the application of the behavioural sciences.

NEW THINKING IN MANAGEMENT

On this project, and others, we have been faced by what may be called the 'new thinking' about designing organizational systems.

Typically this includes the following: job enrichment, participation, management by objectives, management information systems. An interesting feature of these items is that they are in some ways irreconcilable. For example, the aim of job-enrichment programmes would seem to be to delegate decision-taking about the job to the lowest level possible, and the aim of management information systems frequently seems to be to centralize all crucial data at the highest levels.

In the case study there are numerous examples of the ways in which we attempted to relate the interest in the 'new thinking' to the sociological and organizational features of CCE Ltd, and to point to the consequences that might be expected from the adoption of a particular approach. The basic argument is that the structure and processes of the enterprise must be identified and diagnosed as part of the design study. It would follow that the application of some practices might not be appropriate. The ideas that work in the petro-chemicals industry (e.g. sensitivity training) may not be transferrable to an industry like engineering, which is older and is typified by a distinctive history of industrial relations. A major advantage of the Alternatives and Differences Approach is that it places the emphasis upon 'mapping' the existing enterprise and comparing this model with a construction of a future situation. Additionally it allows the behavioural scientist to examine both the existent and the future in the light of propositions about the structure and functioning of enterprises derived from research studies. It is therefore a flexible approach.

THE BEHAVIOURAL SCIENTIST'S ACTIVITIES

At CCE Ltd the primary emphasis was upon the activities of 'mapping' (naming) the sociological and organizational dimensions and upon examining changes to see how far they took account of the probable consequences. In practice the objective was to present a behavioural science perspective on organizational design rather than to carry out counting activities. We have argued that it is the perspective that is the significant contribution.

Inevitably this perspective gave rise to certain tensions for members of CCE Ltd. There were questions about its relevance and attempts to control its diffusion. This created a number of situations that were basically confrontations between the perspective and that of other groups of specialists. Thus one of the activities undertaken was to keep the perspective salient, and this meant handling the attempts to contain it. It has frequently been argued that behavioural scientists should engage in collaborative relationships, but it must not be forgotten that the collaboration involves representatives from various functions with competing perspectives. Consequently the process of joint learning about organizational design resulted in certain kinds of confrontation.

Confrontation is more likely to arise when the behavioural scientist is involved in the decision-taking than when he is used to carry out particular well-defined projects that have been established by management and contracted out. In the latter case managements may frequently be obtaining more data to support their existing beliefs, rather than searching for new and better ways of looking at the human aspect of the enterprise.

WHAT DID AZIMUTH FIND USEFUL?

In this section we consider things the members of the Azimuth Group reported as finding useful to them in the design of the new factory. The following remarks selected from one meeting indicate the general feelings: '... now frightened about groups . . . have become more clued up . . . we all think differently . . . influenced all of us during the design of layouts . . . we are considering parameters not previously considered . . . have given us a new set of values . . . typically conditions not acted on until they are intolerable. The investigations allowed [me] to put the problem on the table. Six months ago people may have denied this . . . getting better at recognizing conflict . . . now are able to present problems to you [i.e., the behavioural scientists] . . . this tells us how people in the conflict actually see it . . . gives another dimension . . .'

A further series of remarks concerns the role they would have preferred us to adopt. It was agreed that the role had been a diagnostic one, but there was some difference of emphasis between Azimuth and ourselves over this. Thus one member of our team argued, 'You may waste the diagnostic skill by using us as advocates . . . [we] recommend you to use some consultants as diagnosticians . . . we have avoided being advocates.' In response a member of Azimuth offered a counter-argument: 'There are two roles of which the first is the diagnostic . . . but there is the more advanced role of protagonist.' This particular discussion led on to an examination of the group's initial feelings in 1967 when they said they felt some disappointment, but now felt that the 'benefit is to create awareness of conditions'. Some members of the group posed a distinction between consulting and our work by suggesting that the latter was 'joint research . . . not used as consulting . . . breaking new ground . . . the difference from consultants is that the research creates . . . awareness'.

These observations are not intended to represent a systematic and detached account by independent researchers looking in from outside. They do however indicate that there are some situations in which members of enterprises feel that it is useful and worth while to involve academic behavioural scientists in a joint relationship of problem definition and solving. It may be noted that many other individuals and groups outside Azimuth had been associated with the project during the first three years. Perhaps one of the most important observations that can be made is that the project may have provided a basis for later and more advanced applications of the behavioural sciences. In practice – as a number of leading enterprises have noted – the introduction of new perspectives take a considerable amount of time. The members of Azimuth seemed to be saying that they found our work relevant to their problems and complementary to the services they could already obtain from other specialists in the field.

HOW MUCH UTILIZATION ?

One of our objectives had been to increase the capability of the enterprise to absorb the behavioural sciences. It therefore seems relevant to pose the question of how much utilization of the behavioural sciences actually occurred. Earlier we suggested that the most appropriate way of examining this was to observe the changes that had taken place along two dimensions: first, the language (naming, or categorizing) used to diagnose the human-organizational aspect and, second, the propositions applied to define and illuminate problems. These add up to examining the ways in which the definitions of reality have been altered, and appraising how long any changes recorded may survive.

In the previous section we reported some observations from the Azimuth group which suggest that they believe they are able to make a finer and more accurate analysis of sociological aspects. In other words, that they had developed a language for talking about organizational design that was believed to be a relevant increment to the 'knowledge' of the firm.

The complete answer to this question lies beyond the present volume and forms the core of a complementary study undertaken by CUSSR of the ways in which the social sciences are utilized by enterprises (Cherns 1968; Clark & Ford 1970). The importance of the question to managers is that it should focus greater attention on what is actually being achieved by including behavioural scientists in decision-making. We hope that the scope will be extended from counting activities into the areas we have suggested are important.

ACHIEVING UTILIZATION

Many experts in the different branches of management services are concerned to obtain a greater utilization of their activities and advice. We were no exception. Our feeling was that this could best be achieved by the kinds of joint investigation and problem-solving set out in the case study. We would be somewhat pessimistic about the advantages of undertaking work where this joint aspect is missing.

The hypothesis about getting application of the behavioural sciences which we are testing is that advanced by Cherns (1968), who argues that research will only be applied if the strategy for its application is built into the original design of the research programme. At a general level, the case study provides tentative evidence to support this hypothesis, though we know from comparisons with other projects that the actual picture is complicated by the distinctive culture and structure of the enterprise. One would expect the strategy to operate differently in the case of, say, banks compared to hospitals.

SUMMARY

There are many other aspects of the case study we shall want to examine in the future but do not have the space to develop in this chapter. For example, an aspect of considerable importance is the role and activities of the linkman. Leaving this kind of problem aside, we would suggest that the case study represents a useful example of the way in which behavioural scientists and enterprises may become entangled in fruitful joint working. The term 'entangled' is appropriate.

In the case study we have attempted to tackle the lines of thinking that a manager might expect behavioural scientists to be undertaking in problem-solving work. We hope we have managed to identify many of the misunderstandings and difficulties that can arise. The base of the case study has been the assumption that enterprises may require a language of concepts and propositions for examining and understanding the human-organizational aspect. We have suggested some of the elements of the language and ways in which it may be developed. This process seems inevitably to involve some confrontation. The Alternatives and Differences Approach is suggested because it is essentially simple to understand, yet it is flexible and is of considerable practical relevance in situations that are undergoing change. An essential feature has been the investigation of the dynamic interplay of individuals and groups in the existing situation. The study and 'mapping' of this cannot be achieved by the application of attitude studies, but requires an approach using a variety of methods within the perspective of the behavioural sciences.

CHAPTER ELEVEN

Operable knowledge

INTRODUCTION

In Chapters 2 and 7 we outlined some of the kinds of thinking that were influential in tackling organizational design at CCE Ltd. The case study demonstrated that the practitioner has to be prepared to relate ideas, concepts, and propositions from the various social sciences to the unique situation of the client. These ideas are utilized both to define the problems that may be anticipated and to suggest the direction in which solutions may be sought. As well as the diffuse personal knowledge of the practitioner, there are the additions that arise from experience in a variety of situations. All this forms the stock of operable knowledge utilized by the practitioner. In this chapter we outline the main features of operable knowledge, then discuss both the task-analysis perspective and that of the 'action frame of reference', indicating their complementarity. Finally we point to some of the problems of 'knowledge utilization'.

OPERABLE KNOWLEDGE

Operable knowledge is the term used to categorize the evidence and data that the practitioner regards as pertinent. In an earlier formulation, Bennis (1964) uses the term 'valid knowledge'. While this has the advantage of emphasizing that Bennis was referring to evidence that both practitioner and client define as appropriate, it had the disadvantage of appearing tautologous. Consequently the term 'operable knowledge' is preferred. For Bennis there are several important features of operable knowledge. For example, it must take account of the behaviour of individuals, of groups, and the organization, as they actually exist in the change situation. It must take account of a variety of levels and include variables which the policy-maker can understand, evaluate, and manipulate. Also, recognition must be given to external variables and their interrelationship with the internal structures, local customs, and values (Bennis 1964).

There are three kinds of operable knowledge covered by the case study. First, there is the knowledge about the client based upon investigations undertaken by the consulting team. Examples would include the investigation of the packing crews in the Making Department (Chapter 5), the operating crews in Processing (Chapter 6), and the study of the three factories in the research phase (Chapters 8 & 9). Second, there are the concepts, general ideas, variables, and propositions drawn from the various disciplines of the behavioural sciences. These may be presented to the client for inclusion in the general 'stock of knowledge' (e.g. autonomous group). However, it may be noted that Clark and Ford argue for caution in assuming that the concepts and propositions presented to the client are precisely those which the practitioner utilizes in his own analysis and diagnosis. Clark and Cherns argue, for example, that 'open sociotechnical systems' is useful both analytically and as a bridging concept linking the practitioner with other in-house experts from management services and with management. Third, there are a small number of 'packaged' forms of behavioural science. The Managerial Grid (see Chapter 12) is a well-known example. These are likely to increase, leading to a need for more accurate documentation about their appropriateness to specific situations (Lippitt 1965).

We cannot leave a discussion of the consultants' definition of operable knowledge without noting that they present this definition within a highly personalized conception of the role of man in society. The beliefs and ideologies of the applied behavioural scientist cannot be ignored. O'Connel argues, for example, that the American behavioural scientist has become a crusader for democratic values. Further, that this particular focus, exemplified in the topics of authentic relationships and risk-taking, has resulted in a restricted use of the behavioural sciences.

The study at CCE Ltd provided evidence of both disagreement and agreement between the consultants and the clients over problem definition (Chapter 5). It was noticeable that the Azimuth Group did not originally present their problems as being amenable to study by social and behavioural scientists. In general, the behavioural scientist cannot really expect this to be the case. Although we do not yet know how British managers perceive the behavioural sciences, it is likely, given the content of post-experience courses, that there will be a high degree of overlap with the perceptions of American managers. Rush (1970), in an extensive study carried out in America, sampled several hundred firms. When respondents were asked to list the names of behavioural scientists they had in mind when they thought of applications, there were twenty names mentioned more than ten times. Of them the 'top nine' were: McGregor, Herzberg, Likert, Argyris, Maslow, Blake & Mouton, Gellerman, and Drucker. It is interesting to contrast these names with the reference at the end of the present book, especially with the frequency of citation. Two important points emerge: first, a heavy referencing of exponents of the 'task-analysis' approach (see next section); second, the contribution of British researchers (e.g. the late Joan Woodward).

We would argue that the practitioner typically aims to create some diffusion of concepts and ideas, but that the presenting frameworks are of necessity simplifications of the actual analytical frameworks. We would also argue that clients are active and selective in deciding the kind of behavioural science they would like to have. Clients are not nearly so passive as many accounts by practitioners would suggest.

TASK-ANALYSIS APPROACH

The approach at CCE Ltd to defining the problems of organization has been influenced by a number of considerations and orientations some of which are in part incompatible. One of the influences has been what is sometimes referred to as the 'task-analysis approach'. This is exemplified, for our purposes, by the work of Burns and Stalker, Emery, Trist, Rice, and Miller from Britain, and of a number of researchers from the United States, including March and Simon, Bell, Perrow, and Dill. In this section we shall set out some of the characteristics of this 'school'. We should first state that the usage of ideas from these researchers has been in the form of 'borrowings' at our discretion; we do not claim to represent their viewpoints, but rather to indicate the influence they have had in the study of CCE Ltd and their general relevance to the analysis of enterprises. In practice, the 'borrowings' have taken the form of a personal selection that has in some ways been difficult to decode (see Clark & Ford 1970; Trist 1968).

The behavioural science practitioner is likely to regard what he reads and experiences as parts of an extending repertoire of approaches, concepts, and propositions forming the source from which he can draw when tackling particular problem-solving projects. One of the interesting features of the task analysis approach is that it has generally been underutilized. An obvious explanation is that it is rather more demanding than a simplistic belief that high morale equals high productivity or that participative management is good. The use of the approach may well require greater rigour in management education and a greater willingness by behavioural scientists to involve themselves in collaborative work with managers.

We shall concentrate on two features of this approach: the analysis of the task, and the influence of the task on the learning experience of the members of the enterprise (Dill 1962). Both are crucial to organizational design and the planning of change.

The idea of examining the kinds of task undertaken by enterprises received considerable support in the 1950s from the work of Tavistock members and from the investigations of Woodward and Burns and Stalker. We have already outlined the main dimensions that Emery formalized from the early studies of his colleagues. This approach to examination of the 'technology' identified some of the features that influence the networks of relationships that the technology facilitates. In this case we are thinking of 'network' as the frequency of contacts between roles, their duration and structuring, sources of initiating interactions, and so on. The work of Woodward suggested reasons for believing that there were particular occupational profiles associated with different kinds of production system. Thus, for example, the ratio of administrators to direct workers varied – apparently systematically – between production systems working on small batch sizes and those on mass production. Woodward also indicated that the nature of the 'management control' system varied systematically with these characteristics.

Woodward's contribution to organizational analysis has been to discredit the treatment of the enterprise as an undifferentiated and homogenous entity and to focus attention upon a more detailed analysis of the interdependence between the 'objectives' of the enterprise in relation to its market (Woodward 1958) and the form of its production system. On the basis of this analysis it is possible to supplement the analysis of Level One in the sociotechnical framework as set out in Chapter 7. (This point is incorporated less directly in Emery's formulation, 1959.) Woodward pointed out some of the grosser features that are of general relevance to organizational analysis.

A major step forward is taken with the work of Burns and Stalker. There are many problems posed by their continuum of management systems from mechanistic to organic, particularly if these concepts are used in a blind and uncritical fashion. All too frequently exposition of their work is limited to the narrow focus upon the continuum. This is to overlook their consideration of the nature of decision-taking, and the political features of the government of enterprises. Burns and Stalker provide a language of concepts and interlinked propositions for exploring and diagnosing the influence of product innovation upon the internal segmentation of tasks. They also provide a framework for anticipating the problems that will face an enterprise if there are changes in the product environment.

The work of the British contributors is complemented by some American studies of product innovation (Lorsch 1965; Lawrence & Lorsch 1967, 1968). They examine the way in which the enterprise is differentiated into segments, and the integration of the activities of these segments. Their concern is to determine how much integration is required in a particular situation, and how it may be introduced (Lawrence & Lorsch 1969). They rightly assert that organizational design must be able to take account of interdependencies of subunits. For example, it may be advantageous to design one department's system of organization to embody the cherished principles of participative management, but the effect may be to make overall coordination more difficult (Miller & Rice 1967). Thus in the case study of CCE Ltd it was necessary to conclude the sociotechnical designs of each group of departments with a number of possibilities leaving the actual choice open until the final period of reconciliation.

The relevance of integration may be noted by recalling the assumptions which underpinned the choice of a production system at CCE Ltd and their connection with changes in the factors influencing the composition of the market. In Chapter 3 we described some of the questions asked to identify the existing forms of integration between Marketing, R & D, and Production, using the example of the introduction of a new product to follow the process.

The nature of the integrative devices is dependent upon the areas of autonomy of the subunits. This is an aspect which should be incorporated into the design. It may mean the examining of new boundaries for activities and also for the sentient groupings, as is illustrated in Chapters 8 and 9. The nature of integration and autonomy is also closely bound in with the leadership styles that are appropriate.

A further important aspect of the analysis of the task of the enterprise is to account for changes over time, as we have noted in projects undertaken by CUSSR in widely differing contexts (e.g., the Services). The designs proposed must include the consideration of the flexibility required by the enterprise (Cherns 1967). This is a difficult aspect to measure (see Pugh *et al.* 1967, 1969), but it has to be tackled by the behavioural science practitioner. There is an increasing awareness that the task of an enterprise influences significantly the learning experiences of its members (Dill 1962). For example, industrial enterprises are unlikely to find it easy to handle the idea of developing a repertoire performance programme to face a new environment. Such rehearsing would assume a level of commitment to the enterprise by its members that is only typically found in the Services.

The task-analysis approach attacked the principle of the *single* one best way to organize (e.g. Woodward 1958), and substituted the argument that the nature of the task undertaken by the enterprise will, and should, be a significant determinant of the organizational structure. This notion helped to direct attention to aspects of the organizational structure, and related this dimension to the predictability of the inputs to the enterprise (e.g. Perrow 1967). Thus a new set of principles was formulated showing that structure and task must be designed jointly, and that different structures will be appropriate for different tasks.

This new approach and its prescriptive principles raises several new problems requiring further research and clarification. Future developments may lead to important changes in the general formulation of the task-analysis approach. First, there is the problem of distinguishing between the general environmental condition of the enterprise as 'objectively' defined by the analyst, and the internal variations between different parts of the enterprise. For example, CCE Ltd could be said to possess an environment with characteristics a, b, c, . . ., but there were considerable differences in the situation of separate departments within the production system alone. Processing may be contrasted with Making and Packing. Second, there is the necessity of incorporating some notion of cycle regulation into organizational design (Haberstroh 1965). For example, the operating cycle of a supermarket is approximately one week, while that of an aero-engine manufacturer is several years. This aspect has considerable implications for both design and the strategy for carrying out design. Third, there is a general simplification of the 'people' aspect. Too much emphasis is given to fitting the organization to the task as objectively defined, and too little recognition is given to the aspirations and motivations of the people involved. It may be argued that the organization should be modified to accommodate both the nature of the task and the characteristics of the members of the enterprise (Morse & Lorsch 1970). This point has considerable relevance to Miller and Rice's formulation of task and sentient boundaries. At CCE Ltd the use of the Alternatives and Differences Approach ensured that the flexibility required was built into the design process. The final point of criticism concerns the neglect of discovering how people defined their own work situation and the nature of the task. This is a considerable criticism, which we attempted to tackle at CCE Ltd. To tackle the point more thoroughly the following section will deal with the Action Frame of Reference.

To summarize: we have suggested that one of the useful sources of ideas for the project at CCE Ltd was the work of a group of researchers who may be broadly termed the task-analysis school. We have outlined some of their work, both in the case study and in Chapter 7 as well as this section. A useful highly compressed account of their ideas is contained in Perrow (1967). The ideas from this school have been utilized to explore the implications of the techno-logical changes proposed by CCE Ltd and to scrutinize their implications for the decision-taking apparatus of the new factory. In the next section we outline some complementary ideas.

ACTION FRAME OF REFERENCE

Action in this context does not refer to decision-taking, but to how the behavioural scientist examines the ways in which the members of an enterprise define the enterprise and the meaning they give to their activities and relationships. Earlier we argued that one of the aims of organizational design is to generate alternative sociotechnical designs and to examine the differences between the alternatives and what exists. In part we were concerned with the application of analytical frameworks from the task-analysis school and in part with a consideration of the principles of the human resources approach (Chapter 2). It is possible to say that we can replace the principles of scientific management by those of the human resources approach. There are examples where this has been done. Such an approach to organizational design neglects the crucial feature of the human-organizational dimension: namely, how those concerned define what management are doing. For example, a proposal for job enrichment by the designer may be seen as an invitation to productivity bargaining.

The application of the action frame of reference is entirely concerned with the discovery of ways in which the members of the enterprise define and give meaning to their work and relationships. The importance of this aspect is hinted at by Miller and Rice when they refer to task systems and sentient systems. In practice this aspect requires considerable investigation, particularly in situations of technological change where the innovations result in changes in the 'rules of the game'.

In Chapter 9 we referred to the importance of identifying the orientations of the members of the enterprise and the individual and group strategies pursued by them. The objective there was to investigate the culture of CCE Ltd. Culture refers to, for example, the characteristic patterns of involvement of the members. These were examined in the study of Factory B and in the investigation of the maintenance workers. These studies included everyone's definitions of his own situation and the relative ability of members and groups (e.g. packing mechanics) to impose their definition upon other groups (e.g. packing crews). Attention is also given to the ways in which members vary in their attachment to the 'rules of the game' and the strategies used to achieve their objectives (Weick 1970).

An important feature of the analysis is the recognition that when members join an enterprise they arrive with particular expectations and ends they would like to pursue. These expectations and ends will be derived from previous experiences in the wider society and in other enterprises (e.g. educational). The first job of the behavioural scientist is to identify the categories used by members in defining the meaning of their own situation. These may be regarded as typifications that provide the individual with a personal frame of reference of meanings. In part the members' own typifications are taken from the common stock in society, the local community, and the enterprise, but the crucial point is the way in which they are sustained. It may be argued that members continually seek for confirmation that their own definition of the situation is established. Looked at more broadly, the enterprise (e.g. CCE Ltd or the military) has sets of definitions that are being continually modified or renewed. This point is particularly important in situations where major changes in the social order are being introduced by one group (e.g. management), because these innovations may transform the definitions already held by those affected. Thus in any situation we must inquire into the established meanings – the culture.

A full exposition of the theory and methodology of this approach is outside the scope of this book, but its application is demonstrated in the investigations described in Chapter 9, and its impact may be gauged from the comments of members of Azimuth (Chapter 10) about the aspects of the consultancy they had found useful.

ORGANIZATION OF KNOWLEDGE

As an increasing proportion of the Gross National Product is allocated the knowledge industry each year, so there is an increasing interest in its performance. An important consequence has been the development of measures of productivity for researchers and renewed attempts to improve the utilization of such research as has already been undertaken. The success of these efforts is almost entirely dependent upon the ability of those who are investigating the knowledge industry to make a meaningful analysis of its structures and processes. This kind of work has been undertaken for some time in America, particularly at the Institute of Social Research, Michigan, in the Centre for Research on the Utilization of Scientific Knowledge (CRUSK). A similar unit was established more recently in this country under the leadership of Professor Albert Cherns.

Cherns has argued that the linkages between various groups of social scientists, the universities and similar institutions, practitioners, and members of enterprises such as managers, are not clearly understood. A major difficulty is that both researchers and administrators do not sufficiently discriminate the various kinds of activities and institution that occur. Clark *et al.* (1969) have shown that practitioners in the behavioural sciences tend to ignore the related activities of researchers because there are certain barriers of hostility and misunderstanding between them. When we look at the relations between research and enterprises we are faced with a picture of many distinct and unconnected groups and individuals pursuing activities that are interrelated. To change this picture requires certain kinds of 'short-circuiting', of which the study of CCE Ltd is an example. For instance, how are we to discover whether the work of behavioural scientists of the task-analysis school is of value, except by attempting to apply it in situations where it seems relevant?

To engage in 'short-circuiting' is to introduce a change in the 'rules of the game' that operate between behavioural scientists and managers. When we look at what has been occurring to date, the overriding impression is that there has been an increasing diffusion of the behavioural sciences through short course, seminars, and articles in such journals as the *Harvard Business Review*. This process has not been matched by much application, so we cannot yet say how far the behavioural sciences have been adopted, or rejected (Rogers 1961). All we can say is that there is not a great deal of evidence yet of adoption, as the survey by Rush (1970) amply demonstrates.

What in fact has happened is that the pace of investment in research in organizational studies has outrun the capability of enterprises to utilize the findings and has not immediately facilitated the creation of a new group of professionally competent practitioners. Much of the output of the behavioural sciences gets no further than the park gateways to management colleges. As Rush has shown, the primary interest of managers is in reading rather than in applications. All this means that the general optimism accompanying the teacher's proclamations about the demise of 'human relations', the passing of 'human resources', and the arrival of 'task analysis' exaggerates the current situation.

In looking at the 'organization of knowledge' it is important to restate the distinctions made earlier between the three activities of counting, categorizing, and propositioning. A further distinction may be drawn between *increments* in the knowledge possessed by enterprises of any or all three of these activities, and *changes*. If we assume that any enterprise (e.g., a retail chain store) has an existing 'stock of knowledge' about the human and sociological aspects, then we can think of increments as small additions that do not in themselves lead to the enterprise acquiring a new way of looking at these topics. It is likely that most of the encounters between behavioural scientists and enterprises lead to incremental alterations in the stock of knowledge. However, perhaps the most important contribution can come by introducing changes in that stock. What form will these take? It is most useful to think of this stock of knowledge as a set of paradigms (Kuhn 1962) or concepts (Schon 1967). A change occurs when an existing paradigm is rejected in favour of a new one.

How can such changes be induced? It might be argued that the management colleges and similar institutions have an important role to play. However, it must be recognized that such bodies have to attempt to survive and they are largely dependent upon the good recommendations of former students. Thus their objective can become to ensure favourable responses from course students rather than to confront existing ways of thinking. Such confrontation as does occur in these contexts tends to be restricted to controversies over which style of management is 'best', rather than an examination of analytical approaches. The reason may be the lack of experience of teachers of the behavioural sciences in actually occupying the role of decision-taker in, for example, an industrual setting, where they would have to justify many of their precepts.

It also seems unlikely that managers on courses would regard the situation in which much of the teaching of the behavioural sciences takes place as one in which they are likely to meet credible practitioners. When they do meet them they are hardly likely to be prepared. The process is a long one. The management colleges clearly do have a role in diffusing the behavioural sciences, but they are unlikely to be seen as significant agents influencing their application and adoption until they engage in more action research and consultancy. This pattern has been followed by Ashridge Management College (Sadler & Barry 1970).

The thorough application of the behavioural sciences requires the establishment of special units that can develop an expertise in handling the practical problems that occur in consulting. The establishment of such units is in part inhibited by the attitudes of some universities, though the pattern varies widely. Recently, a leading American behavioural scientist expressed surprise at the liking of the British manager for 'packages' and suggested that the explanation lay partly in the antipathy between the universities and, for example, industry and the military.

At least one British social scientist working in the advisory/applications field was heard to say: 'I haven't read a book for five years.' That is not necessarily bad, but since there is a need for bridges and new linkages between researchers, practitioners, and managers, it does indicate the difficulties to be faced.

The improved organization of knowledge requires advances in three areas: the research on the ways in which knowledge is utilized; the capabilities of enterprises for utilizing new knowledge; and changes in the approaches of the universities to research, teaching, and applications.

SUMMARY

The organizational design project at CCE Ltd is part of a wider study of the uses of the social sciences. Though it might be argued that members of that Company did not possess a wide knowledge of behavioural sciences, the case study demonstrated that they were able to create a collaborative relationship through which it was possible to interpret and analyse the main organizational issues involved in the design process, and to set the general preferences for participative management in the context of the realities of the situation. Considerable use was made of the task-analysis approach in diagnosis and in the design stage. However, this perspective does not give sufficient attention to the values and beliefs of the members of the enterprise. To take account of these it was necessary to adopt the 'action frame of reference' and undertake detailed researches (Chapters 8 and 9). The success of organizational design as a general activity is dependent upon the rapidity with which the organizational perspective becomes part of the way of thinking of managers and practitioners. When undertaking projects implying wide terms of reference – as was the case at CCE Ltd – management should ensure that they create a capability within the enterprise for receiving the inputs of the behavioural scientist.

CHAPTER TWELVE

Consultant and client

INTRODUCTION

In the previous chapter some of the kinds of knowledge the consultant would regard as valid were outlined and related to the case study. Bennis (1966) argues that the consultant engages with a client to apply this operable knowledge through a *collaborative relationship*. What is the collaborative relationship and why has it been so heavily emphasized? Interestingly enough, there is no evidence that managements place the same weight on the value of 'mutual goal-setting' and the 'equal sharing of power' as is given to these activities by behavioural science practitioners (see O' Connel 1968). It might be that managements prefer their behavioural scientists to do as they are instructed. Therefore it seems sensible to examine the ways in which some behavioural scientists would prefer to consult.

INSTITUTIONAL LEARNING

The model of institutional learning advanced by Revans (1967) has had an important influence in a project involving some ten London hospitals. Revans had conducted a number of research studies into the internal organization of hospitals during the 1950s and 1960s from which he had concluded that one of the most urgent problems in achieving higher morale and better performance, measured in terms of length of patients' stay, was to improve the internal communications. The strategy he suggested for attaining this is an interesting one and may – dependent upon the evaluation of the project he helped to initiate – have considerable implications for oganizational design and the planning of change.

Revans's researches (1962) indicated wide variations in 'morale' between hospitals in the Manchester area. The variations were measured in terms of the length of stay of staff, absenteeism, and similar indices. He found that high or low rates for hospitals were typically spread through all the occupational groups irrespective of status and type of job. From this he concluded that, in the kind of hospital he was studying, there was an organic quality that affected members of the staff at all levels and in every function. In subsequent investigations he established that the rates of labour turnover and the other chosen indices of morale were associated with the length of patients' stay. From this it was inferred that the organic quality of relations among the staff affects the recovery rate of the patient. When examining this aspect in greater detail, Revans and his research team identified significant differences in the kinds of communication between nurses, patients, doctors, and sisters. The content of communications was assessed in terms of frequency and length of contact as well as the kinds of item included. In general, the frequency of contact between the nurse, who was able to observe the patient for long periods, and the doctor, who saw the patient briefly when on his rounds, was a matter of moments or minutes. The important factor seemed to be whether the doctor, the nurse, and the sister were in a situation in which they could pass observations about the patient to one another. Where this was not the case, Revans discovered an association with the measures of morale and length of stay. These findings led Revans to focus upon the importance of internal communications to the morale of the hospital and length of stay of the patient. The next problem he embarked on was to find ways of improving internal communications in hospitals.

The solution Revans proposed was strongly influenced by his own thinking about management education. He conceives management as a problem-solving process in which certain kinds of knowledge are crucial. Management, Revans contends, is best learnt by doing, rather than by reading books and attending lectures. The important element is for the manager to collect the information himself, to make decisions, and to evaluate their outcome.

This line of thinking provided the impetus for the Hospital Internal Communications Project, launched by Revans in collaboration with representatives of the King's Fund Hospital Centre, the (then) Ministry of Health, and ten participating hospitals in the London area. A unique form of organization was devised to enable each hospital to involve its own staff in devising and executing projects related to their own interests and perceived problems. For each hospital, this consisted of a 'supporting' team drawn from senior members of the medical, nursing, and administrative branches (e.g., consultants, matrons, and hospital group secretaries), and an 'operational' team composed of their deputies. Both teams initially attended courses on organization theory and research methods; a three-day appreciation course in the case of the supporting teams, and a one-month course for the operational teams. In addition, the hospital teams were able to draw upon the resources of a central team of social scientists for assistance with survey techniques, data collection, evaluation, and report-writing. The central team played an essential role in coordinating inter-team meetings and encouraging feedback activities within and between hospitals.

One of the boldest elements of the Project was the establishment nine months after its inception of a small independent unit under the direction of Professor George F. Wieland to evaluate the change programmes. Descriptions of this four-year action-research project and its evaluation appear in Wieland and Leigh (1971) and Revans (1972).

This project is an example of a situation in which an experienced researcher – Revans – has identified a problem which he thinks is endemic to hospitals, and proposed a self-learning method as the preferred solution. The emphasis is upon the members of the units affected taking the major part in transforming their own situation. In this case the behavioural scientists played a supporting and indirect role. The next section describes a quite different ideal.

THE EXPERT APPROACH

The Dutch social psychologist and consultant Hutte (1967) is primarily concerned with the role an expert can play within the enterprise in helping 'it' to overcome problems arising from growth and the associated complications of the existing organization. Hutte's focus is upon the behavioural scientist as an expert. Three features of his argument are of relevance. First, his ideas about collaboration between the consultant and the client. Second, the way in which the internal consultant – the expert – distributes information relevant to the adaptation of the enterprise to the problems of growth. Finally, his analysis of the phases of planned change, in which a dominant place is given to the identification of the major centres of power within the enterprise.

Hutte recommends the multidisciplinary approach because he feels that this is one means of handling the realities of the economic, technical, and social dimensions of the situation. He suggests that a multidisciplinary team has a greater capability for adapting to the reformulation of objectives, and adds that the dynamics of interpersonal relations result in 'ever-changing strategies and role-relationships'.

Next, using the principle of the 'strategic pathway', Hutte suggests that the expert maps all the strategic power points in the enterprise. This map is then used in obtaining information and distributing it to ensure that the crucial sources of power are involved. Emphasis is given to recognizing, though not necessarily accepting, the existing power structure. The actual application of this strategy depends, in Hutte's opinion, upon the existence of centres of power in the enterprise and hence the approach is not operable when no such centres exist. This is a point which has considerable implications. For example, a number of behavioural scientists have suggested that their work is centred upon the redistribution of power. Moreover, it would follow from the analytic framework suggested by Burns and Stalker that the idea of power centres would be operable in only a limited number of enterprises.

Hutte identifies five phases in the consulting process, each of which, he contends, should be terminated by a decision at the power centre:

(a) Admittance and introduction. The expert should consult with management and subsystems and aim to obtain collaboration at all levels. Admittance may be at several points, but should always involve high-level management, who provide the introduction. Admittance should be checked before orientation is undertaken.

(b) Orientation. This starts when the expert obtains the reaction to his feedback of the results of the first stage. The reaction is used to plan for the orienting investigation. In this phase the expert follows the strategic pathway, using open-ended interviews based upon fundamental concepts to reveal the picture of the main problems. Because the expert has no knowledge of the strength of the relationship between factors he cannot be specific. The overall picture is then presented to management prior to the localization of the advice. At this stage decisions are made about resources, including finance and staff.

(c) The detailing and localizing of the problem are best achieved from group interviews which provide many insights as well as refining the expert's picture of the organization. In this stage the almost completed diagnosis is fed back to each of the groups consulted, and finally a report is made to management.

(d) It is now possible to make a very carefully prepared presentation to the power centre of the organization. This leads to the drafting of action programmes.

(e) Finally the expert must plan the process of unwinding.

As well as the strategic time phases and pathway, Hutte envisages the expert using a number of tactics from the following eight.

In the first two phases there is an open noncommitted tone to the exercise while the expert is fact-finding. The tactic used is defined as *orientation* and it leads into *localization*, the dominant tactic of the third phase. If group interviews are used, Hutte claims the information will be more relevant and objective. He argues that group interviews lead the organization to experience the action approach and provide direct contacts while at the same time revealing interrelationships between factors and providing a reliable picture of the extent of integration in the task field. Thus a considerable amount of data is collected about major problems. These data and data from the fact-finding should be analysed and presented to management in general terms. The active character of the investigation enables the expert to minipulate the tactic of *facilitation*.

In phase four the main tactic is *participation*, though it may be necessary to confront people with problems. The reference to *confrontation* is of interest, partly because it is omitted by Lewin (1947) and partly because it is included by Blake and Mouton (1964). The aim is to make direct attack on resistance. Both tactics depend on the localization of the problem and the possibility that it can be solved intellectually at the level of the particular group. Participation is generally used, but confrontation is necessary when the problem is not correctly perceived and when the willingness of the group is uncertain.

Hutte refers to three other tactics. *Revelation* refers to disclosing internal problems to the client and is used when open discussion is not possible and the group are involved in emotional aspects. *Co-option* of powerful persons can be used when the group cannot solve problems at their level. *Manipulation* refers to the short-circuiting of official communication channels.

LABORATORY TRAINING

Laboratory training refers to T-groups and similar devices. The origins of this form of training are partly in the work of those American social psychologists who were influenced by Lewin and later founded the National Training Laboratory. It is also likely that the work of British psychologists in this field following the resettlement of former prisoners of war after 1945 played some part in its development (Foulkes & Anthony 1957).

The T-group has emerged as one of the most frequently employed techniques in laboratory training. Initially the focus was upon the individual and providing self-insight, but gradually it has moved away from personal development towards an equally diffuse aim, that of organizational development. In practice this often means that the focus is a particular part of the larger enterprise (Clark & Ford 1970).

In a situation where the individuals composing the 'group' are not known to one another, it is likely that they all enter the situation with two major sets of expectations: a definition of their preferred role and its relative prestige, and a definition of their preferred form of interpersonal relationships. Preferences may vary from loosely structured situations to a firm hierarchized structure. Typically the consultant allows the group to introduce itself and seem to run the session. An interesting experience for the author was to join a group where many of the members had read a little about T-groups. We all began by waiting for someone to 'break', and when that had happened there seemed to be relief that one person was going to 'make the running'. As that particular group emerged over a number of meetings, it was possible to observe individual expectations being altered within the situation. It was surprising to find persons who had seemed resolute and firm showing signs of distress. Certainly the experience made the many concepts used in teaching about group processes assume a deeper meaning, but the major problem that arose was the transferability of the behaviour modifications and their 'insights' to other contexts.

The objective is for members of the laboratory to examine interpersonal relations in the unstructured setting of the 'group'. Thus the emphasis is almost totally upon behaviour experienced by the individual. The members examine bits of data generated by themselves in the group. Topics can include leadership, authority, and communications.

It is argued by exponents of this kind of training that the participants learn to analyse and become more sensitive to interpersonal relations and processes in small groups. Also that they acquire concepts for understanding the situations in which they find them-

OD—S

selves, and these new understandings facilitate a more effective performance. The aim is to achieve change in, for example, the firm, by reconstructing the mental maps of the members. The mechanisms for obtaining this change are the redistribution of power, the increase in trust and mutual confidence, and the resolution of conflicts through joint problem-solving activities.

As the application of the training laboratory has shifted in emphasis from the individual to the organization so there have emerged a number of established practices. Thus the composition of the group formed within an enterprise may represent a diagonal slice through the firm, or the actual work group, or a selection of persons from different functions having the same rank.

The most extensive form of application is that devised by Blake and Mouton (1964, 1967). Their programme, known as the Managerial Grid, has a number of phases and can take several years to apply completely. One of the objectives of this approach is to enable the members to identify the actual strategies they apply in their own work and then to move people towards the 'team management' concept. The Grid is a source of increasing interest for managers and it is one of the few practices that have been explored systematically (Greiner 1967).

FEEDBACK AND ACTION RESEARCH

This example is taken from the early work of Mann (1957). He describes his initial interest in introducing changes in relations between subordinates and their supervisors. In some exploratory and developmental work he experimented with the idea of collecting the perceptions that each group had of the other and feeding the findings of the attitude surveys back to the respondents with the objective of improving relations.

The first attempts seemed to indicate that this approach maximized the acceptance and utilization of the survey. The process is best considered to be one of an interlocking chain of conferences starting with the presentation of the findings to the chief executive and then progressing 'downwards' through the hierarchy. The meetings at the supervisory level were structured to contain the supervisor and his particular work group(s). Each group received the data pertaining to its activities and the members were invited to interpret the findings. They were also asked to indicate how any further analysis of the data might help them in the performance of their tasks. This early experiment encouraged Mann to attempt a more ambitious plan involving an evaluation of the success of the method.

In the early 1950s Mann conducted further investigation in some eight accounting departments, collecting data from both supervisors and some several hundred members. There were some variations in the pattern of feedback between the eight departments and this allowed Mann to conduct a 'natural' experiment by comparing departments in which feedback occurred with a small control group. The departments that conducted feedback varied in the length of the feedback period (13–33 weeks) and the frequency of meetings (9–65). In these departments there were changes in how the employees felt about the work they did, their supervisor, their progress in the company, and the ability of the department to get the work completed.

When looking at the feedback method, Mann suggested that change is most likely to be facilitated by the involvement of those to whom the change is directed. Further, that data can form an objective around which discussion can take place.

Variations in the form and content of feedback have occurred and it has become increasingly utilized (Heller 1969). Sadler and Barry (1970) describe a situation in which they applied Scott's Diagram to a printing firm in order to obtain data on the perceptions of relations between members of management and then utilized the analysed data to suggest changes in organization. Similarly, the Dutch behavioural scientist Hesseling (1968) has investigated managerial communication patterns and described the ways in which information was returned to the respondents as the basic for further action.

COLLABORATIVE RELATIONSHIPS

Each of these examples serves to show that behavioural scientists have varying ideas about the kinds of relationship with clients that are most likely to help the client. We shall use them to examine the case study.

First, we can examine the model of institutional learning. This model is based upon an assumption that a combination of the insights of the members of the hospital and the provision of a joint activity – the selected problem – will be an adequate basis for improving the performance of the hospital. Clearly, the situation at CCE Ltd was very different from that in the ten London hospitals, but it is interesting in so far as the work of the Azimuth Group may be seen to constitute the kind of learning experience that Revans would regard as particularly valuable. That is an aspect we do not wish to question. Rather our focus will be upon what the Azimuth Group reported as finding useful in a relationship with external consultants: this seems to have been the general perspective of the behavioural scientist. Clark (1963) has observed that specialists in particular areas (e.g. operational research) tend to observe and look for particular kinds of clues and information from their visits to enterprises and that the behavioural scientist is similarly likely to make a selective screening of what he sees and hears. Azimuth found the emphasis upon alternative designs, the application of their stated philosophy to their ongoing design work, and similar aspects of the consultancy to be useful. These are all examples of activities that could not easily be generated within the firm. Does this suggest that the consultant should be the expert?

Hutte's analysis does at times tend towards this assertion. His insistence upon the identification of the power centres in the client enterprise is in many senses sensible and practical, but taken out of context it becomes almost obsessive. The idea of a single power centre is totally suspect. The value of Hutte's contribution is its isolation of the phases of a consulting relationship; the weakness is that he does not give sufficient attention to the difference in outlook between behavioural scientists and managers (see Chapter 5).

Both the institutional learning model and that of Hutte give a low priority to the kinds of operable knowledge examined in Chapters 7 and 11. The laboratory training approach developed as a response to an awareness that lectures to managers about individuals and groups did in fact have a low impact, and even this disappeared in a short time. The group experiences were utilized to give the members an awareness of the emergence of group norms and controls by starting them off in an unstructured situation. In their current application to enterprises the emphasis is said to be upon changing cognitive frameworks, but it seems more likely that it will facilitate the crystallization of existing ones. Thus, at the level of the enterprise, the laboratory approach does not seem to include the kinds of knowledge that can help members to analyse their own organizational systems. A similar objection may be brought against the classical use of the feedback method.

Typically the collaborative relationship has been defined by certain American behavioural scientists to be one in which the behavioural scientists helps the client to debureaucratize. If this starting assumption is accepted, the approaches suggested do seem to have some elements of plausibility. However, we cannot assume that all enterprises are equally bureaucratic, or that this condition will be objected to by those involved when it does exist. March and Simon (1958) outline conditions under which relationships are likely to be highly structured because of characteristics of the task, and Crozier (1964) has suggested that the bureaucratic phenomenon can be a source of satisfaction and meaning to those involved. Perhaps the most serious objection to the debureaucratization argument is that very little actual analysis of the client seems to take place before the recommended solution is applied.

The application of organizational analysis to a client almost inevitably introduces tensions between the consultant and the client. The client has established ways of thinking about the organization and justifying the form it takes. The consultant is not necessarily bound by these conventions and can use his analytical skills to map and diagnose the organization. An important feature of this activity is that it draws heavily on the findings of research studies as a source of concepts and ideas. If the client is to develop a competence in this area this will require a major change in the existing ways of looking at the organization. If the consultant is to inject this kind of thinking, it would seem to involve some kinds of confrontation.

An important test of the extent of collaboration between the consultant and the client is to be found in the definition of the problems to be dealt with. At CCE Ltd the opening remarks from the behavioural scientists emphasized the importance of joint investigations and the dialogue. The early phases demonstrated the importance of studying the existing systems. Thus investigations became an important aspect of the relationship. Always there was pressure on us from members of CCE Ltd to take on the role of expert and offer a definitive solution. When we objected, pointing out that this was a joint project, attempts were made to control our activities by requesting us to outline the future of the consultancy in the form of critical path network. Gradually we managed – jointly – to work through this period of tension. In this case collaboration also involved conflict.

There are constant pressures on behavioural scientists to alter their roles once they are in the situation and one of the dangers is that they will attempt to play too many roles. For example, part of the mission of CUSSR is the general establishment within enterprises of an increased ability to utilize the competences of behavioural scientists and the findings of research studies. Great stress is laid upon building a bridge between research findings and problems. This role cannot be sustained if we move too far away from it into, for example, the role of advocate (see Chapter 10).

It has been suggested that the researchers at Western Electric – the scene of the classic Hawthorne studies – made a serious mistake when they moved from a research role into that of action because the research foothold that had been established was undermined. In that case the pioneering research did nothing towards providing Hawthorne with a new theory of organizing.

These observations suggest that not only do behavioural scientists play a variety of roles, but that some kinds of specialization may be appropriate. For example, people who are good at the 'development roles' may not be so proficient at applications. This indicates that the development of an R & D component on human aspect of the enterprise should be a continuous process.

OBTAINING APPLICATIONS

A number of authorities have stressed the need to increase the applications of the behavioural sciences (Cherns 1968; Whyte 1969) and have pointed to the problems that obtaining applications create. Thus Whyte (1962) contends that 'application involves far more than the discovery of bits of knowledge. Application is a social process.' This refers to the fact that organizational design is dependent upon interpersonal and group factors. The behavioural scientist has to give as much attention to the creation of the social milieu of the group as he does to the content of the advice. Good ideas, however logical and elegant, may not be heard if the group to which they are presented is one in which the structure is still emergent. The practitioner always has to observe the group and organizational processes and relate his interventions to his knowledge of them. In the situation where there is a behavioural science team it is possible to split the work within the team and to take turns in intervening and observing. This in itself places various strains on both the consulting team and the clients.

At CCE, for example, we frequently entered into a situation where we were the visitors to Azimuth. They became an established group with particular conventions, which gradually changed as the project developed and the individual careers of those involved altered. In developing a strategy for approaching our major meetings it was usual to divide the tasks so that we were able to contribute in the areas we knew most about, but this was always subject to modification in the actual situation.

An important feature of applications is the linking of ideas and findings with the management organization. Whyte (1962) suggests that those who are involved in applications will 'have learned to organize the flow of research activities and integrate the flow with the structure and process of the management organization'. It is likely that the ease of achieving such a situation will vary widely. There would, for example, seem to have been a number of attempts at applications during the last decade that have lacked both direction and the organizational commitment to achieving a success. There seems to be little point in conducting extensive sociotechnical analyses of particular situations unless managers perceive them to be undertaken in areas that are problematical. Revans's dictum that managers learn best by working on problem-solving stresses the relevance of this point and also suggests the advantage of joint definition of the problems.

There are some situations that may be jointly defined by the practitioner and the manager as problems, but the organizational system may not facilitate a good collaborative relationship. In CCE Ltd, for example, there were a number of factors that made the particular consultancy approach feasible and operable. First, the existence of the Azimuth Group. This was a group charged with examining a future situation. Second, the time commitment of the members to the design of the new factory was high and meant that it was a significant priority. Third, the previous experience of the members of the group was largely associated with a long time perspective (Lawrence & Lorsch 1967). Consequently, they did not (always) expect results the next day. Fourth, members were generally innovative in their thinking.

This situation may be compared with another project in the engineering industry, in which the author was involved as a consultant to establish organizational design. In that situation the major part of the design of the new technology had been subcontracted to a specialist agency, and the internal group was only concerned with the coordination of the move. There was no equivalent to Azimuth. Further, the main members of the enterprise who were directly affected were more closely involved in day-to-day operating and the constraints on thinking which that imposes. In that context the application took a quite different form.

The role of the linkman and internal sponsors to the application is quite crucial. Application can be heavily dependent upon the advice the linkmen are able to provide about timing and the political context. For example, they can play a particularly important part in the formulation of central themes. A good example is the adoption of the 'lay hypothesis' about introducing participative styles into the new production system. They can also give considerable support to the presentation of the proposals for work. This happened in the case study with the planning of the investigations of orientations, when the linkman gave considerable advice on this aspect. The success of the work in the Processing Department was in an important respect due to the dogged determination of the linkman to work systematically with the idea of scenario-writing, and his summaries and questions provided a vital bridge between ourselves and the other members of the project group.

SUMMARY

In this chapter we have compared the relation between the client (CCE Ltd) and the consultant (ourselves) with some 'models' taken from other examples. We have given considerable stress to the importance of making an input of the behavioural science perspective. Given that our main thrust was in the form of the insertion of certain conceptual tools it was necessary to juxtapose these against established forms of thinking. Since incompatible definitions of the situation coexist uneasily, it was inevitable that some conflict would occur. The case study is of particular interest because it represents a serious attempt to apply the ideas developed in broader comparative research studies (Perrow 1970). A final point must be to re-emphasize that the whole case study refers to a specific situation. Utilizing ideas abstracted from it must be undertaken with great caution.

CHAPTER THIRTEEN

Conclusion

1. The objective of the book has been to focus upon the kinds of role that the behavioural science practitioner can play in organizational design.

2. Organizational design is separate from and prior to planned change.

3. Organizational design requires a capability for generating alternative designs for the same sets of tasks.

4. The evaluation of these designs can partly be undertaken by reference to the work of the task-analysis school of theorists and practitioners. (Charles Perrow (1970) has recently published an excellent introduction called *Organizational Analysis: A Sociological View*, which is both readable and relevant.)

5. The evaluation of design also requires researches into the distinctive features of the client's social structure and the systematic comparison of these findings with the planned social structure to reveal the organizational assumptions. This includes an examination of the ways in which members of enterprises define their own situation and the categories they utilize for organizing their ideas.

6. The Alternatives and Differences Approach is particularly relevant to organizational design because it is directed yet flexible. It balances inventiveness with careful investigation.

7. The specific application of the Alternatives and Differences Approach requires careful mapping of the distinctive structure and culture of the enterprise. Its application would be different in the military or in hospitals from that in CCE Ltd.

8. Obtaining the utilization of researches requires that the design of the research strategy includes a strategy for ensuring utilization. This must frequently be done at the start of the project.

9. The choice of the order in which parts of the enterprise are investigated can be crucial. For example, the study of the female packing crews provided a clear example of the impact of the technology, and the investigation of the nature of the automated processes

for the Processing Department provided a structured basis for establishing design as a joint activity.

10. The interests of behavioural scientists and other groups (e.g. operational research) do not necessarily coincide.

11. Organizational design is a multidisciplinary activity in which the role of the behavioural science practitioner is to represent the human-organizational aspect.

12. Thinking about the future requires the establishment of protected project teams who will feel free to experiment with ideas like scenario-writing.

13. Organizational design is a fragmentary, demanding, and exciting activity that requires considerable patience, persistence, and luck.

Research aspect

This book is part of the research programme into the 'Uses of the Social Sciences' with particular reference to uses in non-academic contexts. The programme, which is financed by the Social Science Research Council, United Kingdom (HR. 86/1) commenced in 1967. My part, as co-investigator with Professor A. B. Cherns, has been principally concerned with uses in industrial and military enterprises rather than, for example, government.

Analysis of the literature, and interviews with those involved both in action research/consultancy and the study of it (e.g., Professor G. F. Wieland), demonstrated that many of the accounts had a limited value for secondary analysis. In fact the technique of secondary analysis has been used by, for example, Jones in an extensive context analysis of two hundred published studies, and by Greiner in an examination of eighteen case studies. There are three major problems with many existing studies. First, there are a large number of evaluative studies that take 'before' and 'after' measures and treat consulting as an event rather than a series of interrelated phases (Lippitt *et al.* 1958; Greiner 1967) and subprocesses (Dalton 1970). Second, they are frequently examples of retrospective self-supporting. I have commented in detail elsewhere (Clark & Ford 1970) on the limitations which this introduces, and similar observations have been made by Lake (1968) and by O'Connel (1968). Third, existing accounts represent only a small section of the potential uses of the social sciences. It would seem that the most active practitioners are those imbued with democratic values. Typically, high praise is given to approaches that facilitate the mutual definition of the problem and equal power relationships (Clark & Cherns 1968). This perspective neglects the context of project (e.g. a crisis) and omits a careful consideration of the consultant–client relationship.

Given these problems, Cherns and Clark decided that the most fruitful research strategy would be to adopt the comparative–intensive case-study method. This consists of taking a small number of case studies – we created nine – which are examined intensively on a comparative basis to develop hypotheses and focuses for subsequent testing. It is a descriptive and exploratory approach appropriate to the development of a new field of study. In general there has been remarkably little use of the comparative–intensive case-study method. Lupton (1964), in a study of group norms, and Clark (1965) in the peak-period research, represent examples of individual researchers using this approach. The work of the unit led by the late Joan Woodward is an excellent example of collaboration by several people. The unit-based approach involves considerable problems, particularly in establishing consistency (see Woodward 1970, especially the Methodological Appendix).

Case studies facilitate the use of a wide range of techniques (Wilson 1961) and are particularly useful in exploratory work. Their relevance has been recently highlighted by the work of Weiss and Rein (1970) and Lazarsfeld and Reitz (1970).

At CCE Ltd, I was in the role of participant observer. The distinctive features were that this was a study of a professional activity (the consultant's) and relationship with the client; the situation offered only intermittent exposure to the client, but provided periods for documentation and analysis.

In the case study of CCE Ltd, I have attempted to tackle several of the limitations of earlier studies. First, in general, the organizational context has been neglected. Consequently, it is difficult to assess whether a similar strategy for consulting would have been successful in other contexts such as, for example, speciality unit production, or the Military (see Cherns, Clark, & Parrott 1970).

In dealing with the organizational context we have attended to the antecedent factors (Greiner 1967), especially the expectations of Azimuth regarding the content and form of the consultancy and the existence of a difference of opinion within Azimuth on the subject of participation. Careful consideration has also been given to 'client receptivity' (Jones 1969). Second, the presentation of the case study has been designed to depict the 'unfolding' of events, starting with problem definition and reporting changes in the terms of reference. Careful note is made of the phases and their interdependence (see also Greiner 1967; Dalton 1970). The importance of the longitudinal aspect is stressed by Jones, who demonstrates the gradual routinization of the consultant's activities and a consequent lowering in influence. Third, I have aimed to show the active character of the clients' influence and to point to their selectivity over material and ideas. The client's early control strategies are likely to be typical of this kind of client–consultant relationship. Finally, I have sought to delineate the general political nature of consulting and to record the relationship between the client (Azimuth) and other subgroups within CCE Ltd.

References

AGUILAR, F. J. 1968 *Scanning the Business Environment.* London: Macmillan.

ARGYRIS, C. 1957 *Personality and Organization.* New York: Harper.

ARGYRIS, C. 1964 *Integrating the Individual and the Organization.* New York: Wiley.

ARONOFF, J. 1967 *Psychological Needs and Cultural Systems.* New York: Van Nostrand.

ARONSON, S. H. & SHERWOOD C. C. 1967 Researcher versus Practitioner, Problems in Social Action Research. *Social Work* Oct., 89–96.

ASHBY, W. R. 1956 *Introduction to Cybernetics.* London: Chapman & Hall; New York: Wiley.

BAKKE, E. W. 1950 *Bonds of Organization.* New York: Harper & Row.

BECKHARD, R. 1967 The Confrontation Meeting. *Harvard Business Review* March–April, 45: 149–155.

BECKHARD, R. 1969 *Organization Development: Strategies and Models.* Reading, Mass.: Addison-Wesley.

BELL, G. D. 1967 Formality versus Flexibility in Complex Organizations. In *Organizations and Human Behavior*, Bell (ed.). New York: Prentice-Hall.

BELL, G. D. 1968 Determinants of Spans of Control, *American Journal of Sociology* 73: 100–109.

BENDIX, R. 1947 Bureaucracy: The Problem and its Setting. *American Sociological Review* 12: 493–507.

BENDIX, R. 1956 *Work and Authority in Industry.* New York: Wiley.

BENNIS, W. G. 1964 A New Role for the Behavioural Sciences: Effecting Organizational Change. *Admin. Science Quarterly* 8: 125–165.

BENNIS, W. G. 1966 Theory and Method in Applying Behavioural Science to Planned Organizational Change. In J. R. Lawrence (ed.), *Operational Research and the Social Sciences* London: Tavistock.

BENNIS, W. G. 1969 *Organization Development: Its Nature, Origins, and Prospects.* New York: Addison-Wesley.

BENNIS, W. G., BENNE, K. D., & CHIN, R. 1961, Revised 1969 *The Planning of Change.* New York: Holt, Rinehart & Winston.

VAN BEINUM, H. J. J. 1964 A Field Experiment on Stabilization of Work Groups, Redistribution of Authority and Communications. Paper, XV International Congress of Applied Psychology. Yugoslavia, 1964.

VAN BEINUM, H. J. J. 1966 *The Morale of the Dublin Busmen.* London: Tavistock Institute.

BLAKE, R. R. & MOUTON, J. S. 1964 *The Managerial Grid.* Houston, Tex.: Gulf Publishing Co.

BLAKE, R. R. & MOUTON, J. S. 1968 *Corporate Excellence Through Grid Organization Development*. Houston, Tex.: Gulf Publishing Co.

BLAU, P. M. 1964 *Exchange and Power in Social Life*. New York: Wiley.

BLAUNER, R. 1964 *Alienation and Freedom: the factory worker and his industry*. Chicago: University of Chicago Press.

BLOOD, M. R. & HULIN, C. L. 1967 Alienation, Environmental Characteristics and Worker Responses. *Journal of Applied Psychology* **51** (3).

BOGUSLAW, R. 1966 *The New Utopians*. New York: Prentice-Hall.

BROWN, R. K. 1967 Research and Consultancy in Industrial Enterprises: A review of the Contribution of the Tavistock Institute of Human Relations to the Development of Industrial Sociology. *Sociology* **1** (1): 33–60.

BROWN, R. K. & BRANNEN, P. 1970 Social Relations and Social Perspectives Amongst Shipyard Workers. A Preliminary Statement. *Sociology* **4** (1): 71–84.

BUCKLEY, W. 1967 *Sociology and Modern Systems Theory*. New York: Prentice-Hall.

BUCKLOW, M. 1966 A New Role for the Work Group. *Administrative Science Quarterly* June: 59–78.

BUCKLOW, M. 1969 Readings in Socio-Technical Systems. Paper Tavistock No. HRC 258.

BURNS, T. & STALKER, G. M. 1961 *The Management of Innovation*. London: Tavistock.

BURNS, T. 1966 On the Plurality of Social Systems; in J. R. Lawrence (ed.), *Operational Research and the Social Sciences*. London: Tavistock.

CAREY, A. 1967 The Hawthorne Studies: A Radical Criticism. *American Sociological Review* **32**, 403–416.

CHADWICK-JONES, J. 1970 *Automation and Behavior: A Social Psychological Study*. New York: Wiley.

CHANDLER, A. D. 1962 *Strategy and Structure: Chapters in the History of The Industrial Enterprise*. Boston, Mass.: MIT Press.

CHAPPLE, E. O. & SAYLES, L. R. 1958 *The Measure of Management*. New York: Macmillan.

CHERNS, A. B. 1967 Organization for Change: The Case of the Military. Given to NATO Conference on manpower Research. Published in Wilson, N. A. B. (ed.), *Manpower Research*, 1970. Bath: English Universities Press.

CHERNS, A. B. 1968 Social Research and its Diffusion. *Human Relations* **22** (3): 209–218.

CHERNS, A. B. 1968 The Use of the Useful: Part 2. *Social Science Research Council Newsletter*. London.

CHERNS, A. B., CLARK, P. A., & PARROTT, S. 1970 Sociology and the Military: the Social Organization of training in one service. Paper given to NATO Conference 'The Perceived Role of the Military' at Ile de Bendor, France.

CHERNS, A. B., CLARK, P. A., & SINCLAIR, R. 1970 Aggregates and Structures: Two Complementary Paradigms in Manpower Studies. Given to the Institute of Management Sciences Conference, London.

In A. R. Smith (ed.), *Manpower and Management Science*. London: EUP, 1971.

CHIN, R. 1961 The Utility of Systems Models and Development Models for Practitioners. In Bennis, Benne & Chin (eds.), *The Planning of Change* (1st edition, 1961). New York: Holt, Rinehart & Winston.

CLARK, P. A. 1961 Work Study as an Agent of Bureaucratization. *Time and Motion Study*. August, London.

CLARK, P. A. 1963 A Sociologist in a Work Study Department. *Time and Motion Study*. February, London.

CLARK, P. A. 1964 Productivity Incentives for Knitwear Firms. *Hosiery Trade Journal*. August, Leicester, England.

CLARK, P. A. 1965 Some Sociological Aspects of Peak Periods in Organization. Mimeo.

CLARK, P. A. & CHERNS, A. B. 1968 A Role for Social Scientists in Organizational Design. In G. Heald (ed.), *Approaches to Organizational Behaviour*. London: Tavistock, 1970.

CLARK, P. A., FORD, J. R., & ELING, C. 1969 Planned Organizational Change: Some Current Limitations with Reference to Family and Community. Given to the British Association for the Advancement of Science, Exeter.

CLARK, P. A. & FORD, J. R. 1970 Methodological and Theoretical Problems in the Investigation of Planned Organizational Change. *Sociological Review* 18 (1): 29–52.

CLARK, P. A. 1970b Antecedent Factors and their Influence upon Client Consultant Relations: A Case Study. In preparation.

CLARK, P. A. 1970 Cultural Definitions of Events: The Peak Period Phenomenon. Mimeo. Centre for the Utilization of Social Science Research, Loughborough University of Technology, England.

COCH, L. & FRENCH, J. R. P. 1948 Overcoming Resistance to Change. *Human Relations* 1: 512–533.

CROZIER, M. 1964 *The Bureaucratic Phenomenon*. Chicago: University of Chicago Press; London: Tavistock.

DALTON, G. W. 1970 Influence and Organizational Change. In Dalton, G. W., Lawrence, P. R., & Greiner, L. E. *Organizational Change and Development*. Homewood, Illinois: Irwin-Dorsey.

DALZEIL, S. & KLEIN, L. 1960 *The Human Implications of Work Study*. London: DSIR.

DANIEL, W. W. 1969 Industrial Behaviour and Orientation to Work. *Journal of Management Studies* 3: 366–375.

DAVIS, L. E. 1955 Job Design Research. *Journal of Industrial Engineering* 6: 1–4.

DAVIS, L. E., CANTER, R. R., & HOFFMAN, J. 1955 Current Job Design Criteria. *Journal of Industrial Engineering* March–April, 1–6.

DAVIS, L. E. 1957 Toward a Theory of Job Design. *Journal of Industrial Engineering* Sept.–Oct., 305–309.

DAVIS, L. E. 1957 Toward a Theory of Job Design. *Journal of Industrial Engineering* 8: 8–17.

DAVIS, L. E. 1962 The Effects of Automation of Job Design. *Industrial Relations* 2 (1): 53–71.

DENNIS, H., HENRIQUES, F. M., & SLAUGHTER, C. 1957 *Coal is our Life* (2nd edition 1970). London: Tavistock.

DILL, W. R. 1958 Environment as an Influence on Managerial Autonomy. *Administrative Science Quarterly* 2: 409–443.

DILL, W. R. 1962 The Impact of Environment on Organizational Development. In Mailick, S., & Van Ness, E. H. (eds.), *Concepts and Issues in Administrative Behavior*. New York: Prentice-Hall.

VAN DOORN, J. A. 1966 Conflict in Formal Organizations. In Reuck, A. & Knight, J. (eds.), *Conflict in Society*. London: Churchill.

DORNBUSCH, S. N. 1955 The Military Academy as an Assimilating Institution. *Social Forces* 38 (4).

DROR, Y. 1967 Policy Analysts: A New Professional Role in Government Service. *Public Administration Review* 27: 197–203.

DUBIN, R. 1957 *The World of Work*. New York: Prentice-Hall.

DUBIN, R., HOMANS, G. C., MANN, F. C., & MILLER, D. C. 1965 *Leadership and Productivity*. San Francisco: Chandler.

DUBIN, R. 1965 Supervision and Productivity: Empirical Findings and Theoretical Considerations. In Dubin *et al.*, *Leadership and Productivity*.

EARNSHAW, P. E. 1969 Implications for Organizational Design of the Existing Social System at CCE Ltd. Unpublished Master's dissertation, Loughborough University of Technology.

ELDRIDGE, J. E. T. 1968 *Industrial Disputes; Essays in the Sociology of Industrial Relations*. London: Routledge & Kegan Paul.

EMERY, F. E. 1959 Characteristics of Socio-Technical Systems: A Critical Review of Theories and Facts. Tavistock Institute. TIHR.527.

EMERY, F. & MAREK 1962 Some socio-technical aspects of automation. *Human Relations* 15: 17–26.

EMERY, F. E. & TRIST, E. L. 1965 The Causal Texture of Organizational Environments. *Human Relations* 18: 21–32.

EMERY, F. E. & THORSRUD, E. 1969 *Form and Content in Industrial Democracy*. London: Tavistock.

EMERY, F. E. (ed.) 1969 *Systems Thinking*. Harmondsworth: Penguin.

ETZIONI, A. 1961 *A Comparative Analysis of Complex Organizations*. New York: Free Press.

FAUNCE, W. A. 1967 *Problems of an Industrial Society*. New York: McGraw-Hill.

FELD, M. D. 1964 Military Self-image in a Technological Environment. In Janowitz, M. (ed.), *The New Military*. New York: Russell Sage Foundation.

FIEDLER, F. E. 1965 Engineering the Job to Fit the Manager. *Harvard Business Review* 43 (5): 115–122.

FIEDLER, F. E. 1967 *A Theory of Leadership Effectiveness*. New York: McGraw-Hill.

FLANDERS, A. 1964 *The Fawley Productivity Agreements: A case study of management and collective bargaining*. London: Faber.

FOSTER, M. 1968 Work Involvement and Alienation. *Journal of Manpower and Applied Psychology* 2: 35–48.

FOULKES, S. H. & ANTHONY, E. J. 1957 *Group Psychotherapy: the Psycho-analytic Approach.* Harmondsworth: Penguin.

FRENCH, J. R. P., ISRAEL, J., & ÅS, D. 1960 An Experiment on Participation in a Norwegian Factory. *Human Relations* 13: 3–19.

FRIEDMANN, G. 1955 *Industrial Society.* New York: Free Press.

FRIEDMANN, G. 1961 *The Anatomy of Work.* London: Heinemann.

GARFINKEL, H. 1967 *Studies in Ethnomethodology.* London, New York: Prentice-Hall.

GOFFMAN, E. 1961 *Asylums: Essays on the Social Situation of Mental Patients and other Inmates.* New York: Anchor Books; Harmondsworth: Penguin, 1968.

GLASER, B. G. & STRAUSS, A. L. 1968 *The Discovery of Grounded Theory: Strategies for Qualitative Research.* London: Weidenfeld & Nicolson.

GOLDTHORPE, J. H., LOCKWOOD, D., BECHHOFER, F., & PLATT, J. 1967 *The Affluent Worker; Industrial Attitudes and Behaviour.* Cambridge University Press.

GOLDTHORPE, J. H. 1969 *Social Inequality and Social Integration in Modern Britain.* Presidential Address. Sociology Section. British Association for the Advancement of Science, Exeter.

GOLDTHORPE, J. H., LOCKWOOD, D., BECHHOFFER, F., & PLATT, J. 1970 *The Affluent Worker in the Class Structure.* Cambridge University Press.

GOODMAN, L. L. 1954 *Man and Automation.* Harmondsworth: Penguin.

GOULDNER, A. W. 1954 *Patterns of Industrial Bureaucracy.* Glencoe, Ill.: Free Press.

GOULDNER, A. W. 1957 Theoretical Requirements of the Applied Social Sciences. *American Sociological Review* 22 (1): 92–102.

GOULDNER, A. W. 1959 Reciprocity and Autonomy in Functional Theory. In L. Gross (ed.), *Symposium of Sociological Theory.* New York: Harper & Row.

GOULDNER, A. W. & MILLER, D. 1964 *Applied Sociology.* New York: Free Press

GREINER, L. E. 1967 Antecedents of Planned Organizational Change. *Journal of Applied Behavioural Science* 3 (1): 51–85.

HABERSTROH, C. J. 1965 *Organization Design and Systems Analysis.* In March, J. G., 1965.

HARVEY, E. 1968 Technology and the Structure of Organizations. *American Sociological Review* 33: 247–259.

HEALD, G. (ed.) 1970 *Approaches to the Study of Organizational Behaviour.* London: Tavistock.

HELLER, F. 1971 *Managerial Decision-Making: A Study of Leadership Styles and Power-sharing among Senior Managers.* London: Tavistock.

HERBST, P. G. 1962 *Autonomous Group Functioning.* London: Tavistock.

HERZBERG, F., MAUSNER, B., & SNYDERMAN, B. 1958 *The Motivation to Work.* New York: Wiley.

HESSELING, P. 1968 Communication & Organization Structure in a Large Multi-National Company: A Research Strategy. In Heald, G. (ed.), *Approaches to the Study of Organizational Behaviour*. London: Tavistock, 1970.

HICKSON, D. J., PUGH, D. S., & PHEYSEY, D. C. 1970 Technology and Formal Organization: An Empirical Appraisal. Mimeo.

HJELHOLT, G. 1964 Training for Reality. Paper. Working Paper No. 5. Industrial Management Division. Leeds University. Mimeo.

HOMANS, G. C. 1951 *The Human Group*. London: Routledge & Kegan Paul.

HOROBIN, G. 1957 Community and Occupation in the Hull Fishing Industry. *British Journal of Sociology* 3 (4).

HUTTE, H. 1968 *The Sociatry of Work*. MS.

INTERNATIONAL LABOUR OFFICE 1960 *Introduction to Work Study*. Geneva: ILO.

JANTSCH, E. 1967 *Technological Forecasting in Perspective*. O.E.C.D. Publication.

JAQUES, E. 1951 *The Changing Culture of a Factory*. London: Tavistock/Routledge.

JAQUES, E. 1957 *The Measurement of Responsibility*. London: Tavistock; Cambridge, Mass.: Harvard University Press.

JASINSKI, F. J. 1956 Technological Delimitation of Reciprocal Relationships: A Study of Interaction Patterns in Industry. *Human Organization* 15 (2).

JONES, G. N. 1969 *Planned Organizational Change: An Exploratory Study Using an Empirical Approach*. London: Routledge & Kegan Paul.

KATZ, D. 1955 *Productivity, Supervision and Morale Among Railroad Workers*. New York: Wiley.

KATZ, D. & KAHN, R. L. 1966 *The Social Psychology of Organizations*. New York: Wiley.

KATZ, F. E. 1966 Explaining Informal Work Groups in Complex Organizations: The Case of Autonomy in Structure. *Administrative Science Quarterly* 10: 204–223.

KATZ, F. E. 1968 *Autonomy and Organization*. New York: Random House.

KRUPP, S. 1961 *Pattern in Organization Analysis: A Critical Examination*. New York: Holt, Rinehart & Winston.

KUHN, J. W. 1961 *Bargaining in Grievance Settlement*. Columbia University Press.

KUHN, T. S. 1962 *The Structure of Scientific Revolutions*. Chicago: Chicago University Press.

LAKE, D. 1968 Concepts of Change and Innovation in 1966. *Journal of Applied Behavioral Science* 14 (1): 3–24.

LAWRENCE, J. R. (ed.) 1966 *Operational Research and the Social Sciences*. London: Tavistock.

LAWRENCE, P. R. & LORSCH, J. W. 1967 *Organization and Environment; Managing Differentiation and Integration*. Harvard Business School.

LAWRENCE, P. R. & LORSCH, J. W. 1968 Differentiation and Integration in Complex Organizations. *Administrative Science Quarterly* 12: 1–48.

278   *References*

LAWRENCE, P. R. & LORSCH, J. W. 1969 *Developing Organizations: Diagnosis and Action.* Reading, Mass.: Addison-Wesley.

LAZARSFELD, P. F., SEWELL, W. H., & WILENSKY, H. L. 1967 *The Uses of Sociology.* London: Weidenfeld & Nicolson.

LAZARSFELD, P. F. & REITZ, J. G. 1970 *Towards a Theory of Applied Sociology.* Report Bureau of Applied Social Research, Columbia University.

LEWIN, K. 1947 *Field Theory in Social Science.* New York: Harper; London: Tavistock.

LIKERT, RENSIS 1967 *The Human Organization.* New York: McGraw-Hill.

LIPPITT, R. & LIKERT, R. 1953 The Utilization of the Social Sciences. In Festinger, L. & Katz, D. (eds.), *Research Methods in the Behavioral Sciences.* New York: Holt, Rinehart & Winston, pp. 581–646.

LIPPITT, R., WATSON, J., & WESTLEY, B. 1958 *The Dynamics of Planned Change.* New York: Harcourt Brace.

LIPPITT, R. 1965 The Process Utilization of Social Research to Improve Social Practice. *American Journal of Orthopsychiatry* 25 (4): 663–669.

LORSCH, J. 1965 *Product Innovation and Organization.* London: Macmillan.

LITWAK, E. 1961 Models of Bureaucracy which Permit Conflict. *American Journal of Sociology* 67: 177–184.

LITWIN, G. H. & STRINGER, D. 1968 *Motivation and Organizational Environment.* Boston, Mass.: Harvard University Press.

LUPTON, T. 1964 *On the Shop Floor.* Oxford: Pergamon.

MCGREGOR, D. 1960 *The Human Side of Enterprise.* New York: McGraw-Hill.

MCGREGOR, D. 1966 *Leadership and Motivation.* Boston, Mass.: MIT Press.

MCGREGOR, D. 1970 *The Professional Manager.* Boston, Mass.: MIT Press.

MANN, F. 1957 In Arensberg (ed.), *Studying and Creating Changes in Research in Industrial Human Relations.* New York: Harper.

MARCH, J. G. & SIMON, H. A. 1958 *Organizations.* New York: Wiley.

MARCH, J. G. 1965 *Handbook of Organizations.* New York: Rand McNally.

MARROW, A. L., BOWERS, D. G., & SEASHORE, S. E. 1967 *Management by Participation.* New York: Harper & Row.

MASLOW, A. H. 1954 *Motivation and Personality.* New York: Harper.

MAYO, E. 1949 *The Social Problems of an Industrial Civilization.* London: Routledge & Kegan Paul.

MECHANIC, D. 1962 Sources of Power of Lower Participants in Complex Organizations. *Administrative Science Quarterly* 7: 349–364.

MEISSNER, M. 1969 *Technology and the Worker.* Chandler Publishing.

MERTON, R. K. 1957 The Role Set. *British Journal of Sociology* 8: 106–120.

MILLER, E. J. 1959 Technology Territory, and Time: the Internal Differentiation of Complex Productive Systems. *Human Relations* 12 (3): 243–272.

MILLER, E. J. 1962 Designing and Building a New Organization. Paper given to the British Association for the Advancement of Science.

MILLER, E. J. & RICE, A. K. 1967 *Systems of Organization: The Control of Task and Sentient Boundaries*. London: Tavistock.

MORSE, J. J. & LORSCH, J. W. 1970 Beyond Theory. *Harvard Business Review* May/June: 61–68.

MOUZELIS, N. 1967 *Organization and Bureaucracy: An Analysis of Modern Theories*. London: Routledge & Kegan Paul.

MUMFORD, E. & BANKS, O. 1967 *The Computer and the Clerk*. London: Routledge & Kegan Paul.

MYERS, M. S. 1965 Who are your Motivated Workers? *Harvard Business Review* Jan./Feb.

NADLER, G. 1967 *Work Systems Design: the Ideals Concept*. Homewood, Ill.: Irwin–Dorsey.

NAVILLE, P. 1958 The Social Consequences of Automation. *International Social Science Bulletin* 1: 7–68.

O'CONNEL, J. H. 1968 *Managing Organizational Innovation*. Homewood, Ill.: Irwin–Dorsey.

PALUMBO, D. J. 1969 Power and Role Specificity in Organization Theory. *Public Administration Review* May/July: 237–248.

PATERSON, T. T. 1957 *Morale in War and Work*. London: Parrish.

PAUL, W. J., ROBERTSON, K. B., & HERZBERG, F. 1969 Job Enrichment Pays Off. *Harvard Business Review* March/April: 61–78.

PERROW, C. 1967 A framework for the Comparative Analysis of Organizations. *American Sociological Review* 32: 194–208.

PERROW, C. 1970 *Organizational Analysis: A Sociological View*. Belmont, Calif.: Wadsworth; London: Tavistock.

POPITZ, H., BAHRDT, H. P., JUERES, E. A., & KESTING, A. 1957 Articles originally in German and translated by Ryan as: The Worker's Image of Society. In Burns, T. (ed.), *Industrial Man*. Harmondsworth: Penguin, 1969.

PUGH, D. S., HICKSON, D. J., HININGS, C. R., & TURNER, C. 1969 The Context of Organization Structures. *Administrative Science Quarterly* 14: 91–114.

REDDIN, W. J. 1970 *Managerial Effectiveness*. New York: McGraw-Hill.

REVANS, R. W. 1962 Hospital Attitudes and Communications. *Sociological Review Monograph* (5): 117–143.

REVANS, R. 1967 Studies in Institutional Learning. European Association of Management Training Centres, Brussels.

REVANS, R. W. (ed.) 1972 *Hospitals: Communications, Choice, and Change: The Hospital Internal Communications Project seen from within*. London: Tavistock.

RICE, A. K. 1963 *The Enterprise and its Environment*. London: Tavistock.

RIDGEWAY, D. 1958 Administration of Manufacturer–Dealer Systems. *Administrative Science Quarterly* 2: 464–483.

RIVETT, P. 1969 New Horizons for Operational Research. In N. Farrow (ed.), *Progress of Management Research*. Harmondsworth: Penguin.

ROGERS, E. 1961 *Diffusion of Innovation*. Free Press.

ROSZAK, T. 1970 *The Making of a Counterculture*. London: Faber.

RUSH, H. M. F. 1969 *Behavioral Science: Concepts and Management Applications*. 216. National Industrial Conference Board, New York.

SADLER, P. J. & BARRY, B. A. 1970 *Organisational Development*. London: Longmans.

SAYLES, L. R. 1958 *The Behavior of Industrial Work Groups: Prediction and Control*. Columbia University Press.

SCHON, D. 1963 *Invention and the Evolution of Ideas*. London: Tavistock.

SCHEIN, E. H. 1966 *Organizational Psychology*. New York: Prentice-Hall.

SCOTT, E. L. 1956 *Leadership and Perceptions of Organization*. Research Monograph 82. Bureau of Business Research. Ohio State University.

SCOTT, J. F. & LYNTON, R. P. (eds.) 1952 *Three Studies in Management*. London: Routledge & Kegan Paul.

SCOTT, W. H. 1963 *Coal and Conflict*. Liverpool University Press.

SEILER, J. A. 1966 *Systems Analysis in Organizational Behavior*. Homewood, Ill.: Irwin–Dorsey.

SELZNICK, P. 1954 *T.V.A. and the Grass Roots*. University of California Press.

SELZNICK, P. 1957 *Leadership in Administration*. New York: Harper.

SOFER, C. 1961 *The Organization from Within*. London: Tavistock.

STINCHCOMBE, A. L. 1959 Bureaucratic and Craft Administration of Production: A Comparative Study. *Administrative Science Quarterly* 3 (4): 168–187.

STRAUSS, G. & SAYLES, L. R. 1957 Scanlon Plan: Some Organizational Problems. *Human Organization* 16: 15–27.

STROTHER, G. B. 1962 *Social Sciences Approaches to Business Behavior*. London: Tavistock.

TANNENBAUM, A. S. 1968 *Control in Organizations*. New York: McGraw-Hill.

THOMPSON, J. D. & BATES, F. E. 1957 Technology, Organization and Administration. *Administrative Science Quarterly* 2 (2): 325–343.

THOMPSON, J. D. 1967 *Organization in Action*. New York: Wiley.

THORSRUD, E. 1970 A Strategy for Research and Social Change in Industry: the Industrial Democracy Project in Norway. *Social Science Information* 9 (5): 65–90.

THURLEY, K. E. & HAMBLIN, A. C. 1963 *The Supervisor and His Job*. London: HMSO.

TOURAINE, A. 1965 *Workers' Attitudes to Technical Change*. Paris: OECD.

TRIST, E. L. & BAMFORTH, K. W. 1951 Some Social and Psychological Consequences of the Long-wall Method of Coal-getting. *Human Relations* 4: 3–38.

TRIST, E. L., HIGGIN, G. W., MURRAY, H., & POLLOCK, A. B. 1963 *Organizational Choice: the Loss, Re-discovery and Transformation of a Work Tradition*. London: Tavistock.

TRIST, E. L. 1968 The Professional Facilitation of Planned Change in Organizations. Paper given to 17th International Congress of Applied Psychology, Holland.

TREADGOLD, R. 1963 *Human Relations in Modern Industry*. London: Duckworth.

TURNER, A. N. & LAWRENCE, P. 1965 *Industrial Jobs and the Worker*. Cambridge, Mass.: Harvard University Press.

TURNER, B. A. 1968 The Organization of Production-scheduling in Complex Batch-production Situations: A Comparative View of Organizations as Systems for Getting Work Done. In G. Heald (ed.), *Approaches to the Study of Organizational Behaviour*. London: Tavistock.

TURNER, H. A. & BESCOBY, J. 1961 An Analysis of Post-War Labour Disputes in the British Car Industry. *Manchester School*, May.

TURNER, H. A., CLARK, G., & ROBERTS, G. 1967 *Labour Relations in the Motor Industry*. London: Allen & Unwin.

TURNER, H. A. 1970 *Is Britain really Strike-prone?* Cambridge University Press.

VROOM, V. 1962 Ego-involvement, job satisfaction and job performance. *Personnel Psychology* 15: 159–177.

VROOM, V. H. 1964 *Work and Motivation*. New York: Wiley.

WARNER, W. L. & LOW, J. O. 1947 *The Social System of the Modern Factory*. New Haven, Conn.: Yale University Press.

WEICK, K. E. 1970 *The Social Psychology of Organizing*. Reading, Mass. Addison-Wesley.

WEISS, R. S. & REIN, M. 1970 The Evaluation of Broad Aim Programs. *Administrative Science Quarterly* 15 (3): 97–109.

WHYTE, W. F. 1962 Applying Behavioural Science Research to Management Problems. In Strother, G. B. (ed.), *Social Science Approaches to Business Behaviour*. London: Tavistock.

WHYTE, W. F. 1963 Culture, Industrial Relations and Economic Development: The Case of Peru. *Industrial and Labor Relations Review* 6 (4).

WHYTE, W. F. 1969 *Organizational Behavior: Theory and Application*. Homewood, Ill.: Irwin–Dorsey.

WIELAND, G. F. & LEIGH, H. A. 1971 *Changing Hospitals: The Hospital Internal Communications Project*. London: Tavistock.

WILSON, A. T. M. 1969 The Problems of Implementing Management Research. In Farrow, N. (ed.), *Progress of Management Research*. Harmondsworth: Penguin.

WILSON, B. R. 1961 Institutional Analysis. In A. T. Welford (ed.), *Society: Problems and Methods of Study*. London: Routledge & Kegan Paul.

WOODWARD, J. 1958 *Management and Technology*. London: HMSO.

WOODWARD, J. 1964 Industrial Behaviour: Is there a Science? *New Society* 8 October, London.

WOODWARD, J. 1965 *Industrial Organization: Theory and Practice*. London: Oxford University Press.

WOODWARD, J. (ed.) 1970 *Industrial Organization: Behaviour and Control*. London: Oxford University Press.

WYATT, S. & MARRIOTT, R. 1952 *A Study of Attitudes to Factory Work*. London: Medical Research Council.

YOUNG, M. & WILMOTT, P. 1957 *Family and Kinship in East London.* London: Routledge & Kegan Paul.

ZALEZNIK, A., CHRISTENSEN, C. R., & ROETHLISBERGER, F. J. 1958 *The Motivation, Productivity and Satisfaction of Workers.* Cambridge, Mass.: Harvard University Press.

Name index

Aguilar, F. J., 19, 70
Anthony, E. J., 259
Appleby, B., 67, 68
Argyris, C., 5, 6, 28, 38, 168, 232, 244
Aronoff, J., 17
Ashby, W. R., 155

Bakke, E. W., 223 fn.
Bamforth, K. W., 22, 74, 136
Banks, O., 16, 25–6, 63, 139, 154, 195
Barry, B. A., 188, 252, 261
Bates, F. E., 39
Beckhard, R., 20, 228
Van Beinum, H. J. J., 23
Bell, G. D., 74, 116, 147, 148, 244
Bendix, R., 4, 28, 31, 33, 202
Benne, K. D., 217
Bennis, W. G., 6, 14, 15, 16, 17, 20, 29, 111, 153, 155, 201, 217, 242, 254
Blake, R. R., 13, 22, 54, 244, 258, 260
Blau, P. M., 202
Blauner, R., 37, 38, 39
Boguslaw, R., 155
Brannen, P., 129, 202
Brown, R. K., 4, 129, 202
Buckley, W., 155, 194
Burns, T., 41, 42, 69, 80, 82, 143, 145, 146, 148, 154, 157, 200, 244, 245, 246, 257

Carey, A., 171
Chadwick-Jones, J., 139
Chandler, A. D., 46, 61
Chapple, E. O., 13, 22, 229
Cherns, A. B., 3, 6, 46, 54, 55, 66, 67, 68, 69, 71, 89, 104, 108, 135, 167, 229, 233, 240, 243, 247, 250, 269, 270
Chin, R., 36, 155, 217
Clark, P. A., 3, 4, 5, 6, 15, 33, 66, 67, 71, 83, 89, 104, 129, 135, 138, 145, 155, 167, 196, 215, 217, 229, 233, 240, 243, 244, 250, 259, 262, 269, 270
Coch, L., 17
Crozier, M., 35, 37, 143, 145, 150, 194, 197, 202, 263

Dalton, G. W., 269, 270
Dalzeil, S., 87, 227
Daniel, W. W., 44
Davis, L. E., 21, 27
Dennis, H., 34
Dill, W. R., 42, 43, 145, 159, 244, 245, 247
Van Doorn, J. A., 44, 155, 176
Dornbusch, S. N., 34
Dror, Y., 156, 157
Drucker, P., 244
Dubin, R., 17, 34, 35

Earnshaw, P., 197, 206
Eldridge, J. E. T., 93, 129, 130
Eling, C., 4, 33, 67, 93, 129, 140, 217
Emery, F. E., 30, 110, 123, 127, 132, 137, 138, 140, 141, 142, 154, 195, 199, 244, 245
Etzioni, A., 35, 43, 145, 152

Feld, M. D., 13
Flanders, A., 63, 195
Ford, J. R., 4, 15, 33, 67, 93, 129, 135, 196, 197, 217, 240, 243, 244, 259, 269
Foster, M., 27, 30, 32, 74
Foulkes, S. H., 259
French, J. R. P., 17, 33
Friedmann, G., 27, 28

Garfinkel, H., 208
Gellerman, S. W., 244
Goffman, E., 229
Goldthorpe, J. H., 23, 34, 35, 36, 144, 150–2, 184, 197, 200, 201, 202, 211, 233
Gouldner, A. W., 4, 12, 19, 39, 86, 87, 96, 136, 232
Greiner, L. E., 15, 260, 269, 270

Haberstroh, C. J., 247
Heller, F., 31, 33, 261
Herzberg, F., 6, 29, 32, 46, 104, 181, 244, 261
Hesseling, P., 188
Hickson, D. J., 43, 150

283

Subject index